AJ Rochester is a Sydney-based writer, performer, comedian, film-maker, poet, singer, single mother and goddess. When asked what she wants to be when she grows up she says, 'Young'. She is also the host of the popular SBS series 'Mum's the Word'.

Confessions of a Reformed Dieter

HOW I DROPPED EIGHT DRESS SIZES AND TOOK MY LIFE BACK

A. J. Rochester

arrow books

Published by Arrow Books in 2004

3 5 7 9 10 8 6 4

Copyright © A.J. Rochester 2004

A.J. Rochester has asserted her right under the Copyright, Designs
and Patents Act, 1988, to be identified as the author of this work

Arrow Books Limited
The Random House Group Limited
20 Vauxhall Bridge Road, London, SW1V 2SA

Random House Australia (Pty) Limited
20 Alfred Street, Milsons Point, Sydney,
New South Wales 2061, Australia

Random House New Zealand Limited
18 Poland Road, Glenfield
Auckland 10, New Zealand

Random House South Africa (Pty) Limited
Endulini, 5a Jubilee Road, Parktown 2193, South Africa

The Random House Group Limited Reg. No. 954009

www.randomhouse.co.uk

You can contact A.J. Rochester at ajayrochester@bigpond.com
or look her up at brokenrecords.net.au

A CIP catalogue record for this book is available from the British Library

Papers used by Random House UK are natural, recyclable products made from
wood grown in sustainable forests. The manufacturing processes conform
to the environmental regulations of the country of origin

ISBN 0 09 947149 3

Typeset by SX Composing DTP, Rayleigh, Essex
Printed and bound in Great Britain by
Bookmarque Ltd, Croydon, Surrey

I dedicate this to my birth mother,
Kaylene Beverly Rochester.
RIP

. . . and to all the fat girls

The journey of a thousand miles begins with a single step
(Chinese proverb)

Get off your fat arse and move it!
(AJ Rochester)

Contents

Confession

Okay, so let me start by telling you what I've eaten in the last few days. Yesterday for breakfast I had pancakes with golden syrup. Then for lunch I had Jarlsberg cheese and Kettle chips on white bread, my son's unfinished peanut butter sandwiches, two chocolate bars and some seaweed crackers with cheese. For dinner I had a large BBQ meat lovers pizza (with extra spicy sausage), six deep-fried chicken wings, a garlic bread and bottle of Pepsi. Dessert was ice cream with chocolate and strawberry topping. Today, waking up and telling myself I was going to eat well, I proceeded to have a bacon and egg muffin for breakfast and, as I write, I am still licking the oil off my fingers from the KFC I had for lunch. Can't wait for dinner—I'd better go have a snack.

Hmm, there's nothing quite like putting a piece of fruit 'n' nut chocolate in between two salt and vinegar chips. It's the ultimate in gourmet sandwiches (for those screwing up their noses—try it!) and at least there's fruit in it.

Now some people might say I have an eating problem. Well, I believe my only problem is that scientists are yet to genetically modify deep-fried Mars Bars so they are a fully nutritious, well-balanced meal containing the complete range of vitamins and minerals and are also completely fat-free. Now that would be a perfect world.

But in reality it's not a perfect world and I *do* have an eating problem.

I love food. Even worse, I love junk food. If lard could be double deep-fried I would eat it. If I could deep-fry headache pills I would. If fat could be packaged as a sex aid I would be a very satisfied woman. So it's no wonder I'm now the size of a small yet economically viable continent. When buying jeans I don't buy 501s, I buy 1002s. And I don't get wide leg, I choose wide load. When I work at the cinema, it's as the screen. I'm so big you have to take a train and two buses to get on my good side. I'm so unfit I can't even jump to a conclusion. I don't wear G-strings—I have the whole alphabet. Oh, and my bellybutton no longer collects lint, it makes sweaters.

Now don't get me wrong. I love myself. I think I am a beautiful, gorgeous, energetic and amazing woman. If I could eat whatever I wanted and be whatever size I was, and *still* be able to run after my little boy and be able to play chasey for as long as he wanted without feeling like an elephant was tap dancing on my chest, then I would. But that is not the case, and as a parent (particularly a single one), endangering or unnecessarily shortening my life would be irresponsible and selfish.

I still believe society is cruel and discriminatory and that the media and the general population put too much pressure on people to be thin. I believe women should be allowed to be whoever they are and whatever size they are without being ridiculed, dismissed and treated like second-class citizens.

Having said that, though, for my son's sake I have now decided to DIET. Except that I'm not using the D-word, I'm merely entering the Alfalfa Zone.

Tomorrow I have my first session with a psychiatrist who specialises in eating disorders. I expect her to fill my head with catchy phrases like 'You are what you eat' and 'Your body is a temple', in which case it means I am a church made of deep fried hamburger, full of worshippers who daily bow to the big oil vat and constantly chant, 'Would you like fries with that?'

Next week I am meeting with a personal trainer who henceforth shall be called Crusher, so named because I am sure she will crush my desire to eat junk food, crush my overwhelming urge to drive up to the end of my street to get milk, and therefore crush my will to live. In fitness terms that translates to running me through a range of exercises I will promise to do (and won't), giving me tips on food I will swear to eat (and won't) and inspire me to be a size 12 before my next birthday (which I won't).

I have no idea whether or not I will be successful. I am terrified of either outcome, because as an actress I will have no excuse for not getting work. And what if I get thin and still can't get a boyfriend? Who will I blame then? What if, at the end of eight months, I am bigger than I already am? That's what has usually happened. I am not new to this diet—sorry, Alfalfa Zone—thing. These are just *some* of the diets I have tried:

Jenny Craig was very successful initially. In the first week I lost two, maybe three hundred dollars. My wallet was at least two kilos lighter. I called it my cat food diet because I was always opening a tin or a package to eat. There's nothing as romantic as a dinner for two when your boyfriend's eating the lamb roast you just cooked and you're heating up a tin of tuna, he's on his second case of beer and you're drinking a diet shake. I did actually lose a lot of weight on that one but as soon as I went off it the fat came thundering back to my thighs.

One of my actress friends told me about the Eat Right For Your Type Diet. Not sure what my type was, I thought about the type of guys I liked. Big, gorgeous black men with really big bank accounts. So my type was rich, big and black, therefore I concluded I would simply have to eat chocolate mud cake, choc chip cookies and Lindt dark chocolate, and before I knew it I'd be sleeping with the man of my dreams! Not so, it would seem. Apparently this is eating the right type of food for your blood type. It turned out to be far too complicated. If I can't read about it in ten pages or less, then it's not the diet for me!

Next stop was the Liver Cleansing Diet, which basically meant I would have to give up alcohol, so suffice it to say *that* diet never made its way out of the bookshop.

Then there was the No-Carbohydrate Diet, the All-Carbohydrate Diet and the All-Protein Diet. All of which managed to make me about six kilos heavier. The All-Fruit, All-Prune, All-Chicken, and All-Apple Diets were great for the first two days, but how long can you eat only chicken before growing an extra set of hormone-enhanced breasts?

And let's not forget the All-Egg Diet. On that one I didn't

actually lose any weight but I certainly lost a lot of friends. There's really only a certain number of eggs one person can consume before becoming a national hazard to pollution levels.

I also read an article about these two women in the eighties in America (where else?) who modelled themselves after Barbie. They called themselves the Barbie Twins. When asked to reveal the secret of their successful dieting, they said that before sitting down to a meal they always smothered three-quarters of their dinner in dishwashing liquid, ensuring they would only eat a small portion of what was served. I guess it saved them licking the plate clean.

When Oprah lost all that weight by walking, I went straight out and hired the very last treadmill available in Sydney (Oprah has a way of making things sell). I lost $800 and most of my lounge room. It was the most expensive clotheshorse I have ever owned. Six months later it was returned to the shop, covered in cobwebs. I reasoned that Oprah was rich, she could afford a cook and a trainer and God knows what else it took for her to lose the weight. That old 'It's easy for her' line works every time. After that my motto became 'No Pain—No Pain'. Sure, hard work has a future payoff, but laziness pays off *now*!

Then there were the natural therapies. I went to see a naturopath and past life counsellor. He asked me all sorts of questions and got the answers from my higher brain (what?) by getting me to hold my arm out while he tried to push it back down and I tried to resist. If I said yes but meant no, then the arm would go down by my side (of course it had nothing to do with the fact that he was stronger than me!). If only men used that test to see whether or not I really wanted to sleep with them, chances are I'd still be a virgin. Anyway, he said the reason I was overweight was because in one of my past lives I had been Jewish and held in a concentration camp and that I was eating in this life to compensate for that one (I wish I was kidding!). At least that explained why I didn't like pork. Any wonder I'm the only person I know who liked *Yentl*.

He put some hippy herb drops in water, said by the time I finished those I'd be ready to be thin, and asked for eighty dollars for the ten-minute consultation. As I explained to the police officer later that day, the reason I bit him on the shin was because I'd been a dog in another past life and he'd been my neglectful owner, so I was just responding to my higher brain's memory. All charges were dropped and I continued to pile on the pounds. Weehee.

There was also the psychic who told me I was not fat, it was simply my aura that was overweight and my body was just filling the space. She told me that if I could get my aura to lose a few kilos then the body would follow. I thought that was pretty cool. If I could blame my aura then I could also blame my inner child and my mental giant. I could go to Jenny Craig and say, 'Hi, my inner child's a few kilos overweight—can you help her lose them?' Then I'd get the specially priced children's programme rather than paying the full fee. While I was there my mental giant could go a few rounds on the treadmill, and let's not forget my spiritual guide. He was toting around a few extra kilos as well and it was really weighing me down. At least with so many people to look after, I never felt guilty ordering up big at Macca's— three Big Macs, two Fillet o' Fish and a jumbo fries was the standard order.

My friend Phillippa referred me to *another* psychic counsellor (you'd think I'd learn) who told me to sit opposite her and tell her about the abuse I was subjected to as a child. She sat with her eyes closed and breathed deeply. Then she said that she was breathing in my fat and that in a few days the weight would just start falling off me and that I would never have a problem again. That session cost $120 and by the end of the next week I'd gained another three kilos.

My grandmother felt sorry for me with my obviously ballooning weight so she took me under her wing and introduced me to body wrapping. They wrap you in wet bandages that smell like rotten cabbages, then get a jumbo sized box of Glad Wrap and cover your body in that, then they put a raincoat on you and you sit wrapped up like a mummy thinking there has to be a better way to lose weight. They measure you before and after and you do lose centimetres, and perhaps half a kilo, but as soon as you even drink water, the weight goes back to what it was. I guess when people get sick of the mummy wrap they'll go one step further and offer you the formaldehyde milkshake diet. One sip and you'll stay young forever.

I've tried vegetarianism (my problem was that I love dead flesh and hate vegetables), laxativism, smoking, chewing gum and sexual substitution (that's where if you get hungry you have sex instead. Don't try it—your lover just ends up having a headache twenty times a day). I've tried everything except what I am about to do—get well on the inside (my psychiatrist), get advice for the outside (a nutritionist) and get help for the backside (my personal trainer).

And if all of that fails then I guess I will just have to go back to hiring Moscow Circus to make my dresses, I won't go to the beach for fear of Greenpeace pushing me back out to sea and I'll keep promising myself that next year I am definitely going to lose weight!

YOU ARE NOW ENTERING THE ALFALFA ZONE

(Please leave your thighs at the door.)

The first time I met with my psychiatrist, who I immediately dubbed Dr Nutcase, she didn't tell me my body was a temple or anything like that. She asked me to tell her about myself. Apparently I can't just say 'I have an eating disorder' while they wave a dead chicken (preferably deep fried) in the air doing incantations so that when I walk out of the place I will no longer crave roast chicken and potatoes all smothered in luscious, fat-filled gravy and instead crave beautiful wholemeal pita bread sandwiches stuffed with watercress, alfalfa sprouts and bamboo shoots . . . No, apparently it's not as easy as that. According to her I have to delve into myself a little. Hmm. I have a terrible feeling I'm not going to do too well here.

AJ Rochester's history as requested by Dr Nutcase

Now, I don't want you to laugh, and I know you will think I am joking, but I swear on my birth mother's grave that this is the truth. Since writing that last paragraph I have been to the shops and eaten a hamburger, chips (with extra chicken salt), a couple of chocolate bars and half a packet of chewy sweets. And you know what? It *would* be funny if it weren't so bloody tragic. Have you any idea what it feels like to have no control over how you live your life? To feel trapped in your habits? To not want to know yourself so much that you eat and you eat and you eat until you feel so full and so sick and so disgusted with yourself that your mind is too busy loathing you to have any space left to think about what is really bothering you? Well, I do know what that is like, because that is my life.

Where do I start? Well, I wasn't always fat. When I was a fetus I was a healthy weight. Of course, I still couldn't find a thing to wear but it didn't seem to bother me as much then.

I was born in Sydney on 17 April 1969. My mother was young, single and wanted to be a model so, bowing to the social pressure of the time, she agreed (with a lot of 'help' from the government) to have me adopted out. She tried to get me back but was told I had already gone to my new family. This was not true but she was not to know. Nor did she know she legally had a month to change her mind, something a lot of single mothers were not told back then.

When I was about six weeks of age I was formally adopted by a married, Anglo-Saxon couple some government agency believed would make better parents than my biological grandparents, who had attempted to adopt me but were told the situation was irreversible. I lived in Sydney for eight years and led a very active life. I was a healthy normal- (if not a little under-) weight child with all the usual interests kids have: I did swimming, ballet, physical culture, played tiny tot tennis, rode my bike anywhere I could get away with, and ran around with the neighbourhood kids.

When I was eight my family moved from Sydney to a quaint little town in country New South Wales—not the end of the world, but you could see it from there. It was a dream come true for my father and a nightmare for me.

The first change to my lifestyle was that I no longer engaged in my regular physical activities. Being a city kid, I found that catching pigs, herding cows or chasing the chickens wasn't a substitute for ballet or swimming. In my former world chickens were for eating and they usually came deep fried in a bucket labelled KFC. As far as I knew, chickens grew on trees or in freezers. Pigs were on afternoon cartoon shows and cows, well, they were what you silently called your grandmother after she'd made you eat your sprouts. The only good thing about the country was being able to put a bit of distance between myself and my older brother.

So on top of losing my already hectic exercise schedule, the new school I attended had a teacher who was one of those unlovely creatures called a paedophile. On top of the physical and sexual abuse, which became my daily nightmare, he subjected me to horrific mental abuse. He would sit me in class and pick on me, making comments about my appearance, saying things like the reason I had buckteeth was because of all the hot air issuing from my mouth. I would get into trouble for no reason and he would send me to his office where he could get at me alone and uninterrupted. Apparently, according to information I've read on sexual abuse, it is common for abusers to belittle their victims publicly because of a fear of showing favouritism and quite simply because they are on a very sick and twisted power trip. I have carried a lot of guilt around with me for not saying something to anyone about it then.

The abuse went on from Grade 3 through to Grade 5. He would threaten me each year before the start of the holidays, warning me that if I told anyone about 'our little secret' he would make me repeat a year. Loving school and knowledge as much as I did, my teacher knew that was the very thing that would maintain my silence. My holidays were clouded with fear, worrying about the humiliation of having to repeat, a threat he never came good on.

The saddest part about that episode in my life is I really believed I was special. That's what he told me and when he put his arms around me I felt loved, because physical affection was rarely demonstrated in our house. Hungry for any kind of affection, I was the perfect prey.

Earlier this year I faced my fear and wrote about the abuse for the very first time. Maybe, because of that, I am now ready to let go and lose weight. Maybe, because of that, I no longer need to protect myself with excess flesh. Maybe I've finally let that demon rest.

Anyway, thankfully the abuse stopped when the teacher was suddenly removed from the school. I had one more year of primary left and, under the care of a beautiful man who nurtured my tattered little soul, I found enough confidence to enter the very scary world that is high school.

My high school was near an abattoir, or the meat works as the locals came to call it. Hot summer days, if the wind blew in the right direction, were an experience I could never forget. There's nothing quite like being in science class cutting open a thawed rat while the smell of freshly slaughtered animals mixed with day-old drying blood and exposed offal wafts in on the wind of a 40-degree heat wave. Ah, memories! It's no wonder I constantly lost my appetite.

At high school there was the usual peer group pressure to look good. It was perhaps even stronger where I lived, especially when the ever so glamorous beef queens are crowned. It was every girl's dream to be crowned Miss Hereford or Miss Longhorn, and the pressure to look good started at an early age.

By midway through high school I was already seriously screwed up. I had very low self-esteem, I was convinced I was ugly and I hated myself. My opinion of myself was not helped by the fact that my brother and his gang of mates would call me 'Little Fat Rochester'. At the time I was in no way anything that would even resemble fat. It's just that 'fat' was the hate word of the moment, like 'gay' has been in the past and like 'retard' was when I was in primary school.

Although we lived a long way out of town I convinced my parents to let me return to ballet. From day one the twigs I danced with, including my ballet teacher, constantly urged me to watch my weight because, apparently, I had the potential to have a problem. Boy, were they right!

When girls pulled me aside in high school I knew it was for 'the talk'. They'd say really helpful things like, 'Gary really likes you and thinks that if you lost a little bit of weight he'd probably go out with you.' I'd respond with, 'If I lost a little bit of weight I'd go out with someone better than Gary.' So, as you can see, making friends was not something I did naturally.

I was absolutely terrified of boys and said no to some very sweet ones because I was so scared. By the time my hormones had started coursing through my body, I carried a very terrible secret inside my head. I was not a virgin and in those days a non-virgin was a slut, so I was damaged goods. And on top of that I blamed myself for the abuse. I had obviously encouraged it because I never said no. I was the dirty one.

A few years later with my parents' divorce looming, I moved to Sydney and the strangest thing was that I went completely in the opposite direction sexually. I found myself sleeping with almost everyone who was interested. I could not say no. Anyone who wanted it got it. I didn't feel any better about myself, nor did I enjoy it. And even when I said no I found I had no power. I was raped when I was just eighteen: I said no numerous times, closed my legs and did all but hit and kick my attacker. Instead I just left my body while he did what he wanted then declared I had been the worst of his 378 conquests.

The years passed and despite the pressure to be a stick I continued to maintain a healthy weight and what I consider to be a perfectly normal young woman's body. But the pressure was mounting and the fact that I wanted to become an actress meant I had no alternative but to diet, encouraged heartily by my mother. That's where I found the apples-only diet, then the egg diet. Mum was an endless supply of crash diets guaranteed to help you put on at least two kilos a week. I decided diets didn't work, I would never be thin and therefore I decided I would never be beautiful.

Around 1984 a new craze was taking over the world. I read all about it in the teen magazines. It was the diet all the models and actresses were on, so I figured it must be good, even if it was killing them. It was called anorexia nervosa. And thinly veiled in the articles about the disease were instructions on how to starve yourself to death. I had found my path to beauty.

Off I went to drama college and dance classes, the beginnings of an eating disorder intact, and what did I find?

My classes were full of fellow eating disorder-ettes. We swapped insane diet tips like '101 Ways to Regurgitate Your Meal' and 'How Laxatives Paved the Way for Me!', and did all but declare ourselves a club. The only things missing were our secret handshake (which would have been two fingers down the throat) and a cheer.

The crazy thing is that I was still not fat. I was still dancing, but even the teachers said to me that I would never get gigs if I stayed the way I was—a size 12 was considered overweight.

The first role I scored in a feature film reinforced my belief that I really was fat. I was to play, of all things, the fat girl, even though I was still a size 12. When I met the writer he told me excitedly that I was exactly like the real-life girl I was playing. I was severely depressed and decided I would only ever get to play fat girl roles if I stayed a size 12.

So I literally began to starve myself. It seemed to be the only way. It was obviously working for all the girls who were getting gigs, so I knew it would work for me. I would take speed pills and then not eat for days. Dance classes were often plagued with fits of dizziness but no one seemed concerned— that's just what we did so we could be 'successful'.

I also started to take laxatives every time I ate—just one or two at first, but that quickly turned into taking about fifty a night. I would try to time my laxative sessions so they would be finished by about eight in the morning. Some nights that would mean all-night vigils on the porcelain bus. Occasionally, not having eaten enough to actually digest the pills, the after-effects would hit me later the same day, and I wasn't always in the right place to deal with them.

At the time I was paying the bills by doing clowning (well, we all have to eat! Or at least think about it . . .). Anyway, I remember doing a children's birthday party in Pymble, in Sydney's old money area, daaahling. There I was, Lu-Lu the clown, in the middle of my fun-filled magic show when I was overcome by a powerful urge to go to the toilet. I tried to ignore it but soon realised that if I didn't disappear immediately, the children would see a magic trick they would never forget.

I made my excuses, found my way to the pristine marble bathroom and took ten minutes out to deal with the 'situation'. I splashed cold water on my face, washing off half my make-up in the process, said a quick prayer to the God of Ablutions and went back out to finish the show.

Just as I stepped in front of the kids I knew I had to turn and run for the bathroom again, this time with twenty kids chasing me, thinking it was some new version of hide-and-seek. So there I was, locked in the toilet with a gang of five year olds banging on the door screaming, 'Clown! Clown! Clown! Clown!' only to be interrupted by the parents knocking gently and asking if I was all right. What could I say? Yes, I'm just in the midst of a porcelain purging session, I'll be all right with five years of therapy and a good sense of body image? I remember blaming a bad curry, refusing to take their money and offering to do a freebie for them the following year. Funnily enough, they never called me back.

The thing that really escalated my eating disorder around this time was a disastrous relationship with a man I lived with for over two years. The reason I stayed with him for so long completely eludes me now, because it was totally dysfunctional. From very early in the relationship he would point out how if I lost a little bit of weight I'd have a really good body. He also thought if I did that, then I could actually be quite successful at acting. He said guys would be lining up to go out with me. I should have asked him if he knew a guy from the country called Gary and I should definitely have left him then but alas I did no such thing. Wanting to please him, I said I would go on a diet.

The first wonderful piece of advice he gave me (as my unofficial personal trainer) was that dieting was easy. His philosophy (a man who would always be skinny) was that if I didn't eat I would lose weight. After a few weeks of semi-starvation I stopped eating altogether. It just seemed easier than having to listen to him tell me that eating was why I was fat. He kept telling me he loved the new body I was getting and told me how his friends were already jealous, and how I could do anything I wanted if I could just lose a little more weight. I believed him. I *was* getting more attention, I loved the compliments and the flirting, and I loved my rapidly shrinking body. I felt in control.

A few friends made odd comments about me not eating, but only one person warned me I'd get anorexia if I wasn't careful. The problem was, that's what I wanted. I wanted to be anorexic because that word didn't mean *sick* to me, that word meant being thin, and thin, as every magazine told me, meant *beautiful* and *successful.* I was obsessed with stories of women with anorexia and wished I could be like them. I used to think, if only I had the strength to do what they do. All I wanted was to starve myself to near death. It seemed so attractive. My ambition became: get thin at all costs. I set myself a food limit: half an egg sandwich and one apple a week. Always followed by a box of laxatives.

Of course, I was starving, and I desperately craved certain foods . . . well, food in general. When the desire for food became overwhelming, I would sneak up the road (away from my food Nazi boyfriend) and furtively eat anything I could get my hands on. I would be racked with guilt afterwards. I was a failure. I was a failure because I *had* to eat.

I started just chewing the food and spitting it out but it wasn't enough. I started thinking about how many of the calories still went down my throat even if I didn't swallow the food. I started to think that even if I *touched* food, calories would stick to my fingers and be absorbed into my body. So I decided to start vomiting. If I had to eat then I would make myself throw up.

I was still plagued by the thought of all the extra calories I could not purge soon enough so I kept taking laxatives as a back-up. I would go from chemist to chemist and purchase the biggest box available. I bought so many I had to go to chemists in other suburbs for fear of them knowing my terrible secret. Fifty tablets a night was the norm for me, depending on what I'd eaten that day. I don't know how my partner never found out as I spent most nights getting in and out of bed.

During that time I managed (despite apparently being fat) to score a role in the feature film *The Crossing*. It should have been one of the happiest times of my life but it wasn't. I spent my days on location being a budding movie star and my nights in the bathroom either throwing up, sitting on the toilet or lying on the cold tile floor too weak to move from the toxic damage I was doing to my body. The make-up artists would have a hell of a time trying to disguise the circles under my eyes, pale face and acne from malnutrition. Still, at every break in filming I could be seen doing sit-ups and leg-lifts with 7-kilo weights strapped to my ankles. I was obsessed.

I remember going for my wardrobe fitting and freaking out about a figure-hugging skirt my character was supposed to wear. In a fit of tears I literally begged the wardrobe mistress to change my outfit to something that didn't make me look so fat. They swapped dresses with one of the other actresses but it didn't actually make me feel any better. I felt like an impostor, I felt like I was fat and that everyone knew it and that I didn't really belong on a real movie set because basically I was too fat to be a real actress. Of course, tell that to Camryn Mannheim, Rosie O'Donnell, Kathy Bates and Deborah Mailman and they would laugh in your face, but it wasn't really about what I looked like, it was how I felt about myself. I was not worthy.

I look at photos of myself at that time and I don't remember having such a small body. Why don't they teach you at school how to love yourself and look after your body? If they did it while we were young enough for it to become a part of our consciousness, then so many people would be spared so much grief.

Not long after that film I remember my boyfriend finding chocolate wrappers hidden in the pockets of my jackets and he confronted me with them, saying I'd never have a good body if I ate crap like that. I remember being shamed and desperately wanting to tell him that I thought I might have a problem because I couldn't stop bingeing and purging, but I kept my silence and became even more obsessed.

He went overseas and I launched myself into my eating disorder as far as I could go. I did not eat. I worked out like a maniac. My usual day consisted of swimming for three hours, walking for one hour and doing sit-ups and leg-lifts whenever I could. I took cocktails of speed and laxatives, I drank litres of water and replaced tea with plain hot water. I literally lived (if you could call it that) on nothing. Not surprisingly, I lost weight. Very quickly. And with the rapid weight loss, once again came all the compliments, which just reinforced that I was doing the right thing.

But I didn't just lose weight—I also lost my breasts and my social life. I grew facial hair, had bad breath, I alienated my friends and became a complete and utter walking-talking basket case. I was constantly sick and listless. I spent hours of the daytime sleeping because I had little energy to do anything else; I had chronic stomach cramps from severe malnutrition and overdosing on laxatives. I spent so much time throwing up that I was lucky not to do permanent damage to my teeth (bile rots enamel), my memory was atrocious, I had dizzy spells whenever I stood up, I lost my tolerance for alcohol, I was having muscle spasms and severe cramps in my legs, and suffered heart palpitations. By this point I no longer thought I had a problem. I thought I was the dieting queen.

I caught up with my man overseas, my weight close to 45 kilos, which was too light even for my small 161 cm frame and he greeted me with, 'You are now truly beautiful.' I wasn't convinced. It was my aim to be less than 40 kilos. There are so few photos of me then because I hated my body and didn't want anyone to take photos of it. I had no idea how thin I was. I remember saying to one of my girlfriends on tour, 'Gee, I wish I was as thin as you.' She turned to me with the strangest look on her face and said, 'You're sick.' I had no idea just how right she was.

Two weeks later I collapsed in a hotel bathroom, unable to get out of the bath, severely underweight, at risk of liver failure, having such intense heart palpitations and in so much pain I could not pick myself up off the floor. I was killing myself.

Before flying back to Australia, a nurse the size of the *Titanic* examined me and said, 'Love, you're anorexic, aren't you? It's really simple, darling: if you don't eat you'll die.' And with that little gem, a broken heart and the decision to give up acting, I started to eat—and eat and eat and eat . . . I believed in doing everything as well as I could so instead of starvation, food became my new love. Oh, and that's when I made the decision it would be easier and less heartbreaking to become a lesbian.

I thought it would be safe to be a lesbian. I felt like there was a possibility that I could just be me. I wouldn't have to starve myself to be loved and I wouldn't be sexually harassed. The problem with that rather naïve theory is that lesbians are the same as anyone else and just as many lesbians as men (if not more) made passes at me. After about two years of trying to be a lesbian I had to admit defeat. I had one major problem—I liked boys, a fact which makes life as a lesbian pretty hard.

Not long after that I was on again, off again with the only relationship I have had that was even remotely healthy, and in the midst of trying to make that work I lost my birth mother. That in itself is a complicated story and reads like a soap opera. As I mentioned earlier, I am adopted. When the laws changed I traced my origins only to discover that I already knew my birth mother. My best friend Zoë and I had worked in her theatre restaurant the year before. So, having only just been happily reunited with my real mother, in a cruel twist of fate it was less than a year later when she died. Once again, I was alone and without the mother I had longed to get to know all of my life.

In an attempt to deal with my grief, I pushed away the man I loved, officially sacked my agent, lost contact with friends and family and started to eat and drink my way into obscurity. I look back at that time in my life and think that I was probably having a fairly major nervous breakdown. Pity I couldn't call a mobile mechanic.

After a few years of eating on the run and no longer dancing or exercising at all, I started to pile on the kilos. I didn't care. I was going to eat anything I could get my hands on—especially junk food, because junk food made me happy. I wanted to bury all my hurt and pain in my fat. I wanted to be invisible to men because sexual pressure just made me afraid and in the position of having to defend myself (not always successfully).

Every day was wasted thinking about my next meal. I would eat until no longer hungry and then I would eat some more. I hated myself, and in an attempt to not feel the hatred I just ate more. Pizza, fish and chips, chocolate bars, lollies, hamburgers, red wine, beer, beer, and more beer. Anything to help me forget every problem I'd never faced.

Having turned my back on acting I threw myself into my comedy and writing, with clowning still paying my way. The great thing about clowning was that it was funny to be fat and everybody loved you. I was a natural. Put on the mask and away I went. I realised that if I wanted to be successful at comedy I had to use my fat (and I was very aware that there was only ever fat or thin, with nothing in between). I started to develop some wonderfully hideous fat characters that got big laughs. I had found a way to make people love me!

In an attempt to promote a comedy show I was doing at the Harbourside Brasserie I talked my way into a guest DJ spot on a local radio station, doing a breakfast show on the Central Coast, an hour's drive north of Sydney.

There's a popular expression, 'You've got a great face for TV'. Well, I had a great body for radio. It was kind of funny when people came out to meet the morning crew. They would always be disappointed. The men would say, 'Gee, I thought you'd look different.' Translated: 'You sound thinner on radio.'

Working from 3 am and quite often not finishing till 6 or 7 at night, I lived off McDonald's, and they'd often give us our brekkie for free. I was always too tired to cook so I just ate from the side of the road, and I don't mean roadkill. I mean

I accumulated frequent fryer points. I knew every drive-thru attendant by name, rank and serial number, and even more embarrassingly they knew exactly what I would order. I'd never have to say a word.

Three years of being the takeaway queen, too much loneliness and sadness and 30 more kilos on my small 161 cm frame and I was even more convinced that I was fat, ugly and forever unable to gain control of my life. The one thing I never stopped to think was that no matter what size I was, fat or thin, the only thing that remained a constant was that I thought I was ugly and not good enough to love, least of all by me. That time in my life is marred by a couple of poorly attempted suicides but I couldn't even get that right. I was convinced I was a failure.

I turned my back on radio, burning a few too many bridges, and returned to Sydney in search of the happiness that I thought would save my life. I decided I would do what I had always dreamed of doing: write children's books, teen fiction and outrageous poetry. I thought that if I could just follow my heart then it might lead me back to who I really was and somehow, in amongst all the fear and pain, I might find a way through.

I went on the John Howard Arts Scholarship (dole) and became a writer (professional beer drinker). Figuring I sounded better than I looked, I tried my hand at phone sex. I failed miserably, only able to breathlessly pant things like, 'Your hands wander down to my area of luurve' instead of the naughty bits the paying customers wanted to talk about. I remember one day saying, very Marilyn Monroe-ish, 'Your hands caress my big, voluminous melon-like breasts—' And the customer cut in with 'Not that big.' I realised then that, even over the phone, I was still way too fat.

With the last of my radio money I decided to go to Bali for 'the holiday of a lifetime'. After years of friends telling me what a great party place it was, so relaxed, so much fun, beautiful friendly people, I finally succumbed and ended up there with the ten thousand other drunken Aussies we saw frequenting the pool bars. It was a nightmare. Wherever I went I was pointed at by the Balinese men. They would puff out their cheeks, laugh, mimic my fat walk and exclaim loudly, 'Hey, sumo! Very fat sumo! Hey, sumo lady, you very fat!'

I was feeling so bad that I couldn't bring myself even to lie by the poolside to get one of those great five-dollar massages. After much nagging by my friend Alicia I agreed to have the 'ten-dollar in the privacy of your hotel room' deal. Ten minutes into my forty-five minute massage the size 6 woman says to me, 'You very fat. Something the matter with you?'

In tears that night I promised myself I would never come to Bali again and that I would finally lose some weight. I put on quite a few more kilos before I actually decided to honour that promise.

Unfortunately, when I came back to Sydney I fell in with a pack of performance poets. I spent three years drinking heavily, eating hot dogs and meat pies in the wee hours of the morning, living off two-minute noodles and writing some really good poetry (at least, after fifteen beers it sounded really good). The beer added another ten or twenty kilos (I'm not sure—I threw out my scales five dress sizes ago) and in the midst of too many late-night binge-drinking sessions and telling everyone 'I love you . . .' I fell pregnant with the little man who is my son Kai. This was not what I had planned for my life!

Funnily enough, that's when my life started to turn around. Sounds like a great dieting tip: just get pregnant and you'll get off your fat bum and do something with yourself. There is nothing like being responsible for the life of an innocent child to help you get your shit together. The first thing I did was stop drinking. I started to eat healthily for the first time in my life and throughout most of my pregnancy, without meaning to, I actually lost weight. I remember that during my labour I said to my best friend Zoë the same thing I'd said every year of my fat life: 'I promise you, I am going to get fit. I am going to get so healthy. You just wait and see.' Zoë had heard this a million times and, true to form, it turned out to be another hollow promise.

My relationship with Kai's dad was not going well and I handled it the way I had handled every other problem in my life: I tried to eat it away. My daily diet consisted of spring rolls, dim sims, prawn toast, hot chips, roast chicken, pizza, lollies, cheesecake, French toast, chocolate, potato gems, fish-finger sandwiches (eight at a time), no fruit, no vegetables and definitely no self-respect. I hated myself, I hated my lack of control, I hated the fact that not only was I going to be single (again) I was now going to be a single mum. I felt a complete and utter failure and had I not had my son to live for, it is highly likely I may have tried to kill myself a little more quickly than by eating myself to death.

For the last few years I've made a living (if you could call it that) singing in my band, doing spoken word (performance poetry), selling articles to magazines, and doing corporate comedy shows, the odd clown gig and any television I could talk my way into.

I was due to give birth to Kai the day I performed my poetry at the Basement jazz club in Sydney, September 1999, when talent scouted by Lina Safro, a producer from SBSTV. She was doing a series on motherhood called 'Mum's the Word', was looking for a host and wondered if I'd like the job. Of course I said yes immediately, but was plagued by the fear that she presumed I was just fat because I was pregnant and once she realised I was *really* fat then I'd lose my part in the show.

I would often joke to my friends that SBS hired me not because of ethnicity but because I was fat and in television terms that definitely made me a minority. God bless equal opportunity employers.

To her credit, Lina hired me for my talent and not the size of my body. We filmed eight episodes, each on a different aspect of motherhood. I introduced and closed the show, filmed links to various segments and best of all, it was my job to interview famous dads.

I was constantly haunted by the thought of what I would look like on screen given that, apart from already being over one hundred kilos, the camera makes you look a stone (7 kilos) heavier than you actually are. I wondered whether they shot me with a wide angle lens.

When the show finally aired in May 2001 I saw myself on

screen and cringed. I did a photo shoot for *TV Week* and when I saw the article I realised why they had only used a head shot. If they'd done a full body shot they'd have needed a double-page spread. I was desperately ashamed but tried to make the best of a bad situation.

I decided to throw a publicity stunt halfway through the series. Being fat, I knew the odds were against me being offered any more jobs in TV. I wanted my own comedy show and thought that if I embraced the fact that I am fat then someone might say, 'Oh, she's the next big thing in comedy and everyone knows fat girls are funny!' Rather than being embarrassed by my size, I thought I'd act all proud and empowered (note the word 'act'—I didn't feel empowered at all.) I declared a national Flesh is Best Day and imagined 'A Current Affair' not doing their usual 'Mary lost 100 kilos and gained a life and two husbands' story but instead showing a group of big girls who were proud to be fat and wanted to stay that way. Women celebrating their flesh!

I staged the stunt at Sydney Town Hall. I had a huge chocolate bar built for the occasion. 'Fatbury's dairy milk chocolate . . . an arse and a half in every bar'. I had belly-dancers, body-painters, a waif begging for chocolate donations and various fat comedy characters all running around asking guys if they'd been with a big woman before. I declared myself to be big, beautiful and here to stay! To the passers-by I sang a song I had written called 'White African Queen': 'I am a woman, I have flesh to spare, I'd be a goddess anywhere but here, I'm a size sixteen, an African Queen, but because I'm white my size is not right . . .' The funny thing was that I was not a size 16. I was a size 26! But I was intent on creating a positive image of fat girls.

We formed a picket line and carried placards that declared 'My boobs and chest are Rubenesque', 'I shop at Big Flesh', 'I'm Fat-tastic' and 'Don't put a Fatwah on me'. I wore a fabulous red 'fashioned for the big girl' piece of lingerie (some people might call it a curtain). We handed out petitions to dress manufacturers to increase their sizing, to airlines to increase the width of their seats and to television execs to show more *real* women on TV (i.e. women like me!).

It was great fun. Lots of women came up and said, 'Yeah, big girls rule!' Lots of older men came up for a cuddle and a kiss. Many women shared their personal horror stories of being overweight and suffering from eating disorders, and a film crew even turned up. They were from the Lifestyle Channel on Foxtel and they were doing a show on obesity (such a dirty word) with the lovely working title of 'The Fat Trap'. They filmed my stunt and said they would meet with me next week to do a full length interview.

The film crew were interested in talking with someone who was obese, which came as really shocking news to me. Had I really become *that* fat? This was the ultimate moment of realisation and truth. I was fat, everyone knew I was fat, and the question was, did I really want to stay that way for the rest of my life?

That word—OBESE—kept going around and around inside my head. Other people were obese, surely I wasn't that fat?! Obese meant out of control, dangerously overweight, socially unacceptable and completely, well, FAT. I'd been so busy calling myself a goddess that I'd lost sight of the bigger picture—I was slowly but surely killing myself. How could I possibly be proud of that?

I realised I was at crisis point. I looked at my son and saw his little double chins developing and wondered what I was doing to him. I seriously questioned whether this was the way I wanted to live (or half live) the rest of my life.

Which Way are the Choccy Biccies?

The next time I did a supermarket shop, I was determined to make healthy choices—how hard can it be? Okay, very. I remember reading somewhere that you shouldn't shop when you're hungry, so I stopped off at the food hall and had a Chinese all-you-can-eat plate of food plus two dim sims, a can of Coke and a piece of chocolate mud cake. I'm not sure that's what they meant but I was now ready to shop.

I started off okay in the fruit and veggie section. I got mushrooms, figuring I could make some kind of healthy pasta dish with those and I also threw in two bananas, one orange and I nearly bought an avocado but then I thought it might be full of fat.

I successfully passed the deli section and refrained from buying twiggy sticks, frankfurters and bacon. Then I entered the cereal aisle.

Oh my God, I was not prepared for the sea of information on the backs of the cereal packets. Any more info and it'd be the bloody Encyclopedia Britannica. First there were the fat-free fruit bricks with four added vitamins, the iron-enriched flakes that were high in fibre, the Heart Foundation approved cereal with added folate and antioxidants (What are they? Bran flakes that stop body odour?), ones with added minerals, added vitamins, added iron, added fruit, added additives, cholesterol free, fat free, calorie free and I'm sure the ones that are best for me are also flavour free. I was lost, dazed, confused. Surely the packets that had the word 'sport' on them were the ones for me. I had to make a decision. Was I a netballer, canoeist, runner, iron man or tennis ace?

Why didn't they have a picture of a fatty like me sitting in front of a television, remote control in hand, eating pizza and Coke? They could call it 'National Heart Foundation approved, Putrid Grain! 'Cause after all that fat in the body, anything healthy is sure to taste bad. Better get the heart monitor, we got ourselves a candidate. Putrid Grain. For those too lazy to know better.'

I shook my head, wiped the sweat from my brow, took a deep breath, panicked again and, making a quick decision, reached for the cereal of my choice—Coco Pops!

Downcast and disillusioned I got out of there as quickly as possible. I did buy some fat-free yoghurt, I didn't buy cheese or fish fingers, I did buy four tins of peaches and came home with broken spirits and the realisation that I am in deep, deep trouble. It was time to call in the cavalry.

The day before the Lifestyle Channel were due to film me I came up with a cunning plan. I figured that with the promise of publicity I would be able to access the resources I would not normally be able to afford. I rang my best friend's sister who also happens to run a personal training business. I've known her for sixteen years and she has seen me thin/fat/thin/fat/thin and finally obese. I asked (begged) her if she would do it for free, in return for a mention on the TV show. To her credit she said she would have done it for me a long time ago and all I needed to do was ask. She would be there for me.

I went to my doctor and shamefacedly admitted my history of eating disorders and asked her to refer me to a shrink who specialises in that area. I made an appointment, knowing I couldn't afford to pay her but after I told her my story and begged her to help me finally save my life, she agreed to bulk bill me. It's amazing the support you can find when you need it.

I realised that if I didn't do something now then I might not get another opportunity like this again. I also figured that if I had a camera following my bum around all the time, then there was no way I would stop doing this. Failing your diet is one thing (something I mastered a long time ago), doing it publicly is a whole other ball game. This was the moment of truth. If they agreed to my plan there would be a camera in my house from day one and if I didn't lose weight every week then I would be labelled a loser (or a non-loser) for the rest of my life. No more excuses!

With the resources I would need set in place I then put it to the producer. I told her I was about to get fit (uhuh). I was going to see a personal trainer (of course I would) and a shrink (oh really?), I was going to change my life (yeah sure!)

and asked her if she wanted to film it. She jumped at the chance and added that she had a friend who was a nutritionist so she said she would get her to advise me on what and how to eat/cook and before I had time to say, 'Pass the choccy biccies', this is where I have ended up.

So there it is. My story. That wasn't so bad after all. I wish I hadn't eaten the hamburger now. And I can't believe tomorrow is D-Day. The day I truly enter the Alfalfa Zone. Crusher, my personal trainer, has rung a few times and told me to keep all my food in the fridge. She's coming over to tell me what and how to eat—not that I've ever had any trouble in the how-to department, just in the what and how much.

It's been funny knowing that after tomorrow chocolate will be a distant memory as I power-walk my way to physical freedom. I suppose I'll have to get a real boyfriend if I no longer have chocolate. Oh dear, I'm not sure I'm ready for that kind of commitment. At least Mars Bars never get you pregnant and never ask you for your best friend's phone number!

Apparently I have to wear a sports top for her evaluation of my body. I'm not sure why. One look at the circus tent dress I'd be wearing should be enough for her. How can I possibly go and buy a sports top? Surely the sales assistant will just laugh, hand me a bag of donuts, point across the shopping mall and say, 'The only thing in your size is in the Kmart camping section. But the good news is, hammocks are on special today!'

Crusher also mentioned I'd be doing something called a food diary. Does that mean I actually have to admit to someone else all the rubbish I eat? That would change everything. Everybody knows the food you eat when no one's watching has absolutely no calories in it! Now what am I going to do? I can see the entries in my diary now:

'Dear Diary, I had a nightmare last night. I was a giant piece of cabanossi lying in a huge Jacuzzi filled with tomato sauce. Then this huge mouth came looming towards me and at that precise moment—'

Somehow I don't think this is what she meant. Oh well, I guess I'll find out tomorrow. Right now I have to throw out the dried-up mushrooms, rancid yoghurt and rotten bananas I bought the other day having promised myself I'd eat more healthily. And I'd better just finish the chocolate mud cake before Crusher comes over and throws it out. I'd also better get rid of the seven empty pizza boxes, the twelve empty long-necked beer bottles and the five Chinese takeaway containers.

Just in case she checks my rubbish.

109 KILOS

(240 lb)

19 July 2001:   Week 1, Day 1

I started the day off well by eating a bagel, which I absolutely smothered in butter (hey, even Jesus ate well at the Last Supper!). I met the film crew from the Lifestyle Channel and did an interview. We would do one now, one half way through my weight loss and one at the end of thirty kilos. In the meantime, they have given me a camera and shown me how to use it. Every week I am to do a diary update of what my week has been like—highs, lows, revelations, confessions, exercise I have done and habits I have learnt and/or broken. I'll film my weigh-ins with Crusher and anything else I think is important. Realised just how big this thing is. There is absolutely no way I can back out of this now. Imagine failing on national television. It's not going to happen!

The first interview went well. It was a bit weird talking so openly about my life—painful childhood, sexual abuse, rape, the bulimia—but I tried to think of it in a positive way. By getting it out of my head, I no longer need to carry it around and by admitting that I'm obese, that I have a problem and that I need help, well, I just can't ignore it any more. Hopefully this means I am finally ready to deal with it. And if it can help other people in my situation then it has to be a good thing, huh?

After that we all got in the car and went to Crusher's gym. The meeting was not anywhere near as bad as I had imagined. Okay, so I was completely shamed, humiliated and disgusted that I had let myself get to this point, but apart from that I walked away with the vague belief I could do this thing.

First of all I had to sign some papers including one with a rider to the effect that I wouldn't sue her if she kills me. Trying not to dwell on that, I then had to complete a health questionnaire detailing my medical history. If you have experienced any of the following conditions please tick appropriate box:

Anorexia   ☑
Bulimia   ☑
Obesity   ☑
Epilepsy   ☑
High blood pressure   ☑
Heart palpitations   ☑
Dizziness   ☑
And so on . . .

It may have been easier to tick what I didn't have. Now I know why she made me sign the indemnity form.

Crusher then did what they call a fat test. This is where they use a tricky little instrument to measure just how much fat you are actually hauling around. Well, my arse is so big that, apart from having its own postcode, we were unable to test how much body fat I have—there was just too much. Crusher tried to get a reading in three or four places but the verdict was the same. I was simply too fat.

Trying to not burst into tears I pretended to laugh (and not think about the camera as it zoomed in on the flabby stretchmarked overhang) and continued on, telling myself it would make good TV. Then it was time to check the blood pressure. Unfortunately my arm was also too fat for the elasticised band and we couldn't get a reading. Not making as many jokes now, it was time to see how much I weighed.

The last time I had weighed myself was two years ago when I was eight months pregnant with my four and a half kilo baby. I had been 110 kilos. Crusher was happy to inform me I had indeed lost weight since giving birth. Yay! I was now 109 kilos. Okay, so I have some work to do.

Next was the tape measure test. The results? As expected: 36–24–36. All right, that was my thigh, arm and ankle, but at least I've got *something* in proportion. Actually I've blocked out my actual measurements because once I saw 108 cm around my waist I started seeing alfalfa sprouts in a whole new light.

I didn't even get to the fitness test (which would have me exercising with an elevated heart rate) because, once again, I am dangerously overweight (sigh). So what we have decided (Crusher decides—I do) is that for now, I am to concentrate on eating well and moving more. No gyms (thank God!) and no huge exercise regimes yet. Thinking I had got out of this easily, she then introduced me to Mr String: she made me suck in my gut, which I did (suddenly in Asia there was more room to move), told me to hold my breath, then tied a piece of string just below my ribs and then instructed me to relax. As you can imagine, the string cut off most of the circulation to my heart, which actually forced me to suck in my tummy again and hold it there. I did it on and off for twenty seconds, and after five minutes of this I was starting to breathe a little heavier.

She then got me to do bum squeezes, which I did for five minutes, which basically had me clenching my buttocks together as hard as they will go (imagine trying to hold a fifty cent piece in there), holding it for ten seconds then resting for ten seconds. Then she had me doing them both together, bum squeezes and tummy tucks. My heart rate was up—I was exercising and there wasn't even one anorexic blonde bimbo gym junkie in sight!

Next came the food diary. Each day I am supposed to make a list of exactly what I have had to eat and drink and any exercise I have done, including running after my son. I have to fax that to her at the end of the week. This system, I came to realise, works primarily on honesty and guilt. The mere thought of putting down the words 'bacon and egg muffin' makes me put on a thousand kilos and I know what Crusher would say if she read that next week so I intend to opt instead for the healthy please-my-mistress kind of deal.

I'm not sure how long that will last and I'm sure I will find some way to cheat. I guess if I went out and had five beers I could say I had five yeast drinks. I don't know how often I could get away with that. I guess it depends on how trusting Crusher is. I have a feeling I haven't seen the worst of her yet. She's just lulling me into a deep sense of security, after which she will reveal her true unforgiving, driven, die-hard bastard self that will crush me and bend me to her will. Well, I guess that's what people pay her to do.

We (she) decided I could lose up to 45 kilos but we would aim at 30 for now. Very generous of her, don't you think? She told me that this task was not an easy one and it would be up to me whether I succeeded or failed. She said she would advise and support me through it but at the end of the day I was the one who had to commit to making the changes. I made a pledge, hand over heart, which went something like I promise to . . . actually I can't really remember *what* I pledged because I'd been in her office for two hours and I hadn't had a chocolate hit so I think my blood sugar was low, but I'm sure that whatever it was I promised is bound to hurt and if that doesn't kill me then the complete lack of fat in my life will.

What if my body goes into shock? Maybe I'll go through withdrawals. Maybe I'll have to go on some programme that allows me to go to the chemist, get my legal and not second-grade portion of fat and head to my local ingesting room, where I can guzzle it down and lie there heavy lidded and sated for fifteen minutes before going out and mugging a granny for her hamburger mince. We didn't discuss that. Note to self: ask about fat-attacks.

We then came back to my place and she showed me a range of 'exercises' I could do around the home. She showed me how to pick up all the toys while doing aerobically beneficial squats and lunges. She also said that every time I had to go up my stairs (except when busting for a wee) I was to do three sets of twenty up and down the first step. I gave it a go and by the second set my heart was out of my chest and hitching its way to a transplant patient, my legs had turned to jelly and I realised why she hadn't done the fitness test. I had to sit down.

She showed me some great snack foods I could have that

are fat free, including fruit, jelly snakes (yippee!), sultanas, fruit, rice crackers, licorice, fruit, low-fat yoghurt, seaweed rice crisps and . . . fruit. She stressed that fruit was better than the jelly snakes but then, noticing the crestfallen look on my face, added that it was a big change so I am to take it slowly and do the best I can. She quickly went through my fridge and cupboards and threw out the cakes, Coke, cheese, ice cream, chips, boxes and boxes of macaroni cheese, four cheese pastas and my precious stock of beer (aaah!).

She explained to me that first of all I need to cut most of the fat out of my diet. She told me that a woman's body generally uses up about 40 grams of fat per day in a normal day's activity. So if I only eat 20 grams of fat over the day, then my body will burn 20 grams of stored fat. This is *before* doing any exercise. So that means I have to switch from full-cream to skim milk, from full-fat to low-fat cheese. I am to eat lots of fresh fruit, vegetables and salads, and snack on the foods she has already listed for me.

I have to eat a total of around 1400 calories per day (as opposed to my normal tally of about 14 000 000). I am to get my metabolism firing. From years of anorexia my body has gone into survival mode, which means it stores everything as fat. If I feed my body regularly it will soon learn that it is going to be fed and will start burning fat. To get it to do this I need to eat six meals a day. Breakfast, snack, lunch, snack, dinner, snack. She recommended I have fruit and cereal for breakfast and a salad sandwich for lunch as well as a low-fat yoghurt. I have to eat two serves of dairy and at least four pieces of fruit every day. I need to drink at least six glasses of water a day, to flush the toxins from my body, avoid dehydration and to fill me up between meals. Alcohol is not on the list of recommended foods and beverages. I'm surprised she didn't just hand me a gun and tell me to get the job over and done with right now.

To encourage my body to burn even more fat, I have to start moving. I'm to try and do a twenty-minute walk at least twice a week, and I have to do the squats, the tummy tucks, bum squeezes and stair exercises every day of the week. She reminded me not to shop when I am hungry, and to walk to the shops instead of driving.

She told me it was important to set small goals and to reward myself once a week with something yummy, be it a piece of chocolate cake or a little piece of chocolate or whatever will work as an incentive to stick to the plan. She explained that this was a big change of life. This was not going to begin and end as most diets do. This new way of eating is (apparently) the way I am going to live the rest of my life.

She gave me a hug, told me she believed in me and said I deserved a healthy body and it was time I took back my life. I agreed (having a bit of a cry but trying to be brave for the camera) and resisted telling her that despite the fact that I hadn't actually done much physical stuff with her I was beginning to feel sore already.

Finally left alone I had a really good cry, felt better after having a long soak in the bath, went to bed, and couldn't sleep as I was too excited/terrified by the prospect that I was actually going to do this thing. I promised myself I would walk Kai to child care first thing in the morning.

Getting Started
- You want to change your life? First thing you do is check your health with your doctor.
- Throw out all your junk/processed/pre-packaged food. Don't leave things like biscuits and cakes in the cupboard in case guests come around, because chances are that in moments of weakness you will raid the cupboard and eat them yourself.
- Have a fat photo. As you lose weight, bring it out and remind yourself what a good job you are doing.
- Always wear the same clothes at measure time/weigh-in. It does make a difference.
- Similarly, always use the same set of scales. They all vary and you set yourself up for disappointment ('failure') by changing the scales.
- Don't expect miracles but know that if you keep going, they will happen! Believe in yourself!

20 July 2001
Arse: bigger than England

10 am: Woke up feeling thinner already. Realised I was dreaming. Woke up. Looked at myself in the mirror and realised the enormity of my arse . . . no, sorry, I mean the enormity of the task I have set myself.

I plan to lose at least a third of my body in around nine months. Surely this can't be done? The reality hits me and I feel a little despondent knowing that I always start off with the best of intentions but then a few days—or in some cases minutes—later I give in to the craving for junk food and the feeling that the job is too big to finish (or even start). Still, if I just do a couple of hours at a time rather than think that I will never again be a preferred customer at KFC then I might just make it through the first day. God, is it really only ten o'clock? When is lunch?

11.30 am: I didn't walk my boy to child care—it was too cold (who said I was too lazy?). I'll do it this afternoon. I have already done the stair thingy three times. Kai just stood at the bottom of the stairs laughing at me. Then again, if I could see my bum bobbing up and down the stairwell I'd think it was pretty hilarious too.

I had muesli for breakfast, a muesli bar for a snack and right now I am desperately looking at the clock so I can break for lunch. The funny thing is, I know I can cover breakfast and lunch but when it comes to making a decision about what to do for dinner, I am definitely out of my league. I know fish is good for you, but the only fish I ever cook is fish fingers or deep fried, and I know Crusher will have a seizure if that's on my diary first day in.

Later: I had the yummiest ham and salad sandwich for lunch and am currently feeling okay about this. The knowledge that I am allowed to have jelly snakes gives me some small comfort. Maybe I'll just carry them around in my purse as a kind of sugary security blanket. Anyway, I have my second appointment with Dr Nutcase today so I guess we'll wait and see what she has to say.

21 July   Alcoholic carrots

Spoke with Dr Nutcase yesterday and still no talk of eating disorders. She keeps asking questions about my life history, getting to know me and what makes me tick. I talked a lot about past relationships, relations between me and my family and what I am doing with my life. Feels weird telling a complete stranger everything about yourself. I don't know quite what I expected but I thought it would be a bit like school, where she says, 'Okay, class, now today we're learning what to do when we want to stick our fingers down our throat. Any suggestions? No, AJ, we don't drink a bottle of Draino in the hope we might throw up, and for goodness sake, stop counting how many calories in the air you are breathing . . . we are trying to get well here!'

I hope we touch on it soon though as I feel quite isolated here in the Alfalfa Zone. Now that I can't have chocolate I am craving it even more (if that is actually possible).

Spoke with Crusher about preparing meals. I just don't know how to cook. She said if I freak out at dinner time and don't know what to cook, then to have a Lean Cuisine and vegetables or a salad until I learn some recipes. Am keeping things simple, at the moment sticking to cereal with juice and a piece of fruit for breakfast, muesli bar and fruit for morning tea, ham and salad sandwich for lunch, low-fat yoghurt and fruit for afternoon tea and for dinner a Lean Cuisine and added vegetables (corn, potato and peas).

It's only the second day and already I'm bored. I've taken to opening the fridge just so I can stare in there and imagine what I could be eating if I wasn't doing this fitness thing. Oh my God, is it really only Day 2?

When I told Crusher what I'd eaten yesterday she said I had to eat more. My previous concept of dieting was to eat less but apparently this is not the way to thin thighs. She assured me that if I ate all the food she recommended then I would actually lose weight. I've just got to get off my fat arse and walk some-where. The problem with that is that I will probably pass the shops and then be faced with the dilemma of eating chocolate or buying beer—both of which are strictly prohibited.

Just before Crusher hung up she said if I was going to have a big night out on the booze then there were ways of preparing for that. I'm looking forward to that little dangling carrot. The very last thing she said (apart from 'Call me if you're about to crumble') was, 'AJ, stick to this thing one day at a time and you *will* lose weight. You can do it!' I can't imagine doing this for nine days let alone nine months but I'm going to do my best.

22 July
How long is this thing going to take?

Whatever you do, don't think of a white polar bear.

You thought of one, didn't you? Try it again.

Don't think of a white polar bear.

Hah, you can't do it, can you? The minute anyone tells us not to think about something, we can't help but think about precisely that thing. My polar bear is chocolate, chips, pizza, hamburgers, any outlet with a drive-thru and ice cream. Worst of all, I see chocolate everywhere. Why do so many shops have it at the counter? I woke up in a pool of drool, chewing my sheet, thinking (wishing) it was chocolate.

It's only Day 4 and already I'm getting a bit shirty. I decided to brave the supermarket again. The expedition itself was quite successful. At least I think it was. I usually buy lollies, biscuits and chips for Kai but knowing I have zero willpower I have decided he will just have to learn to like my food 'cause I can't have that stuff in my house. And how did I choose my wonderfully nutritious fat-free food? Basically I bought everything in the shop that said it was anything between 97 and 100 per cent fat free.

These days food manufacturers realise that many people (women mostly) want to know how much fat they are consuming. Crusher has said I can have around 20–40 grammes of fat per day, so I should choose foods with less than approximately five per cent fat. It's easy to work out if you check out the little label on the back of the packs. It's called Nutrition Information. It tells you how much fat or how many calories there is per serving. The fat column will list the total fat content and the saturated fat content. It's saturated fat that's the baddie, because it increases the risk of heart disease. The other fats are okay (within reason).

Crusher also said to keep an eye on the energy content—

in other words, how many calories are in the food—because even if something is low in fat, it might be high in calories. She explained it was important to keep a balance of fat/calories and to try to reduce both of those in my diet. She reminded me to be careful when reading the label because usually the package contains more than one serving, so make sure you check how many servings are in each pack and read the label appropriately.

She told me to watch out for terms like 'light' or 'lite' because they don't always mean light in fat—they might mean light in colour or salt. And 'reduced fat' doesn't mean something is low fat but that it has approximately 25% less fat than the full-fat version. So once again I just have to check the fat content carefully. Bloody tricky, this diet, oops, Alfalfa Zone, thing!

Anyway, with that as my method of judging what was good for me, I got heaps of Lean Cuisines, cup-a-soups, Hokkien noodles, the biggest bag of jelly snakes, diet jelly, diet yoghurt, two apples, a bag of potatoes, a bag of mush-rooms and two carrots.

Yes, I know what you're thinking . . . it's pretty light on the fresh fruit and veggies. Well, that's where I need to let you in on a little secret of mine. I hate vegetables. I can't stand them. I am strictly carnivorous by nature. If everything I ate previously had a heartbeat I would be more than happy to shove it down my throat. Hey, wait a minute, what's that? Oh, it's just the vegans picketing outside my door. Don't worry, they don't have enough strength to knock on the door let alone break it down.

Anyway, Day 4 is at a close and maybe tomorrow will be a little easier. I will definitely go for a walk then (it was raining today—I don't want to get a cold).

23 July   There was movement . . .

5 pm: Day 5 and I actually moved! I did more than walk to the television to pick up the remote control. I actually walked out of the house and up the street. For twenty minutes. Okay, so Heather Turland is in no danger of me taking her spot in the limelight but I actually did something that resembles exercise. Tomorrow I will *definitely* walk my boy to child care!

And just for the record, to compensate for the twenty-minute walk I have done no stair thingies and no tummy tucks. I don't want to put too much strain on the heart.

I ate crumpets for breakfast, muesli bars for snacks, ham and salad sandwich for lunch and a Healthy Choice meal from the freezer for dinner. I can't believe it is more than half a week and I haven't broken the diet—oops, I mean I haven't left the Alfalfa Zone. Oh well, I did have a couple of Kai's chicken nuggets tonight but they were leftovers and as such actually contain no fat or calories (I'm sure I read that somewhere). I also failed to mention them in my diary. See, I'm cheating already.

I have decided to trawl through the girlie magazines for recipes because they are sure to have fat-free meal tips—they wouldn't want to fatten up the future breeders of our country. God forbid all our mothers should be fat!

Oh, and the walk I went on was on the way to the bottle

shop but by the time I got home I was inspired enough not to drink anything.

. . . Well, almost. I'd better go; the wine's just chilled. Now, now—Crusher said I could have two glasses of wine a day. I just won't mention the glass I'm using is the tankard I bought at Oktoberfest.

9.56 pm: Make that three glasses of wine. Okay, I know I've now exceeded my limit, but I have to have a life and I'm thinking, if I can have two glasses of wine per day, then that equals fourteen a week, so if I save them up and earn interest on them, then I can drink a lot more in one session. That system works for me, how about you?

10.08 pm: Okay, back again, but like I (hic) said, I've saved them up. This is (hic) my foutrth glass, but only becauyse there's somebthing good (hic) on tele. I won't have anny more (hic).

10.28 pm: The true test is . . . will I surb=vive the drunken munchkies (I think my computer spell check is drubnk too) . . . subddenly my resolve is nobn-existent isn't this where most of my wbeight has abccumulated—the midnight kbebabs, the drunbken 'let's cook chips' episodes? Oh dear, I am in big trbouble, I better habve another glazss of wine.

25 July   Pool of drool

I can't believe it but I survived the munchies. No late-night snackies for me! It's Day 7 now and I still haven't walked (if you don't count the walk to the bottle shop!). I'm dreading weigh-in day tomorrow as I've even been slack on the stair thingy. No exercise but I have mostly stuck to the fat-free food regime. Yesterday was hard for me because I went to the shopping mall and forgot to take a snack and so made the decision to have a sushi roll. I won't know until tomorrow whether it was allowed but it was the best choice I could make. Okay, I could have gone to the fruit shop and had an apple but that would mean walking past Wendy's ice-cream and Charlie's chicken shop and I'm sorry, but I'm not that strong.

I was busted staring at a woman eating hot chips. It wasn't so much that I was following the chips from the bag to her mouth but more the bucket of drool coursing down my chin and flooding the floor. Maybe I'll just avoid anywhere with food for the next six months.

26 July   Week 2

Today is weigh-in day. I have no idea if what I have done has been effective but my skin is in better condition and I actually feel a little healthier and certainly more energetic. Okay, obviously not energetic enough to actually do any exercise, but at least I've considered it! I'm feeling strong-ish and I may even make it through Week 2.

Summary of Week 1

These are the changes I made:

- Thought about doing some exercise.
- Cut out all junk food.

- Ate at regular intervals and instituted proper meal times which were breakfast, snack, lunch, snack, dinner, snack.
- Thought about doing some exercise.
- Everything I ate was 97–100% fat free (I think).
- I wrote (almost) everything I ate in my food diary.
- Went from full-cream to skim milk.
- Cut down alcohol intake and drank no beer (I said cut down not cut out!) and thought about doing some exercise.

Things Crusher will say I should have done:
- Exercised.
- Eaten more fresh fruit and vegetables.
- Exercised.

Did I lose weight? I feel as if I have, but I have to wait until this afternoon to find out. Until then, I will think thin and continue on in the Alfalfa Zone.

Later: Crusher has been and gone and these are the results: I lost 1 kilogram, which for me was disappointing because previously when I have used the laxative/starvation/excessive exercise diet I have lost about 5 kilos in one week. I have to come to terms with the fact that doing it the healthy way takes longer but lasts longer, and the final outcome will not end up killing me. (Health experts recommend a loss of between half to 1 kilo per week.) My disappointment didn't last for long because Crusher took out her tape measure and declared my body to indeed be shrinking.

I have lost 2.5 centimetres off my neck, 4.5 off my waist, 2 off my hips, 4 off my thighs, 2 off my mid thigh and 3.5 off my triceps/biceps! So excited was I by my success I was ready to go out and buy myself some lycra hot pants, until I realised that I was only 1 kilogram down with 29 to go (not counting the extra 15 kilos I really need to lose!). Hmm, I might just stick to one day at a time.

Crusher did tell me to eat more fruit. She pored over my food diary and asked a thousand questions, like did I have butter on my bread, what kind of mayonnaise did I use, how many eggs in the scrambled eggs and what cordial did I drink? She told me I had done a great job (maybe she should become a politician) then set some new goals, which seem reasonable to achieve.

This week's goals
- Eat more fruit. At least three or four pieces of fresh fruit per day.
- Eat two serves of dairy a day—low-fat yoghurt and a smoothie, or a piece of low-fat cheese.
- Cut out fruit juice/cordial and replace with water/low-joule cordial.
- Drink at least eight glasses of water per day.
- Cut out butter. Replace with low-fat mayo/diet jam etc.
- When making scrambled eggs, use two whites and only one yolk.
- When making an egg sandwich do the same and use low-fat mayo and low-fat milk.
- When drinking tea, cut down the sugar (out altogether if I can) and only use low-fat milk.

- Don't miss the snacks. Eat every three hours or so. Religiously.
- Eat more food!

I was surprised when she said I hadn't eaten enough, because it felt like I was forever putting something in my mouth. She also recommended snacks like sultanas, salsa, diet jelly and pretzels, all of which are mostly fat free.

Crusher totally lived up to her name when she saw that on one of the nights I'd exceeded my limit of alcohol. I reasoned that if you can lie on the floor without having to hold on, then you haven't had enough to drink. She replied: 'AJ, the reason you have a fat arse is because you drink too much alcohol. If you want to change that, then listen to what I say!' She certainly wouldn't win any awards for diplomacy but one glance at the size 26 underpants I have to buy from the local Nana factory was enough to stop me from being a smartarse (although my compulsively smart arse is certainly big enough to house every member of Mensa). So the deal with alcohol is, if I am going to make a night of it, I have to have done a huge amount of walking and all my other exercises before I even contemplate a night on the grog. Somebody stop this bus—I want to get off.

Crusher also upped my exercise quotient (I knew it was too good to be true!). She gave me squats, lunges and leg-lifts to do in front of the television. I'm to continue the Mr String tummy tucks and butt squeezes. I have to continue doing the stair thingy every time I go upstairs and I'm to try walking my boy to kindy (Day 8 and I still haven't done more than think about it!).

Thought for the day: Why do today what you can put off till tomorrow?

27 July   Veggie phobia

All in all, you could say yesterday was a good day. As soon as Crusher walked out the door I immediately celebrated by eating six jelly snakes and three fat-free crackers. Did my first to camera diary entry (all happy having lost a kilo). I had to go to my band rehearsal, which meant I had to drive past KFC. Knowing my weakness, I took the long way round, thus avoiding the temptation altogether.

I was on a high all night and am now inspired to last until the end of Week 2 (that's easy for me to say this side of the week). Best of all, Crusher has insisted I work with the Reward System. If I am good and stay in the Alfalfa Zone all week, on Day 14 I am allowed to have . . . wait for it . . . a piece of chocolate mud cake! Yeehaa! Guilt free. So with the food diary keeping me honest, I know this is the way to go. With that little chocolate carrot dangling on my path to thinner thighs, I'm off to do Mr String and stairs, then off to see Dr Nutcase.

Later: I did see Dr Nutcase (though I didn't do the stairs). Today we actually started to cover some ground. It's still mostly me talking and telling her about myself. I definitely thought she'd talk more or have some great tricks to help me lose weight. She's basically still just getting to know me. I started by telling her I'd actually entered the Alfalfa Zone and as a result have lost 1 kilo and collectively 19 centimetres. She asked me if I wanted to be thin and it took me ten minutes of saying things like, 'No, I just want to be healthy and fit' and 'I just want to eat well and respect myself' etc etc until I stopped, looked her in the eye and said, 'Ah, yes, actually, I do want to be thin.'

She asked me why and I said I was sick of hating myself and treating my body with little or no respect. I wouldn't feed my son all the rubbish I eat, so why do it to myself? She told me that was a good thing to remember when reaching for the junk. Say to myself, 'Would I feed this to my son?' If the answer is no, then say, 'Well, why feed it to myself? I deserve a healthy body just as much as my son does!'

We talked a lot about the moment I decided to get fat. At the time I was doing stand-up comedy and ten years ago very few women could tolerate the boys-only club attitude that goes on backstage. So when a female comic actually stayed around for more than three weeks, the penises were out and fighting for first kiss. The female comics were a trophy for whichever male had the most comedic credibility (i.e. the one who could get them in the sack first). They were like seagulls fighting over the very last chip, desperate to add your name to their list of conquests.

Admittedly it wasn't just the comedians. It was every guy I knew. I found I couldn't have any male friends without going through the 'I can't believe we slept together' phase. Then I discovered that if I slept with every guy who asked, I was called a slut, and if I said no, I was called a stuck-up slut. It was a lose–lose situation. I was so sick of their constant unwanted attention and their inability to understand the word NO.

In desperation to simply be left alone I decided I had no other option than to get fat. Already eating to bury my pain it simply gave me another excuse to keep shovelling food into my gob. That way, I reasoned I would never be sexually harassed again (which is stupid because then I just found men who loved big women. Aaah!). So just like that, I decided to really work on getting fat.

I wanted to become invisible. I wanted to feel safe. I wanted to be left alone to just be me. I wanted people to like me not because I had a great set of legs that would go perfectly around their neck but because I was funny, creative, sensitive and a little scared of life. I desperately wanted to disappear. The problem with getting fat was that in many ways I became even more visible and was then a direct target for hatred and discrimination. The number of times I've had the words 'Jenny Craig' yelled at me by passing cars is outrageous. Not to mention numerous road rage incidents labelling me a fat slut. See, fat, thin, sexually active, virginal, abstaining or just driving around in my car, I still get labelled a slut. And I know it's not what I'm wearing because I've never seen a slut in a potato sack, which is about all I can get to fit me these days.

Add to that the restrictions that being fat placed on my health, lifestyle and career and I realise now it was probably not the most effective solution to my problems. However, with the help of Dr Nutcase I may just learn to feel safe and comfortable in my body, whatever size it is.

She sat there and listened, nodded her head, and made the occasional note—probably just adding to her shopping list while thinking, God, this girl is boring! I told her I had been disappointed with losing only 1 kilo but she told me I should be very happy with that. She reminded me that health professionals recommend a weight loss of around a kilo per week at the absolute maximum. She said I need to start telling myself that I do things differently now. I am going to do this healthily and the more slowly I do it the more long term the results will be.

The other thing we touched on was my severe hatred of vegetables—a mild obstacle if good health is on the agenda. This particular psychosis of mine stems from my childhood. Like most Skippy families in the seventies, mine supped on steak and three veg seven days a week. My mother came from the cookbook age that recommended 'if vegetables are left boiling for forty minutes, just pop in a little bi-carb soda and the colour will come rushing back'. Believe me, colour is not everything. If I took a Kandinsky painting, ripped it from its frame and ate it, I would almost guarantee it would be more flavoursome than the best of my mother's cooking. Let's just say it was a little bland. The most creative meal we ever had was when Dad gave Mum a crockpot for Christmas, which meant the meat and vegetables could be left cooking all day long. Yum!

To make matters worse, I simply refused to eat my vegetables, which meant I had to sit at the table until I finished what was on my plate. Usually around midnight my mother's resolve crumbled and I went to bed hungry. All this left me with a mild veggie phobia that I have not yet been able to kick. The good thing is, Dr Nutcase thinks it is possible. What I have to do is draw a pyramid and put the vegetable I hate more than my thighs at the top of the pyramid and the vegetable I hate the least at the bottom. Then I am to start at the bottom and look for ways to eat them that allow me to develop a liking for the taste, ultimately teaching myself to eat a range of vegetables cooked in many ways.

Now obviously I've never had a problem with potatoes—as long as they're deep fried and smothered in oil, I could eat buckets of the buggers. So, with peas being second from the bottom of my pyramid, today for lunch I am attempting to have 99.9 per cent fat-free pea and ham soup. We'll see how it goes . . .

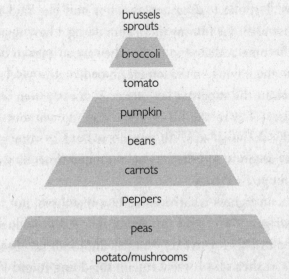

brussels
sprouts

broccoli

tomato

pumpkin

beans

carrots

peppers

peas

potato/mushrooms

29 July   Sausage grease

Okay, whoever invented diet cordials was evil. What the hell is phenylalanine anyway? Sounds like the name of some hillbilly from the movie *Deliverance*. It tastes completely disgusting. Maybe in a few weeks when my taste buds have shrivelled up and died from boredom it might not taste too bad. But I am doing as Crusher instructed and attempting to replace yummy naturally sweetened by God's rays of sunlight fruit juice with manufactured in a lab and sweetened by phenylalanine (whatever that is) diet cordial. Euh! At least it makes me want to drink more water.

It is Day 10 in the Alfalfa Zone and I'm feeling okay. I definitely feel thinner and the shape of my gut is changing. Instead of it being one big slab of fat hanging down around my thighs it now only hangs around my hips and is kind of lumpy. I spoke to Crusher about it and she said it was because of all the tummy tucks I am doing. I have to admit I have become addicted to them. They are so easy to do, you can do them lying on the lounge, in bed, on the toilet, in the shower, in the supermarket queue. It doesn't even feel like exercise. They're the sit-ups you can do without doing actually doing sit-ups. All you do is hold in your gut for twenty seconds and then let go. As many times as you can without getting dizzy.

Oh, and guess what? I actually walked! No, not just to the refrigerator to pour myself another glass of wine, but I walked briskly for twenty minutes and, wait for it—in the rain! Crusher said I was a legend for doing it and I know she's just trying to pump me up but I did it. And it felt great!

The way I am eating at the moment, I have enough calories to fuel my body to get through my day and because I am constantly adding fuel to my body, it is no longer storing anything as fat, so any exercise I do will burn off the fat from my body. I have this image of the fat monster being woken up whenever I do some exercise. Hope he's hungry—he's got the Homer Simpson all-you-can-eat meal deal!

Knowing that I am the sloth from hell, though, I am not looking at it as exercise. For instance, instead of saying I'm going to do three sets of twenty of all the exercises Crusher has set me, I try to catch myself off guard. I'll get up to go to the toilet in an ad break and do one set of squats. Then next ad break I'll do the same. So throughout the day I might actually do six sets of squats, four sets of lunges and four sets of stairs. Add to that a twenty-minute walk once a week (which is all I've done so far) and it is more exercise and toning than I have done in about eight years.

I had this realisation the other night. Okay, I was a little bit tipsy at the time but it seemed to make sense then. Let me just get it clear in my head. When Crusher showed me how to do my exercises while doing my housework (for example, doing the squats to pick up the toys) and if I actually do it, instead of bending from the waist every time, then during my normal day I'd have actually done the same number of squats as someone who went to the gym. So if I incorporate that into my life as a *habit*, then my whole lifestyle changes and everything I do benefits my health and my body.

Okay, not everything in my life benefits my health. The gigantic piss-up I'm planning on the weekend certainly won't do that but I have a plan. Crusher said if I was planning to drink alcohol I have to have walked and exercised that day. Now what I plan to do is not take my chocolate cake reward and transfer it into alcohol points. Then what I will do is walk Thursday, Friday and Saturday (hey, don't look so sceptical), I will stick strictly to my eating plan and, on the night in question, instead of wine or beer I am going to drink vodka and soda. I'm not sure if that makes a difference calorie-wise but it's my plan and I'm sticking to it. At least the soda is like water wearing a dinner suit, so I will at least reach my quota of water for the day.

Anyway, I've been so good. All week I've only had four glasses of wine, which for me is a record. It's not that I've ever had a drinking problem. I've only ever drunk on certain days of the week—those ending in 'y'. So give me a break!

And with that naughty session ahead of me, I now need to confess a few sins from this past week. Today I fell out of the Alfalfa Zone and into a fish and chip shop where I purchased and proceeded to eat a battered sav and chips. And you know what? They were fantastic. They were better than any orgasm I've had (sorry, lads!). Every bite of every chip tasted as if it was my last meal on death row and I'd been served caviar and smoked salmon on gold platters. The sausage grease dribbling down my chin was like the tongue of Antonio Banderas, licking me lustily in some kind of Barbara Cartland romance novel. Each chip was like biting into a little piece of Pierce Brosnan, each little bit of Irish Catholic flesh gliding down my throat and filling my belly with the love and the luck of the Irish. Okay, so I might have been hallucinating just a little bit but it has been ten days since I had fat!

I'm not sure how it happened. It was a moment of weakness . . . okay, it was a few moments of weakness as it did take me about fifteen minutes to walk to the shop . . . oh, okay, seeing as how I'm confessing I might as well be completely honest. I drove to the shop and it was three suburbs away, with plenty of time in between to turn around and heat up a Lean Cuisine but let me just say this. I did feel guilty about eating it. I felt guilty when I ordered it, when I paid for it, when I opened up the butcher's paper and saw it glistening there, begging me to devour it. I also felt guilty when I stuffed it down my throat and savoured every greasy, fat-filled, calorie-laden moment. Heaven is deep fried and fatty and Elvis is sure to be God's right hand man, so, Lord, take me now!

The phone has just rung and it was Crusher telling me she can't do the weigh-in tomorrow. You have no idea how happy I am. That gives me a few days to work off the sav. She caught me off guard and I found myself confessing my battered sav and chips sin. Surprisingly she was okay about it. She said that I had made amazing changes to my eating habits and that eating junk is a part of life and if done in moderation then it is okay. She banned me from doing it again and told me to keep doing the walks and my home exercises but she said I needed to stop feeling guilty and move on.

Because I come from an eating disorder background, all I had wanted to do was either throw up, take some laxatives or starve myself today to make up for my blunder. I did none of these and stuck strictly to the regime. Is this what it is going to be like for the next nine months? Me constantly trying not to throw up or take laxatives? I don't know that I am strong enough to resist that temptation.

Nutcase reminded me to say out loud to myself that 'I don't do that kind of behaviour any more. I am healthy and do not need to harm myself in that way. What I am doing is healthy and responsible and I will lose weight and keep it off. I just need to stick to one day at a time.' Yeah, it's one thing to say it but to believe it is another. Oh well, looks like I've got a very long way to go.

31 July   Dinner parties

I have always been a very social person. I am renowned for my roast dinners and have missed throwing my weekly dinner parties. So today I got on the Internet and found heaps of recipes for fat-free meals and have decided I am going to host a fat-free dinner party. I have decided to cook rice paper rolls with pork and Chinese cabbage for entree and a low-fat frittata for main. Dessert is simply strawberries and I am not going to have any wine (yeah, sure!).

1 August   Absolutely guilt free

The first thing that happened was one of my guests walked in the door and admitted to having eaten two fried chicken drumsticks before coming to dinner because he knew he would be eating 'rabbit food'. Having cooked all afternoon I was so angry with him I made him pledge that he would eat everything on his plate including any leftovers there may be.

First course was the pork rice paper rolls served with lime and sweet chilli sauce. Oh my God, could fat-free food really taste that good? I had no idea. This is something I am going to make often. The lads gobbled them up and couldn't believe they were healthy. Recommended serving was three rolls each: I had one.

Having not cooked these things before, I was not sure about the timing and the second course took much longer to cook than I had anticipated so I served a salad as a mini course in itself. I'm sure there's a fancy word for it in dining vocab but it tasted great all the same. I had both regular and fat-free dressing but in a show of support the boys threw caution to the wind and decided to throw the fat-filled dressing away. I had friends and compatriots on my journey to health and well-being!

Of course it was easy to do that with the salad dressing but I didn't see them doing the same with the expensive Merlot I was refusing to drink. I had one glass and no, it wasn't an oil barrel sized glass, it was a small goblet and I savoured every single drop of that fruity elixir. Then I clung to my tankard of water the whole night, fearful of letting go and ending the night standing on my balcony, flashing my tits at every passing pedestrian—something I have been known to do (and I do apologise to the City of Orange. I had fallen off the wagon after six weeks of sobriety. Not a pretty sight!).

Next course was the potato and asparagus frittata and having eaten slowly over the evening, when the time came to have the main I was mostly full of salad, pork roll and water, so I ate nearly all of my reduced portion, relished the taste and went to bed absolutely guilt free, apart from the fact that I had eaten so late in the evening. I'm not sure whether that affects your metabolism, so that's another question for Crusher.

Anyway, my guests were drunk, happy and more than sated and went away shaking their heads that good low-fat food could taste so yummy. I was equally if not more surprised. I've promised myself I'm going to learn to cook one new dish a week.

2 August   End of Week 2—phew!

Today, Day 14 in the Alfalfa Zone, I walked my boy to kindy! It's a fifty-minute walk (half up a steep hill). It took me more time to actually decide to do the walk than it did to do the bloody thing. I paced around the house convincing myself that it was too cold, that I was too tired, that I had too much to do. I finally did it and I've got to tell you it was not a pleasant sight, my Mt Everest arse wobbling down the hill,

Pork rice paper rolls
360 g low-fat minced pork
1 teaspoon Vietnamese or Chinese spice
1 clove of garlic, crushed
1 teaspoon fresh ginger, grated
360 g Chinese cabbage, shredded
5 green onions, sliced

1 tablespoon soy sauce

4 tablespoons oyster sauce

bunch coriander leaves, chopped

12 rice paper sheets

DIPPING SAUCE:

100 ml sweet chilli sauce

5 tablespoons lime juice

1 tablespoon coriander leaves, coarsely chopped

Cook the pork with no oil in a fry pan with the spice, garlic and ginger until the pork is cooked. Add the cabbage, onions, soy sauce, oyster sauce, and coriander. Cook until the cabbage goes soft and kind of translucent.

Put a sheet of rice paper in a bowl of warm water until it goes soft and pliable, lift the sheet from the water and place it on the bench. Pat dry with a paper towel. Place 2 heaped tablespoons of the mixture in the centre, fold in the sides and roll up. This should make approximately 10 rolls.

Place the rolls in a single layer in a steamer set over a large saucepan of simmering water and steam for about 4–5 minutes. To make the dipping sauce, combine all the ingredients in a bowl and serve with the rolls.

Serves 3–4; contains 7g fat.

me puffing and panting, coughing up buckets of phlegm that had lain dormant in my lungs from the time I had the flu when I was six and a half. I'm surprised I didn't cough up the plastic Bambi I swallowed when I was five (and which, to my knowledge, is yet to pass through my system!).

I made a promise to myself that I will do some sort of exercise three days in a row in preparation for my big night out this weekend, so that's one down, only two more to go. I'm sure I'll have a really good excuse not to go tomorrow. I could have written the book on why not to exercise. I've spent most of my life procrastinating, why not another day of it?

Not quite 101 excuses to not exercise

1. Because I couldn't be bothered (I didn't say they'd be good excuses!).
2. I have to watch paint dry.
3. The simple activity of thinking burns up calories, so, thinking about *not* exercising is kind of like doing a mental workout and is bound to burn at least a few calories and every one off my bum counts!
4. I have to write a list of excuses for not exercising.
5. The circus comes to town next week and I want to save my energy for when I audition for the job as the fat lady.
6. Because I love the fact that all my underpants have signs on them declaring DANGER! WIDE LOAD!
7. I love going into McDonald's, ordering my oversized meal and being asked by some skinny twelve year old, 'Are you *sure* you want fries with that?'

Hmm, maybe I should just do them. I'll just check what's on TV, and then I'll get straight to it . . .

3 pm: Now, I don't want you to get too excited, but the undies I bought two weeks ago are hanging around my arse. They are loose! That's not to say my arse is no longer the size of a small African country, but every little bit counts. And I do believe I am walking a little taller. I have to admit I haven't done stairs in days and this week is going to have too much alcohol in it so I'm dreading the next weigh-in day, but today I am happy. Not only am I planning a HUGE night of alcohol consumption on Saturday night, but I also have this boy, or should I say *man*, I'm hoping to throw into the mix. So apart from looking forward to my big night out on the grog I'm also hoping to end the night with an invigorating session of bedroom aerobics. At least sex is considered exercise (and don't you dare tell me otherwise!).

Crusher told me not to drink too much and remembering her words—'AJ, your arse is so big because you drink too much'—can't help but instil in me some sense of diet-like sobriety. I hereby promise to try not to get totally legless.

It's not that I have a drinking problem, but let's just say if there's a nip in the air, I'll drink it. I'm a party girl, I always have been, always will be. I'll just have to find new ways of keeping up. And new ways of making ugly men attractive, 'cause everyone knows the magic of beer—the more you drink the better they look. The problem is, after staying sober while your friends drink their ten to fifteen beers, you suddenly realise that they are full of shit and not really very interesting after all. Then you begin to wonder if you sound like that when you are drunk . . . Oh dear, I think I need a drink.

3 August
How much do brain cells weigh?

Today is the day. National Get Trashed Day! I have had two hard weeks in the Alfalfa Zone and tonight I enter the 'Owthefugarya Zone' (loosely translated: the drink until you pass out or end up with somebody in your bed zone). I've been preparing for days. I had to negotiate this day with Crusher and, let me tell you, if Hannibal Lecter had been discussing what (and more importantly who) to have for dinner he would have gone very, very hungry. This was the deal.

Three days leading up to the event I had to do my normal sets of exercises *and* a forty-minute walk. I had to give up my chocolate cake treat in lieu of the calories I would be consuming through alcohol. I had to stick to my eating programme religiously and I was not to drink any alcohol the days before. On the day of the event I had to walk another forty minutes, drink lots of water and promise not to drink beer or wine and to stick to vodka and soda.

So I did all the preparation and now I'm all dressed up and ready to go out. Already my lace-up corset has to be tightened and I feel bloody good about myself. I think this eating plan is actually working!

Oh, and guess what? I don't know why, but since I've been

eating well, I have stopped chewing my fingernails. I'm such a chronic nail-biter, I'm lucky not to be tapping this keyboard with my nose. I don't know whether it's because I'm actually eating enough to satisfy myself, or because I'm getting vitamins and minerals I haven't had since Heinz baby foods were my staple diet, or whether it's just because I feel good, so I don't need to eat myself up with self-loathing.

Anyway, all dressed up and ready to paint the town red. I'm going out for cocktails first, then going to see this guy I've been stalking (lusting after) in a play and then I'm going to take him home and shag him until he either has a heart attack or begs to be let free. Or maybe I'll be the one who has the heart attack. I don't care as long as in the morning most of my body is in pain. You know, the kind of pain you get after you've been a naughty girl and even though you can't remember, it must have been good cause it hurts so much. Or is that just me?

I have a confession to make and Crusher is going to kill me. I have decided not to have dinner. Now, I know this is wrong, but let me just explain why. Normally on my nights out on the grog, I have to drain a wino of his blood before I even feel mildly tipsy. Tonight, though, I figure if I don't have dinner then I will get drunk more easily and won't have to drink as much, therefore I won't ingest as many calories and my rigid self-control will make me stop *before* I drink too much or get the munchies and end up at Harry's Café de Wheels pigging out on fifteen pies and a dozen sausage rolls before actually getting hungry and feasting on any lost sailors who may be wandering around Woolloomooloo.

Anyway, before I go, let me make a pledge not to get too plastered, to only drink vodka and soda, and not to answer the call of the midnight munchies. See you tomorrow!

7 August   Long Island legless

Okay, well I'm not sure where to start but let me say this. Not having had dinner may have been a little bit foolish. On the bright side, I did get very drunk very quickly. I also discovered that when ordering Long Island Iced Teas you can have cranberry juice instead of Coca Cola, which must save thousands of calories! And yes I know I promised to drink only vodka and soda but Long Island Iced Teas have vodka in them, so it's *kind of* the same thing. And cranberries are fruit, so it's kind of like a health drink, really. Anyway, I was embarrassingly drunk after the first drink, so of course I lost *all* resolve to be in any semblance of control.

The good thing was, I did not succumb to the midnight munchies. No freshly baked pies at 3 am, no chippies with my drinkies, no scrumptious five-day-old hot dog jammed between week-old buns—at least I don't remember eating any of those things, but then I don't really remember much past the second drink. Apart from a vague memory of balancing beers on my breasts for free drinks . . . but I'm sure that wasn't me. Just a girl who looked like me!

I do remember one thing vividly. Waking up in *someone else's* bed. Prince Alfred's, no less. That would be bed fifteen in E Block North. Of the Royal Prince Alfred Hospital. Oh, didn't I mention my severely broken leg? And the plate and seven pins they have just put in it? The only good thing is, I had to fast for two days before they operated on me so at least I'm likely to reach my goal weight this week.

And the stupid thing is, it all happened because I was trying to be sensible. (Stop laughing!) Being drunk (okay, mildly paralytic) and wanting to get home safely and in one piece I decided to catch a cab even though I was only a ten-minute walk from my house. Bad choice. Got home, went to pay the five dollar cab fare and realised I had no money. Knowing I had cash upstairs I told the cabby I'd be back in a couple of minutes. He made me leave my bag and mobile phone in the car while I ran upstairs to my apartment. 'No problem, be back in a sec,' I said.

Ran upstairs, got the money, tripped on my skirt, slid off the top step and tumbled head first the rest of the way down the stairs. All twenty of them. Actually twenty-two to be exact. I know 'cause I count them with my son every day of the week. Lying at the foot of the hallway stairs, I am one door and six feet away from the cabby. I am lying there in pain, unable to move, barely able to breathe (I am in a tight corset) and so drunk I don't know what to do. Then I hear the cab drive off and I am stranded. I call out for help but none of my neighbours hear me. By this stage I am in big trouble. Deep shit, some might say.

I somehow manage to unclip the corset (it took me about ten minutes and a lot of holding my breath), drag myself up the stairs, my breasts banging on each step, and spill inelegantly into my apartment. Then in my drunken wisdom, after raiding the freezer for something to put on my leg, I somehow managed to drag myself up another twenty stairs to my bedroom and thankfully I passed out.

I wake up in the morning surrounded by now-thawed peas, corn and cubed carrot spilling out of the partially opened packet and my leg is still very, very sore. I feel like death warmed up and I cannot walk. I can barely move but somehow I crawl downstairs to the phone, ring the friend who has my son and tell her I'm off to hospital, I might have broken my leg.

So here I am sitting in hospital, doped up to the eyeballs on morphine, and I feel positive and confident that this is not going to stop me from losing weight and getting healthy. And no, it's not the morphine talking, that has barely affected me at all. It has, however, made the three-headed tap-dancing leprechaun at the end of my bed rather annoying but the huge blue caterpillar said she would eat him if he caused any trouble so I'm sure it's not the drugs when I say I *am still committed to getting fit.*

So, where was I? Ah yes, the Alfalfa Zone. I'm serious, though. I'm sure that there are things I can do while lying down or even sitting in a wheelchair (which is where I'm going to be for the next two months). There must be incapacitated people who for various reasons (i.e. health) have to lose weight and/or improve their fitness.

So today is my first day of being able to eat and I am getting straight back on the horse. I asked a friend to bring in my low-fat bikkies, my muesli bars and fruit. I'm only drinking water, and I get my visitors to bring me ham and salad sandwiches for lunch and sushi for dinner. So I'm eating well, all things considered.

8 August   Where are the drugs?

Okay, I've been in hospital four days, I'm missing Kai dreadfully, and feeling stupid and guilty for being so irresponsible. Have cried for about one hundred hours and I can't believe I could do something so bloody dumb. I finally start to move my arse and I get myself completely incapacitated. I'm so lucky that Kai's dad is not working at the moment as he has come to the rescue and has moved into my house so he can look after Kai.

I rang the producer of the 'Lifestyle Show' and assured her this was not going to stop me from getting fit. It sounded like she didn't believe me and frankly, why should she?

As if I didn't feel bad enough, I have to tell you something. I asked my friend Phillippa to bring in my video camera and we did an update of my diary entries . . . last thing I filmed was me all dressed up and ready for my big night out, doing the corset up a little tighter, promising not to get too drunk. Next thing you see is me lying in a hospital bed, broken leg, looking like shit, saying God knows what on God knows how many drugs. But wait, there's more!

Phillippa then abducted me from my hospital bed and spirited me off to the cafeteria where I ate a chicken schnitzel and chips covered in gravy and, oh my God, it was a little slice of heaven. Now I'm not making excuses here, but I have a broken leg! This is where I should be eating chocolates and lollies and yummy cakes that people bring to me out of sympathy. The two boxes of chocolates I was given I presented to the nurses (that way when I want morphine,

I get morphine!). But there's only so much good in me. I'm also doing my stomach crunches lying here in bed. I do about fifty a day so it must be having some effect.

Zoë rang and told me an incredibly inspiring story. Heather Turland, who is Australia's number one female marathon runner, was due to compete in the Commonwealth Games when she was hit by a car in Rome and broke her leg. She got a fibreglass cast and trained in a pool and on an exercise bike. She had the cast removed, competed in the games and went on to win gold for Australia. Now, I'm no marathon runner, but I'm sure the same principles apply to me. If I eat well, and do some sort of exercise, then I will lose weight and get fit despite being in a wheelchair. Now, where's the nurse who dishes out the drugs?

11 August Kai's human jungle gym

I'm finally home. Have missed a few sessions with Nutcase—being hospitalised does that to you, I suppose. I'm now in Week 4 of the Alfalfa Zone and this week has been the strangest yet. I'm going mad just lying around but I am eating well. The good thing about being a prisoner in your own home is that there is absolutely no temptation. When I was able bodied, every time I ventured up the street I would be tempted to buy junk food. I live in the heart of Newtown, in Sydney's inner west district, with fifty-six Thai restaurants, forty kebab joints and too many takeaway places offering the best hamburgers in town. Even buying petrol is an exercise in strength and willpower. Okay, it's not the petrol that is the problem, it's the lolly counter. It's bad enough being a parent of a two-year-old and dealing with the 'I want a Caramello Koala and I want it now' tantrums without being addicted to junk food yourself. I would always buy myself a chocolate, sometimes three or four, sometimes even a huge 250-gram block of Fruit 'n' Nut. Now, being stuck at home, I can only eat what's here.

The other good thing is that I haven't had a drink since That Night and am not too keen to go back to it. One broken leg is enough for a lifetime. I just hope Crusher comes soon as I have to do something other than the tragic leg-lifts I'm currently doing. I am pushing myself around in the wheelchair and have discovered I have absolutely no upper body strength! Either that or I am just too heavy to lift. Even Kai's dad, who is a big man, has trouble lifting me up from the lounge room floor (which has become my new bed). I've got to be honest, I have never been so humiliated in my entire life. I'm so fat I can't even drag my sorry arse up my own stairs to have a shower or sleep in my comfy bed. It's even more incentive to actually make this thing happen!

Crusher is going to bring hand weights so I can get strong enough to lift my jumbo-sized bum out of the wheelchair.

Kai loves the fact that I am home and confined to the lounge room as I have become his little human jungle gym.

12 August   Prison

Oh my God, I have the worst craving for Pizza Hut. I am pacing the house, well, wheeling up and down the hallway, fingers on the phone ready to dial that sweet little number to fat heaven. I keep thinking how well I've done and reason with myself that I can't just walk it off. I'm going to try to reason with myself . . .

Why I should get BBQ meat lovers pizza

- Because I want to.
- Pizza makes the world go around.
- Because I deserve it.
- Pizza tastes great.
- Because the craving won't go away and I'm beginning to obsess.
- Pizza doesn't tell you that if you lost some weight he'd go out with you.
- Pizza never ever breaks up with you.
- Pizza never leaves the toilet seat up.
- Because the box is made of cardboard, so I'm making sure a forest has not been culled in vain.
- I want pizza!

Why I shouldn't get BBQ meat lovers pizza

- Because it's full of fat and I will hate myself for eating it.
- Because I deserve to be happy and healthy and that kind of food will do neither for me.
- Because I have no way of walking it off.
- Because when it comes time to buy myself a bikini I don't want a Pizza Hut thigh hanging around my ankles.
- Because I have done so well, why spoil it now?
- Because if I have pizza I'll never be able to go out with

anyone better than Gary who is probably still dating girls
from country high schools and telling them they're just
too fat.

Okay, okay, I've managed to convince myself not to have IT
for dinner. I also rang Crusher and told her I was obsessing. I
only got her answering machine but it felt better to admit it
to someone who I know would never eat that kind of food.

13 August   Pizza pizza pizza

8 am: Oh dear, have woken up thinking about pizza. I can't
get it out of my pizza, I mean my head. I don't know what to
pizza, I mean do. No amount of pizza, sorry, sensible
thinking can convince me to not order it. I desperately need
to see pizza, um, Dr Nutcase about it but my next appointment isn't until the end of the pizza, oops, week. Pizza Pizza
Pizza Pizza aaah!

1 pm: Okay, the universe is conspiring to get me healthy. I
crumbled at lunchtime and rang Pizza Hut to order the
whole works—pizza, deep-fried chicken wings with ranch
style dressing, garlic bread *and* a Sara Lee chocolate cheesecake, but the computers were down and they couldn't home
deliver. I tried to convince them I was an eighty-year-old
pensioner who had fallen down and couldn't get up and had
eaten nothing but kitty litter and the tyres from my wheelchair for the last three weeks, and that Pizza Hut were my
only hope but they just said ring back in an hour, by which

time I had eaten my ham and salad sandwich and my 40-calorie cup-a-soup and I no longer wanted their beautiful, greasy, scrumptious, fat-filled meat lovers pizza. So thank you, universe, you saved my now not so fat arse!

8 pm: It was bound to happen sooner or later, and you don't have to point out it was sooner rather than later, thanks. I did it. I fell off the wagon. I just couldn't stand it any longer. I had to get it out of my system and now I have to confess my sin. I did the home delivery thing and had four huge slices of BBQ meat lovers pizza, with three deep-fried devil wings with ranch style sauce and garlic bread. I did say no to the cheesecake. You have to save calories where you can! Oh, and don't think it didn't taste great! I savoured every single greasy mouthful. I even went so far as to cover my pizza in the ranch style sauce which is normally used for the chicken wings, but us people with eating disorders do not stuff around and I made that meal so good it could have been my last and I would have died a very happy person.

14 August
Definitely heavier than yesterday

Have woken up feeling sooooo guilty. But I just have to get back on the horse. Problem is, I think I ate that too. Have had my cereal for breakfast and today I am not going to let one mouthful go astray. Have realised I have no way of exercising the excess calories off and I am now totally dreading weigh-in day. Rang Crusher and confessed my sins. She said I did well ignoring it for a day and asked, 'Did you really feel obsessed?' I said yes and she replied, 'Well, then, you did the right thing. You would normally have the leftovers for lunch, right?' I admitted I would normally have the leftovers for breakfast. She said 'Well, you're not doing that, are you?' I said no and she said, 'Well, then, you've changed another bad habit, haven't you? Congratulations!'

The worst moment was when she said, 'What, so you had two pieces of pizza, right?' I mumbled that I'd actually had four pieces and then there was nothing but silence down the other end of the phone. Planes flew overhead. Frogs croaked. Bees buzzed. More silence. Then she very casually said that I had consumed over 80 grams of fat and that I didn't actually have any way of walking it off and to try not to do it again. I could tell she was disappointed. So was I.

Thought it was strange that Crusher was so good about it. Felt even more guilty for her not having yelled at me. Rang Zoë to tell her. Maybe I could get her to tell me off. She agreed that I needed to satisfy my craving but she also gave me some great advice. (Zoë has also struggled with an eating disorder and lost 20 kilos through changing her eating habits and becoming a marathon runner.) She said to create a list of all the things I could do *instead* of breaking the diet—sorry, leaving the Alfalfa Zone. That way, if I feel like a chocolate bar or a cake or a beer, I just go to the list and find something I could do that would not only take my mind off the craving but would make me feel better.

So this is my list.

Things to do when I get hungry for food I don't need

1. Read a book
2. Go for a walk
3. Stick photos in albums
4. Clean out a drawer
5. Go window shopping
6. Write a letter to a friend
7. Update Kai's baby book
8. Surf the net
9. Brush and condition my hair
10. Ring someone I haven't spoken to in ages
11. Write a poem
12. Do my exercises
13. Paint
14. Practise my poetry
15. Have a bubble bath
16. Give myself a mud mask
17. Write a comedy skit
18. File and paint my nails
19. Get a massage
20. Write a story for Kai
21. Sort out paperwork
22. Write some of my book
23. Write a song
24. Go to an art gallery
25. Go for a swim
26. Eat a piece of fruit
27. Sort out CD rack
28. Give myself a foot spa

29. Paint
30. Have sex

So there it is. I'll be interested to see how it works next time the craving hits. Oh yes, there will be a next time, I'm sure.

16 August   Slap that thigh

Crusher comes tomorrow. That will be the end of the fifth week in the Alfalfa Zone. One whole month. I'm getting a little paranoid. The battered sav, hot chips, chicken schnitzel, gravy, chicken wings and pizza have come back to haunt me. God, did I really have that much junk? Not to mention the alcohol that got me the broken leg! Although in the past that could easily have been just one day's food, so there has been progress!

I'm madly doing tummy tucks and leg-lifts and I now realise it is too late for redemption. The fat has already gone to my legs and there will be nothing for me to do but slap the thigh and ride the wave in.

17 August   Praying Mantras

10 am: Supposed to go to Nutcase today but she told me to stay home because it is too hard for me to get there with my leg all smashed to pieces. Phew! It's not that I'm avoiding her or anything, but I don't really want to go. Afraid of how depressed it's going to make me dredging up all the horrible things from my past.

Anyway, this is it! The moment of truth. The last month has been amazing for me. I have drastically altered my eating habits, I feel more healthy than I have in years, my skin is glowing and almost pimple free, and I no longer chew my fingernails because they have stopped splitting and are now growing strong and healthy.

In the past month these are the changes I have made

- I now eat three meals and three snacks per day.
- I no longer eat butter or margarine.
- I don't drink cordial or fruit juice.
- I only drink diet cordial and, yes, my taste buds are adjusting.
- I drink 1–2 litres of water each day.
- When I snack I have low-fat crackers, muesli bars or fruit.
- I have severely cut down my drinking of alcohol.
- I choose foods with little or no fat (well, mostly . . .)
- I think about exercising more than I do.
- I exercise more than I did.

These are the improvements I want to make

- Learn to cook low-fat recipes.
- Not think about pizza and hot chips with battered savs.
- Eat more fruit.
- Exercise more.
- Cut out alcohol completely.
- Not think about pizza and hot chips with battered savs.
- Discover new low-fat snacks.
- Find new and tasty ways to cook veggies.

- Not crumble at the first sign of a craving but find effective ways of resisting the temptation.
- Not snack as much in between meals.
- And not think about pizza and hot chips with battered savs.

The hardest time for me is when I'm cooking Kai's dinner. I nibble on what I'm cooking him, I open and close the fridge. I have a couple of biscuits, then see the cheese and have a piece of that, then a few lollies, until I've had my total snack allowance for the week before I've even had my dinner.

I still crave chocolate desperately. Why can't I have two pieces of white bread, smothered in real butter, with fruit and nut chocolate and salt and vinegar chips? Why not? Because my arse is inches away from being declared an independent nation and I do not want some explorer sticking a flag up it declaring his intention to colonise (excuse the pun).

I'm getting very bored with the same old lunch and dinners as I generally have a ham and salad sandwich and Lean Cuisines. Next month I want to learn some low-fat recipes, interesting snacks and different lunch options. I am meeting my nutritionist soon so she'll be able to point me in the right direction, I'm sure.

Crusher is due here any minute so I'll talk to you after I find out how much (if any) lard I might have lost from my humungous bum in the last few weeks.

3 pm: Before I tell you the news, I have to let you know that we had to slightly guestimate my weight because I have a huge plaster cast on my leg. The physiotherapist at the hospital said it weighs around three kilos. When I started in the Alfalfa Zone I was 109 kilograms. Today (with the plaster leg) I weighed in at 106. So take off the weight of the plaster and I now weigh 103, which means I have lost six kilos in one month. Yeah!

Crusher has given me a range of upper body exercises to do every day while laid up in bed, most of them using a thin piece of rubber tubing. It takes about forty minutes to get through them all and feels like working on a home gym without it taking up all the space in my house. Of course I look like a wounded bull elephant that needs to be put out of its misery but I reason to myself that, no matter how bad I look, if I just keep doing them, then one day (although from here it seems unlikely) I might not look quite so fat.

Crusher once again quite clearly explained to me that because I have no way of atoning for my food sins then I must stay focused and not eat food filled with fat (pizza!). Because we burn calories in our normal activities through-out the day and because I am doing nothing but lying on my back all day, then I am expending very little energy, thus burning very few calories. So no more pizza! (Of course, that doesn't mean no *less* pizza. I'm sure one a month would be okay . . . wouldn't it?)

Crusher also stressed it was important for me to continue the reward system. So once a week I give myself a food reward. Maybe a piece of cake or some chocolate. Something that will make me feel like I'm not going to miss out on life's little luxuries forever.

She read over my food diary and I am amazed to find I am still not eating enough. On top of what I am already eating she reminded me that she wants me to have *at least* four pieces of fruit a day (something she told me three weeks ago!). I have to add one low-fat yoghurt a day as well. It's quite strange because I am already eating more regularly than I have ever eaten. It was not uncommon for me to miss breakfast and lunch and then grab a hamburger at three or four in the afternoon. This is one major factor in my having put on so much weight. My metabolism has learnt to store food for later, thus turning most of what I eat to fat. So if I get my metabolism firing and keep adding fuel, it will have no need to store fat and as I burn kilojoules, it will burn my body fat away. All I have to do now is get moving.

We had trouble doing my measurements because I wasn't wearing the same clothes as my first weigh-in. I was wearing thicker trousers than I had last time, which meant my thighs didn't read as having become smaller, which was disappointing. Crusher said it was important to wear the same clothes at each weigh-in to avoid unnecessary disappointments like that. I did lose another two centimetres off my boobs, though. They're still huge, but let's just say Anna Nicole Smith no longer has any competition in the wet t-shirt stakes, at least not from me.

I definitely feel thinner but I do have moments of paranoia where I think I couldn't possibly be losing weight eating this much food. Crusher said, 'AJ, you can't change your eating habits the way you have and not lose weight!' So that has become one of six mantras I say every day.

My Mantras

- The reason your arse is so big is because you drink too much.
- You have no way of walking off that kind of food (pizza).
- You can't change your eating habits the way you have without losing weight.
- One day at a time.
- Beer is not my life.
- Battered savs are not God's gift to me.

Speaking of eating disorders (was I?), I am now entering the zone where in the past I would start cutting out meals. I just have to stick to the regime and talk about it with Dr Nutcase because it is definitely something I will have to address.

19 August   Too fat for crutches!

Well, if there was ever reason enough to lose weight then this is it. I got my new cast and was hoping I'd be able to get some crutches and actually get moving. Well, I got the crutches but I am too heavy to hold my own body up. What embarrassment! That means I am confined to a wheelchair for at least another month. Oh my God. How could I have let myself go like this?

20 August   Dancing on table tops

So far this week I've stuck to the eating plan, I've done my exercises every day, except the horrible tummy arch ones which I wimped out on first go and haven't gone back to since and, yes, I know I'm not supposed to shirk any of them but I'm not perfect and I don't want to go to extremes. I do have a broken leg, you know!

I was so good yesterday. I was absolutely starving around three o'clock so I snacked on three jelly snakes and two popped rice crackers (not the little hors d'oeuvre size but the big chunky round ones) with Promite. It filled me up enough to get me through to dinner time but more importantly I felt really good about myself for having made a relatively healthy choice. Oh yes, I can hear all the vegetarians saying, 'Oh, a celery stick would have been better for you, or maybe you should have had a fruit salad!' but to be honest I'd had enough fruit and I really felt like having chocolate bars, hot chips and fifteen beers until I was naked and dancing on the table top to the karaoke version of 'American Pie'... well, maybe not. I have gone cold turkey on all junk food and apart from a few slips have drastically changed what I eat and sometimes enough is enough.

I think the difference is that when dieting in the past, I would falter and have some junk, then I'd get disheartened and just give up altogether. Alternatively, I'd eat the junk and then starve myself or take laxatives. Now, I pick myself up, dust the cake crumbs from my mouth and just keep going. I try not to feel guilty (notice the *try*). I move on and stop obsessing about what I ate yesterday and concentrate on what I'm eating today.

Having Dr Nutcase and Crusher helps keep me honest. The food diary, apart from encouraging me to make healthy choices, definitely stops me from starving myself because I don't want to be caught out doing something as silly as not eating. Knowing Crusher has also struggled with an eating disorder makes me feel like it *is* possible to lose weight slowly and turn my life around, finding a way to enjoy food, eat well, and live life to the fullest. I'm a long way off, but on good days I can see it in my future . . . oh God, you can tell I'm on drugs! Even if they are just painkillers.

21 August   Oh God, not again!

Had the craving yesterday and I still have it today. Hot chips. Hot chips. Hot chips. This is what happened with the pizza and I am determined to do something different about it. I know! I'll go to the list.

I washed my hair.

I still want chips. Go back to the list of things to do when craving food.

I have now, despite being in a wheelchair, cleaned every corner of my house. Have gone through every bit of paperwork, filed things, made phone calls, written a letter to a friend and am still thinking about chips. Maybe I need another list.

Alternative list of things to do when craving crap food

1. Poke eyes out with a blunt stick.
2. Go to bathroom, remove undies, clench buttocks tightly. Inspect. If it doesn't look like cottage cheese then eat

whatever you want. Otherwise refer back to List One and don't eat the chips.

3. Remove all clothing, stand in bright sunlight. Imagine having sex in this state. Put the chips down and run as far away as possible.

4. Get on the Internet, make a booking for a nudist colony. Refer back to List One.

5. Go swimwear shopping anywhere that provides fluorescent lighting. Take anti-depressants in copious quantities.

6. Using a mirror, assume favourite sexual position and evaluate objectively. Never crave hot chips again.

7. Place one $8.95 plate of fried chicken in front of you. Call liposuction clinic on quote to get $8.95 plate of chicken sucked *out* of your arse. Realise it is more than you owe on your car. Refer to List One.

No, that list didn't do any good either. It's a good thing I've got a broken leg because I'd have been to the chip shop and back by now. Maybe I'll call this the Broken Leg Diet. Break both your legs and your arms, then you'll have to be spoonfed. Better still, break all your bones and eat through a tube!

Not able to rid myself of the craving for potato, I got on the Internet and found a recipe for fat-free wedges. I made them, gave a lot of them to Kai and had a few with my Lean Cuisine and surprisingly they tasted great! I'm sure the chip craving will come back but for now I'm feeling good having made the healthy choice.

22 August   Crusher harassing AJ

I am going well. I'm sticking to the good food, have done most of my exercises every day (yes, I did say most!) and am feeling pretty focused. Crusher, sensing my lack of interest in doing my exercises, has taken to ringing me every day, saying she will ring back in forty minutes and doesn't want to hear I haven't done the work.

I've been a little bored with the food and have been looking for some interesting snacks. Have found crispbread with tuna to be very satisfying, especially with a dash of fat-free mayo. A small tin of baked beans is a good pick-me-up and I've just discovered Parker's sun dried tomato and basil pretzels. They are 98 per cent fat free and bloody delicious. I ate the whole pack, only 164 calories, and loved every one of them.

Just when I thought I'd managed to get through the chip craving, my friend Juzzy turned up on my doorstep with three pieces of crispy, succulent, fatty fried chicken and a big box of chips smothered in chicken salt. My mouth is drooling as I type this. I sat next to her watching the chicken travel from the box into her mouth. I stared longingly as she made her way through the entire three pieces of chicken. She was three-quarters of the way through the chips when I crumbled.

I couldn't resist. It was not as if I'd gone out and actually paid for the chips myself. But there they were, glistening brightly in the box, right at the end of my fingertips. Before I knew it I'd had six and I was compelled to write them in my diary. At least I didn't eat the chicken! Especially since fried chicken is my weakness (and pizza isn't?). Oh, okay, anything with fat in it is my weakness—in my worst moments I have been known to buy an eight-piece pack from KFC and simply eat the skin off all eight pieces, then follow it with a chicken fillet burger with bacon and cheese, large fries, corn and a chocolate mousse. So compare that to six measly little chippies and I have conquered Goliath. Okay, well maybe not conquered, but definitely winded him a good bit.

23 August
Right off the Richter scale

Today Nutcase asked me more questions about my child-hood, my extended/adopted family, past relationships with all the losers I have let into my life—sorry, I mean boyfriends I have had—my birth mother's death, the sexual abuse at the hands of my schoolteacher, and of course a million questions about when I was anorexic.

She didn't give me any tips or hints or say anything really, just listened and nodded and made notes. I think she is just getting to know me and my history, getting names and dates right and getting a picture of me in her head. I'm sure she's got some kind of sliding scale where she looks up what has happened to you and how mad you are because of it and I'm sure I would send it right off the Richter scale—white-coated, thumb-sucking future here I come. Actually, it's pretty easy. Not as bad as I thought it would be.

Told her about the cravings and the pizza episode. She

explained that I can't expect to make all the changes overnight and if I used to eat three pizzas a week and I've now only had one in a month then I have done a good job. She said I have years and years of bad eating habits to change and it will take years and years to do that. She said I need to congratulate myself for doing such a good job and to concentrate on the positives. She also said I could just remind myself that I don't do that anymore. I don't need junk food. I don't need to comfort eat. I treat my body with respect and love and the pizza will not do anything for me other than make me unhappy.

She said Zoë's list idea was a good one and to try it out next time. She told me to keep sticking to the food diary and the eating plan and to remember that if I take one day at a time, then everything will be okay.

1 September   Are you skinny?

Crusher dropped in for a quick surprise visit and checked my food diary. She saw the chips on the list and had a complete freak-out. When I explained to her it wasn't me who had bought them but my friend Juzzy, she went even more ballistic. She told me to call Juzzy immediately. I did and Crusher grabbed the phone from my hands. She said, 'Hi, Juzzy. It's Crusher here. Are you skinny? Yes, I thought you might be. And are you AJ's friend? Yes? Well, what the hell are you doing bringing food like that to her house? Next time you come bring a salad or stay at home. AJ does not need friends like you.'

Open mouthed I marvelled at Crusher's ability to . . . crush. This girl's good.

Tomorrow, I meet my nutritionist. I'll call her Beansprout as I'm sure all she eats are lentils, beansprouts and prune juice—all totally organic, of course!

2 September
Beansprout's big adventure

Beansprout met me and the film crew at the supermarket. I should have been in a wheelchair but I managed to hobble around on crutches so it was easier to film. Laid up and unable to do any work I am so broke I jumped at the chance to do a day's filming, even though the last thing I need to do is drag myself up and down the horrific stairs to my apartment. But I need the money and the show must go on! Ah, the consummate professional!

Poor Beansprout nearly fainted when, as we passed the deli section, I admitted my usual weekly shopping list consisted of eight rashers of bacon, ten twiggy sticks, eight cocktail frankfurters, ham, bacon bits, salami, Jarlsberg cheese and a huge wedge of King Island cheddar. She seemed nauseous when I admitted that by the time I'd wobble my way to the checkout the twiggy sticks, salami and frankfurters would be nothing but empty packets. I blamed the disappearance of the food on my two-year-old toddler—even when I *didn't* have a kid. I'd just mumble something lame like, 'Oh, he's just gone to get me something from the bottle shop . . .'

How to shop

- Shop with a written list in mind. Don't shop when you are hungry. Take a bottle of water and when you *are* tempted to buy things off the list, drink that and keep walking past those counters. At all costs avoid the lolly aisle or whichever aisles house your food weaknesses. Try shopping on the Internet (less temptation).

- Try not to run out of food at home. That's when you're tempted to go to the corner shop and buy junk food or order takeaway.

- If you are entering the premenstrual zone then be prepared. Have the cupboard/fridge stocked with diet chocky mousse, jelly snakes and potatoes so you can make fat-free wedges (see p. 265). Have a relatively healthy PMT pig-out. Eat lots of fruit during this time as it will reduce the chances of acne and will make you less likely to binge.

- Have a treat every now and then. Once a week have a small piece of chocky. And don't buy a big bar and think you'll ration it out. Go to the shop and buy a chocolate frog or a milky bar— nice and small and nothing left over to binge on.

The object of getting together was to debunk some preconceived ideas of dieting, look at making healthy choices for snacks and to give me a couple of healthy low-fat meals that are quick and easy to cook. She said that my producer had told her how much pre-packaged food there had been in my cupboards and freezer and she told me to remember that fresh food is best.

First stop was the fruit and veggie section and she reiterated what Crusher had said. I should aim at eating three to four pieces of fruit every day and *at least* one meal with vegetables or salad. (And no, dating a vegetarian who loves having his ears nibbled does not qualify as eating vegetarian.)

Caesar salads are out. Bacon, anchovies, eggs, Parmesan, the dressing and quite often the croutons are full of fat! Ricotta cheese is a great low-fat cheese and is excellent to cook with (see recipe for spinach pie on p. 120). Normal cheddar has around 36 grams of fat per 110 grams compared to ricotta's 8 grams, so it's definitely the one I need to be eating.

When she recommended almonds as a snack I asked if they were full of fat. Beansprout explained not all fats were bad and that if you choose your fats and have them in the right amounts they can help you feel full for longer by keeping the blood sugar levels nice and constant, so you don't get those evil afternoon hunger pains. She said don't get too paranoid about fat, but learn to read the labels on food and make sure you make an informed choice about how much fat you are consuming.

Cooking oil sprays are a better alternative to cook with than traditional vegetable oil. You use a lot less with a light spray on the pan as opposed to frying food a centimetre deep in oil. Beansprout also reiterated what Crusher had told me before: that extra light olive oil does not mean extra light in calories. It means extra light in colour and flavour!

Beansprout recommended beans for breakfast as a great way to get through the day without getting the three o'clock urge to binge. Proteins (eggs, beans or sardines) metabolise more slowly and therefore create a more stable building block for the day. And when you want to snack on something sweet (like lollies), she said, always eat something more substantial first, like tuna on crackers or a piece of fruit, but never just have the sugar as it will not ease the hunger. Save it for a treat *after* you've eaten and you won't have the temptation to keep eating until the next meal time, or be tempted to eat a whole packet of sweets.

She recommended some great low-fat snacks such as pretzels, licorice, almonds, hummus on rice thins and tinned peaches. I love all of these things and it's good to know that I can vary my food intake as long as I have reasonable quantities.

Beansprout said it was important to make life choices rather than temporary weight loss choices. So, eating a little bit of hummus on a cracker is not going to make me fat and it will ensure I have enough variety in my diet to not get bored and want to eat the whole tub with a full slab of Turkish bread and butter—which I have been known to do. The life choice is to make smart decisions and to eat healthy, tasty food in moderation.

She came back to my house and cooked two fantastic recipes, both of which I have included. One is Spinach and Ricotta Pie (see page 120) and the other Tuna Surprise. You

---

Beansprout's Tuna Surprise

200 g brown rice, cooked

1 onion, chopped

2 tablespoons plain flour

125 ml skimmed milk

400 g tuna in springwater

100 g frozen peas

100 g sweetcorn

100 g mushrooms, sliced

Preheat the oven to 200 degrees. Using cooking spray, brown the onion in a frying pan. Add the flour and stir for 1–2 minutes, then add the milk and stir continuously until the mixture thickens (3–4 minutes). In a casserole dish mix the onion mixture with the remaining ingredients and cook in the oven for 20 minutes. Serve with rice.

Serves 3; contains 3g fat.

---

may ask why I called it Tuna Surprise. It's because for someone who hates vegetables, I thought it tasted great. It looked a little boring, but believe me, it really is tasty!

Beansprout had a quick look in my cupboards and recommended I choose fruit over muesli bars and save them as a treat or put them in my handbag for when I get caught out somewhere in between meals. She also suggested I use a low-fat milk with added calcium, not only because I have a broken leg but to avoid osteoporosis in later years. She left me eating my yummy red licorice strips and suddenly I felt very alone.

5 September   Bored bored bored!

It's nearly Week 8 and I am in a slump. Have been crying all afternoon and I can't seem to stop. I'm sick of eating healthy food, I'm sick of exercising, I'm sick of not drinking beer, I'm sick of counting calories, I'm sick of thinking about whether or not something has fat in it and how many grams, I'm sick of rice crackers, lettuce and carrot, I wish vegetables didn't exist and I wish I worked in a fish and chip shop where I could eat all the battered savs my body could take. I just want to eat whatever I want, whenever I want and I don't want to obsess about whether my thighs are in fact thinner than they were a month ago. I want chippies and I want to get drunk and I want to eat like a normal person. I don't want to think about everything that goes into my mouth. I want to go for a walk or a swim. I'm sick of being confined to bed, I'm sick of doing the same boring exercises and staring at the same boring spot on the wall.

I spent a teary hour on the phone to Crusher (actually I was bawling my eyes out while Kai's dad filmed it for the TV show—why did I ever agree to this?!) telling her I couldn't see my way out. I can't imagine doing this for the rest of my life. I'm obsessing about everything that passes through my lips and I can't cope! I want to know if I will ever eat like a normal person—and I don't even know what a normal person eats, so even that is a dilemma!

Apparently this is a natural slump, and my frustration is increased because I also have the broken leg. She mentioned that if I was able bodied I could walk my frustration off, get the heart pumping, and enjoy the adrenaline rush from an accelerated heart rate. But all I can do are my exercises lying in bed or staring at the same boring wall or the same boring door.

I mentioned that I felt like I was being controlled. Crusher said, 'AJ, it doesn't matter what you eat, *you* are in control. It's *you* who chooses to eat well and look after yourself or *you* who makes the choice to eat food that is of absolutely no benefit to you, but *you are in control.*' I think I will add that to my list of mantras: 'I am in control!' (Yeah, in control of a ten tonne ice-cream truck heading straight for a one hundred foot cliff that plunges into a raging volcano! Not that I'm being negative at all!)

Control is an important issue in my life and one I intend to discuss with Dr Nutcase. Crusher tried to reiterate that it is time *I* took control of my body and that I deserve to have my body as healthy as it could possibly be. She said that I would not be watching what I eat forever. It is only until I get down to my goal weight, by which time my metabolism will be burning at such a high rate I will be able to eat normally (normal meaning I could have the occasional piece of pizza etc, not my previous 'normal' eating patterns). By that time I will simply have to maintain my weight rather than work so hard to lose it.

I have also realised that when I was a child, food was not fun or very enjoyable at all. I spent so many nights sitting at the dinner table with my over-boiled vegetables, supposedly good food (i.e. vegetables) feels like a punishment to me. I need to reprogramme my brain into feeling as if I am rewarding myself when I eat well. I'm hoping that will come with better fitness and an ability to fit into something other than a size 26.

I also explained that it has finally hit me that this *is* forever. This is not a diet I start and stop and that freaks me out because I don't quite know how to make those changes. I am addicted to eating crap food. It's all I've ever done since I left home. I don't know how to live any other way. And I know that this time it is forever. There is no way on God's earth that I am going to fail at this, particularly with it being filmed. I can just see it now, a picture of my ginormous bum wobbling down the street with a voiceover: '. . . and AJ still struggles with her battle of the bulge—a bout she may never win!' Euh! It's not just because of that, though. If I fail this time, then I will never ever do this. I can't keep living my life this way. It has to change.

Crusher said to think of it not as a loss but as a lifestyle change—a positive one. I am learning how to live my life healthily. She said that I need to believe that I am beautiful on the inside and the outside and I need to remember that I am not punishing myself, I am getting myself healthy, which is the way I deserve to be. We did the pledge again, which basically said I commit to having the best body I could possibly have, that I deserve to be healthy, I deserve to feel good and enjoy life, I deserve to eat well and I am a wonderfully talented, empowered woman who can do anything I set my mind to. Thank God I didn't have to sign in blood because I didn't really feel like I meant it.

I got off the phone and did my exercises and I did feel good about that. Crusher also said that after I see Dr Nutcase on Friday, I can eat whatever I want. It's funny, though. Now that I've slept on it, the thought of having hot chip sandwiches doesn't really fill me with the excitement I thought it would. Maybe I should do it anyway and get it out of my system.

I do feel recommitted to my cause. As Crusher says, don't think of it as eight months of sacrifice, think of it as a few weeks of making healthy choices. It's only three weeks until the cast comes off, then I'll be able to walk off my frustration, so until then I'll just stare at that same spot on the ceiling as I do my sit-ups and think myself thin!

7 September
Reward and punishment

8 am: Woke up feeling a little lost. Being a robot and just sticking to the plan. Crusher rang and made me promise to do my exercises. I did them. She told me to eat—I did. Today is Treat Day. Having looked forward to this day all week, I feel a little strange not actually being excited by the prospect of eating my treat. I don't really feel as if it will make me feel any better and have realised it will probably only make me feel guilty. Am really glad I am seeing Dr Nutcase today. I feel as if we're just about to get onto the good (hard/juicy) stuff.

2 pm: The first thing she said was, 'How are you?'

After I had picked myself up off the floor, wiped up the two-foot puddle of tears and reassured the patients in the waiting room that I hadn't gone completely mad, I eventually started to open up. I described how each day this week had been a struggle. I admitted to fluctuating between wanting to starve myself, wanting to quit, wanting to starve myself, wanting to continue eating and exercising, wanting to starve myself, wanting to binge eat anything I could get my hands on, including my furniture, and even wondering what Kai would taste like double deep fried and covered in BBQ sauce.

I also explained that I had finally realised that I have been abused or totally abused myself all my life. I have done it with bad food, too much food, not enough food, drugs, alcohol, lack of exercise, too much exercise, vomiting, starvation, laxatives, diet pills. I am thirty-two years of age and I have spent most of my life abusing myself. Worst of all, I can't see that there will ever be any other way. I don't know the way out of this.

She didn't look too frightened, apart from the stun gun she placed in her lap and the little red button on the wall she pressed repeatedly, but she did say I was reacting exactly as expected. Because food was either forbidden or seen as a punishment throughout my entire childhood, with biscuits and cakes locked away in the cupboard which I was not allowed to open without asking permission, I have developed patterns of either punishing or rewarding myself with food. Having done that all my life, it is not something I can change overnight. The good thing was, she said I am young enough to change my life habits and simply facing them is the hardest step to take.

She reminded me that these are early days and if I keep eating well and regularly, the way Crusher has told me to, then eventually it *will* become a habit for me. Habits are hard to break but easier to create. Eventually it will happen but I have to let go and trust and keep rewarding myself for the small victories I achieve rather than dwelling on the final outcome.

I mentioned that the thought of rewarding myself with junk food doesn't make me feel that good and she recommended I find some other reward system, like having my hair done, or getting a massage or facial. She also said that if I change my mind and decide to have the food reward, then to try to remember the feeling I had when I realised that the food will not make me any happier than I already am, then not to worry about it and to simply do it and get on with eating well. She also said that because I have used food to handle stress, it is natural, especially with a broken leg, to want to revert back to the only habits I know and instead of dwelling on the guilt, I need to give myself a break and applaud myself for doing such a good job. I have to dwell on the positive side of what I am doing rather than the moments of 'weakness'—or, in her words, 'learned habits'—which in time will not be a controlling factor of my life.

She taught me a technique for dealing with the moments of weakness, be they wanting to binge or starve. She described how sometimes when we are walking down the street we think we hear someone calling our name. Without even thinking, we automatically turn, realise it wasn't us being addressed, and then we continue on as we had been. Well, it's exactly the same with learned eating habits. There I am, moving along really well, exercising, eating good food at all the right times, when suddenly I am compelled to either eat something unhealthy or simply not eat at all. At that time I need to take a moment out, become quite still and recognise it as a learned behaviour and one that is not correct, healthy or good for me. Then I need to remind myself that I deserve better, and that I no longer behave that way, and then simply keep moving forward. If it persists, then she suggested I have a mantra and do a meditation on it, visualising something that relaxes me or focuses me. I could positively see myself in the future, happy and healthy, or I could distract myself by visualising a cloud or stars, or I could repeat a phrase like 'I don't do that any more' or 'I deserve better than that'.

She simplified the technique by using the words Recognise, Challenge and Distract. Recognise the learned response, challenge it with a new mantra and distract it with a meditation or visualisation. I have decided to say: 'I don't need to do that any more, I deserve to be as healthy as I could possibly be, I deserve better.' I will visualise myself in a healthy body. She also suggested I write them out and stick them on the walls, cupboards and fridge, which I am definitely going to do.

She also said that without continuing my therapy and dealing with things as they come up, that alone would not work long term, but she stressed it's important to work slowly and effectively and to take each week as it comes. She said she knew I could do it and it's only a matter of time before it starts to work. The more you say it, the more you believe it. Retrain your brain. Oh my god, that sounds *so* Anthony Robbins.

Straight after therapy I went to the chip shop and had my 'treat'—a battered sav and chips. I revelled in every mouthful and realised it had been a while since I had done anything like that, so, as instructed by Nutcase, I applauded my changed eating habits, including the cutting out of alcohol, then simply got on with the job of changing my life. I am just about to have a snack and do my exercises and feel as if I am able to conquer the next few weeks. It's time to move through the slump. Come on, bum, let's go!

8 pm: Since the battered sav I have not been hungry all day and I remember Crusher and Beansprout telling me that fat fills you up for longer, so I have made a point of sticking to the plan: breakfast, snack, lunch, snack, dinner, snack.

Remembering Crusher's words—'Just do it until it becomes a habit!' Okay!

Weigh-in day is sometime next week so I have a goal to focus on.

8 September   No big squeeze

I have just had my first clothing victory! A few years ago Zoë gave me a beautiful linen shirt I have never been able to fit into (a shirt she wore while pregnant, I might add—it would go over my head but wouldn't get past my hips). I've held onto it (and many of my thin clothes) in the desperate hope that one day I might be able to squeeze myself into it.

I was just staring in at the range of caftans I had to choose from when the shirt caught my eye and I thought, oh well, what the hell, I'll give it a try. Not only did it fit but it is loose! Not loose as in 'I've been to India and suffered three months of dysentery' kind of loose, but it does go over my hips and it doesn't look like I'm trying to squeeze an elephant into a mouse hole. So onward, Alfalfa Zone, onward!

9 September   A brainwave

6 pm: Craving beer. Beautiful beer. Sweet, frothy at the top of the frosted glass tastes better than sex beer. The first beer of the day. Sweet nectar of the yeast gods. The golden drink of happiness, guzzled by many gold medal winning athletes, or at least that's what the ads imply. And if sports people drink it then it must be good for you. Oh, beer, beer, glorious beer. I'm not a heavy drinker, but there was a time in my past, in one session of about eight hours, when I downed 27 schooners and still managed to stand upright.

Think about it. Where would we be without alcohol? I would most certainly still be a virgin and just how would Aussie men communicate their feelings for each other if they no longer had the option of throwing up in the back of Jacko's car? Beer is everybody's friend and I want one now!

Since entering the Alfalfa Zone I have barely had any alcohol at all (not counting the night of the dilapidated leg) and I have not so much as even looked at a beer (wine, vodka and Long Island Teas, perhaps, but beer—definitely not!) and I have decided the time has come to submit. But I will be good and only have one. Okay, so I might have two, but definitely no more than three! And, yes, I know what you're thinking. I know that beer is fattening and that I'm more likely to binge on junk food if I'm drunk but things are different now. This is my eighth week—give me some credit for at least having a *little* willpower!

Anyway, this is my theory. A lite beer has only around 100 calories and otherwise is almost all water. The rest is carbohydrates, which are highly beneficial and easy to burn off. The average diet recommends a daily intake of approximately 1400 calories. This means that I can have around twelve beers a day, which is more than enough for me.

Alcohol always makes you want to go to the loo more often than normal so the flushing of the liquid from your body creates a gentle workout routine of fast walking (to the bathroom), on the spot running (waiting for a cubicle) and the squat and hover (if you're like me and have been taught not to actually sit on the public toilet seat). And there's the added single leg lift if there's no latch on the toilet door. Let's also not forget to mention the repetitions of the bicep curls in getting the beer to the mouth and back onto the table, up to the mouth and back onto the table, to the mouth and back onto the table.

On this diet you can eat whatever you want but only after consuming the requisite number of daily beers. This way, it is highly likely the food will only remain in your body a short amount of time before you once again do the circuit training of the walk, run, squat, and now the added 'lose the contents of your tummy' crunches. If you consume enough alcohol you may also be seen furthering your exercise programme on the dance floor, and perhaps after a few days of this, your stamina will have increased enough for you to actually go back to someone's house to get really aerobic.

On your second day of the Drink Yourself Skinny Diet you are guaranteed not to want to go anywhere near food and will have no further appetite problems except when drunk, which doesn't count 'cause anything you can't remember eating has absolutely no calories. Keep doing that until you find yourself rake thin, in detox and feeding through a tube. A look that's sure to be seen on the runways sometime soon.

9 pm: Nbow, beforeb I say anybthink, I just neebd to tell you, I had a fewb moreb beers than just three. I lost count after the roast lamb and potatoes but I think the Drink Yourself Skinny Diet is a btrainwave. I haveb come up with the ultimate diet. Don't laugh! I maty be oneto something here. (Why cam't I type when I'm drink, soorry, I mean drunk.) So bwhat do you thinkb? Oh dear, I think I'd better bgo to bed.

10 September   Shhh!

Okay, so I do have a minor headache and I am feeling just a teensy bit guilty but I had fun and losing weight is one thing but living your life is another and if I can't do both then I'm not interested. This is where I've gone wrong in the past. Not seeing it as a life change, acting all pure for however many weeks it is until I crumble, then throwing it all in because it seems completely unachievable. This way, I have my odd night out, and then I get straight back to being healthy and looking after myself. The whole thing seems so much more possible psychologically.

Yesterday I took Kai to the RSL to see Hi-Five (a kids' band). Because I am in a wheelchair and can't get up and dance (or even chase after him if he runs off) and because I couldn't get any more tickets, I sent him in with his dad and I waited outside playing the fruit machines and drinking too much beer with the rest of the dads. We had dinner afterwards, and rather than eating fish and chips or schnitzel and wedges, I chose lean roast lamb and oven baked potatoes with peas and corn. It was great to conquer that little battle and I did it by doing the Recognise, Challenge and Distract thing Nutcase told me about. I recognised that I was craving chips, I challenged the craving with the thought that I don't eat that kind of food any more, that I deserve better, then I distracted the thought by ordering something healthier and by the time I'd eaten it I had moved on. I felt better for making a good choice. And maybe in six months I'll be making even better choices like salad (yeah, right) but for now, I have made an improvement on my life habits.

It's quite surreal working so hard on myself, trying desperately to train myself in how to eat, what to eat, when to eat, trying to change my body, my health, my life and seeing Kai just plod along, completely unaware of what I am doing, not just for me but for him too. He will be healthier, he won't know the struggle I have had learning to live a 'normal' life, and hopefully, if this goes according to plan, he will just know me as a normal-sized, non-food-obsessed mum. We will definitely have a more active lifestyle and hopefully that will translate into making his life a lot easier than mine has been.

14 September   Keep pretending

Dr Nutcase was amazing this week. I explained to her that most of the time I am so conscious of everything I eat and whether or not I exercise and obsessing about how much and how long etc etc etc that most of the time I actually feel like I'm pretending and that it's not real at all—I am kidding myself that I am getting healthy and changing my life. She explained that this was normal for people who have been abused in various forms. All I have ever really known is abusive behaviour, so when it came time to look after myself I just continued the pattern of abuse. What I need to do is keep 'pretending' until I have done it for so long that eating well and being healthy simply becomes my new pattern of behaviour, one I will not think about every minute of the day.

I also said that most of the time I only remembered the catchphrase Recognise, Challenge and Distract *after* I had made a bad food choice. She explained it this way. When we ride a bicycle, something most of us have done since we were children, we don't get on it and think, I am holding the handle bars, I am now using the pedals, I am balancing and watching where I am going etc. We do this when we are learning but after that we simply get on it and go, and we only stop to think about it if there is something wrong.

Similarly, when it comes to food, I make unhealthy choices. I just eat the way I have always done (it has become habit to eat in an abusive way) and I've never had to think about it because it's the only way I know. Now that I know this is unhealthy and abusive to me I have to remind myself that this is so and that takes time and repetition. She suggested that afterwards I remind myself of the catchphrase and make a pledge to myself that next time I will remember. She said eventually this would begin to work and soon I would recognise my craving for what it was before I acted upon it and eventually, I won't need to do so as I will be eating healthily. I just need to keep doing it until it becomes the way I naturally live my life.

I left feeling great and then found out Crusher had decided to do a surprise inspection. Eek! I hadn't done my exercises for two days and I'd had the beer! Very paranoid. Looked at my belly, decided I looked eight months pregnant, realised I hadn't lost any weight at all and maybe the shirt I now thought fitted me better had never been too tight and I was just kidding myself.

She forgot her scales (thank God!) but we did a body measure. Realised with horror I could probably suck my gut in but could do nothing about the size of my thighs. She walked in the door and immediately said, 'I can see you've lost weight.' I suspected she was lulling me into a false sense of confidence and started imagining her reading the tape measure in horror, then pushing me up against the table, grabbing hold of my ginormous arse, slapping it, wobbling it and screaming witch-like, 'I'll get you, my Fatty! Just you wait.'

Oh my God, I thought in desperation. What if I've put weight on?

She whipped out the measure the way a cowgirl cracks a whip. I was the fattened lamb being led to slaughter. She compared my measurements to the ones I had done two months ago in her gym, my first day in the Alfalfa Zone. And this is how it went:

	Then	Now
Neck	41 cm	36.5 cm
Chest	125 cm	116.5 cm
Arm	46 cm	36.5 cm
Waist	108 cm	97.5 cm
Hips	140 cm	130 cm
Thigh	82 cm	64.5 cm

Total lost: 60.5 cm. Yeehaa! I think I'll celebrate by having a beer. Note to self: don't you dare!

17 September
I can walk! Kind of . . .

The cast is off! This is it! D-Day for real. Time to get on the scales and see if I've actually lost any kilos . . .

I waited until I'd gone to the toilet first, stepped on and I am now 101.5 kilos! I have lost 7.5 kilos! Yeeehaa! This has totally inspired me and I am going to swim every day for the rest of my life. I'll start later today.

8 pm: Okay. Wasn't quite ready today. Definitely tomorrow. I promise.

Crusher rang and said it was time to get serious. I have to do forty minutes of exercise every day and because I am struggling to walk (I now have a walking stick), for now I am confined to the pool. She said I have to do laps and to think about finding some aqua classes. It was time to start burning that fat. So step aside, Dawn Fraser—here I come!

23 September   Water babe

I know it's hard to believe but I did it. I swam every day this week! I'd drop Kai at child care and head straight for the pool. Or I'd invite friends over for coffee and then ask them if they'd mind him for an hour while I went and did my laps. It's so hard being a single mum. You always feel like you're stealing from your child's life just to get some time for yourself. It's times like this I wish my birth mum was around.

Anyway, with the cast a thing of the past I got to the pool at last! Ooh, that's a poem! Sorry about that, purely unintentional. Anyway, initially it was a bit daunting. Finding a swimming costume that didn't have a skirt on it was hard enough not to mention the fact that any costume over a size 16 only comes in big floral print, sports something that looks like a hula skirt on it and has embarrassing cardboard like scaffolding in the bra section. Who designs these things? Does somebody decide that when women get this fat they just don't care what they look like and as punishment for being that size they have to wear the worst kind of fashions—those only ever found in nightmares or circuses? Or do they make the swimmers look that hideous so no one notices the fat? It is very, very scary in the plus size section of Kmart. I will be happy never to go there again! Despite that little hurdle, I did eventually get to the pool.

I noticed the lanes had little signs at the end. Fast, Medium, Slow or Leisure Swimmers. I chose the slowest of them. I started doing my laps but quickly discovered it's really hard to do freestyle when the water's only one foot deep. Got kicked out of the kiddies' pool after nearly drowning a one year old. Decided it was time to try the big pool.

I surprised myself by doing forty minutes worth of laps and only found it mildly boring going up and down, up and down. I just took it easy, was a bit out of breath, but I kept going. I fuelled myself on by repeating, 'One hundred kilos, one hundred kilos, one hundred kilos' every stroke I took. I also entertained myself by trying to check out the picnic hampers of the guys who wore Speedos. Hey, a girl's gotta have some fun!

A few days into laps I discovered aquarobics, which I absolutely adore even though I look like a birthing southern right whale and am forever looking around for fear of Planet Ark people trying to tag and rescue me. My previous image of aquarobics was overweight eighty-year-old blue-rinsed grannies floating around with the aid of their plastic hips, walking frames parked at the edge of the pool, the old dears not so gracefully drowning to beefed-up versions of Burt Bacharach.

It's not like that at all. It's kind of funky, and doesn't really feel like exercise because you're so worried about the amount of water you're swallowing you don't have time to think you might actually be burning calories. What I like most apart from the fact that no one can see your body is the weightlessness. It's really easy to do the work and there's absolutely no impact on my healing limb, or the rest of my oversized body for that matter.

I have discovered that aerobics teachers (aqua included) cannot count and they love to lie. They delight in counting you down. 'Come on, ten more to go. I'll count them with you. Ten, nine, eight, seven, seven, seven, six, five, four, three, three, three, two, two, one.' And a word of warning: 'One more time' does not mean *one* more time. We all know it's only men who, when talking genitalia, can turn three inches into eight. Well, it's only aerobics instructors who can turn one more time into four and a mild heart attack!

Still, it must be doing me some good because after seven days of super aquatic fitness I am now 100 kilos! Exercising definitely puts me in the right frame of mind for eating well. The heart gets pumping, I feel fit, and therefore I want to treat my body well so I exercise some more. It's kind of like a not-so-vicious circle.

My preferred breakfast is cereal with fruit juice, fruit salad and yoghurt, or a poached egg on toast. My favourite snacks are licorice, pretzels, crackers or fruit. My fave lunches are soup, ham and salad sandwiches, baked beans on toast or sardines on rice crisps. For dinner I'll occasionally do the Lean Cuisine thing, but I have ventured out and now at least

The Killer Spinach and Ricotta Pie

I couldn't be bothered using fresh spinach but if you do, you'll need about a ½ kilo, maybe more, of chopped steamed spinach. I use two boxes of frozen chopped spinach (make sure you squeeze out all the water). Mix the spinach together with 350 g ricotta cheese, 4 chopped mushrooms, 1 table-spoon of pinenuts, a small tin of sweetcorn and a teaspoon of finely chopped garlic. Spoon the mixture into a greased baking dish (using cooking oil spray). Sprinkle a teaspoon of Parmesan on top, cook at 210 degrees (don't forget to preheat the oven) for about 15–20 minutes. Very scrummy. Serves 3–4. Or you can try Beansprout's version, which is slightly simpler:

Beansprout's Spinach and Ricotta Pie

Preheat the oven to 200 degrees. Steam 500 g of fresh spinach (or you can cheat and use 2 boxes of the frozen stuff). Mix the spinach with 350 g ricotta cheese and a tablespoon of Parmesan cheese. Spoon the mixture into a lightly sprayed pie dish and place in the oven for approximately 25 minutes or until golden brown on top. Squeeze a quarter of a lemon over the dish and serve with a salad.

Serves 3–4; contains 9 g fat.

three times a week I do a stir-fry with Hokkien noodles, a pasta with a tomato-based sauce, grilled fish with vegetables and rice, or spinach and ricotta pie. I've a long way to go but I feel like it is possible.

My clothes are starting to feel and look a lot looser than they have done for quite a while. My bra has had to be adjusted from the longest strap to the shortest, and I now fit in the bath a little easier. I am looking forward to weighing in under one hundred and that should be next week.

2 October   Mouth-to-mouth

Oh dear, oh dear, oh dear. I blame beer! With Kai spending the weekend at his godmother's house I seized the opportunity to get away to a writers festival for a few days and thought I was so clever. I packed all my diet food, paid extra for a room with a microwave, even took litres of bottled water with me. I started off all right but didn't factor in the meeting up with boozy friends, drinking beer all night and ending up at a cafe early the next morning ordering bacon, eggs, sausages and an overflow bucket for all the extra fat I was consuming. Then the 'Oh well, I'm on holiday' excuse kicked in and I found myself eating KFC (twice, I might add!). Then I had an attack of the 'I'll start back tomorrow so I might as well order pizza, eat chocolate and drink more beer' then the 'oh God, somebody stop this bus, I want to throw up' scenario. Just your typical long weekend away, really. Or is that just me? Hmm.

I am now most definitely too afraid to step onto the scales. I can't call Crusher for fear of what she might say. I want to go into hiding except they don't make bunkers big enough to house my arse so I'm going to have to keep going.

I can't go back to my local pool because I had an argument with the pool attendant—as you do! He said I couldn't wear a t-shirt in the pool because it clogs the filter. I asked why cotton t-shirts clog it and not cotton swimmers or board shorts. He told me to shut up, called me Quacky and told me to waddle waddle waddle away. And no, I am not joking.

This is a serious dilemma. I *have* to wear a t-shirt! This could become a major trauma for me. My swimmers are now so loose around my breasts they are constantly slipping out and floating to the top of the pool. The last thing I need is the life-saving attendant thinking there was a drowned child in the pool and attempting mouth-to-mouth on my left breast. Of course, it could be quite thrilling but it's not an experience I really need right now. I *have* to wear a t-shirt to keep them in place! Not to mention, I am just not confident enough to wear body-hugging swimmers. Think of 100 kilos of pig fat wrapped in plastic and that is how I feel in anything Lycra. I look like one of those rolled roasts with the string tied around them to keep the meat in place. I'm telling you, I just look too damned fat! And who says I have a negative body image?! I'm going to have to change pools. Where to now? Might check on the pools in Siberia. At least they'd be a little secluded.

5 October   T-shirts rule

I found another pool and really had to push myself to go swimming. I knew I would feel better but I had to make the first move. And not surprisingly, I do feel much better.

And joy of joys! I have found a pool that not only allows people like me—fatties—to wear t-shirts but it also has a creche, a gym and aquarobics. I am going to become a member and get my fat pizza-filled arse back into gear. I just have to wait till payday!

8 October   Sergeant Bilko

Still doing lots of laps, at least forty minutes every day. What I do is I make myself stay in the pool for at least that time. Even on days when I'm so bored I could poke my eyes out for entertainment, I stay there. Some days I'll do thirty minutes of laps and have a fun splash around for the rest of it, but I don't want to break my rule. It's a precedent I've set and I'm going to stick with it! My mantra as I swim is now 'under one hundred, under one hundred, under one hundred'. I really want to get over that psychological barrier of breaking the century.

Haven't tried the creche yet, but I took Kai down to have a look and have started talking about it, calling it the kids' room and trying to get him to like the concept of going there. Don't know how he'll go but I don't have a choice unless I find an instant family—just add water!

I emailed Crusher my list of food sins and she said she wouldn't come and weigh or measure me if I didn't get focused again. She didn't say much at all. There was none of the 'oh well, you did your best' kind of thing. Just a stony demand that I get focused. I fear she is going to start getting tough on me. It was what she didn't say that made me feel so guilty. My mind just filled in the blanks. I could see her, Sergeant Bilko style, yelling at me to stop wasting her time and to get off my fat arse and *move it*!

Every single day is a struggle to eat well. Constantly feel the urge to buy laxatives but just remind myself that I don't do that any more (remember the little red caboose? *I think I can, I think I can, I know I can etc etc etc*). Nutcase said to remember that what I am doing works. Doing it slowly means doing it forever and a healthy body is what I deserve and one day at a time will get me closer to that goal . . . Of course, I don't believe a bloody word of it but Nutcase assures me that eventually I will!

99 KILOS

(218 lb)

13 October   Queen of the world

Checked in with Dr Nutcase. I love how she always starts the sessions with, 'How are you?' I refrain from replying: 'Well, apart from being completely psychotic about food, maniacally counting fat content *and* calories *and* obsessing about the size of my thighs, and constantly trying to convince myself *not* to skol fifty laxatives for breakfast, and trying hard not to give up and go back to being fat and unhappy and out of control for the rest of my life and being depressed about how I could have let myself go like this, um, yeah, apart from that I'm fine. Thanks for asking.'

It took me all of about five seconds to confess my sins of the weekend away and her response surprised me. She pulled me up on saying I need to get back on track. She explained how that sets me up with a preconceived idea that there is a good and a bad track to be on. She said, 'There is no track. It's all one track and it's called living. Healthy people go on holiday; they eat pizza, drink beer and have bacon and eggs for breakfast. Then they go back home and live life like they do most of the time. If you fall into despair about what you eat while on holidays, you fall back into the pattern of thinking you have failed, therefore there's no point continuing.'

She also explained that I don't fail any more as I simply live my life. I am developing new strategies around food, eating and body image and as I create this new way of living I simply do it. And when I eat crap, I do that, enjoy it as a treat and then get on with eating healthily. The more healthy (and possibly thinner) I become, the more likely I am not to panic and feel as if I'm going to be trapped in my fat body forever, because if I put a kilo on when I am on holidays, it will be easier to work off than the 30-plus I am currently working on losing.

I also said when I hear good news about my weight loss it sends me into a panic and I eat almost as if I am afraid of reaching my goal. She said it was because the real me will be more visible and feel more exposed, but that I need to remember I am a strong, capable, articulate woman and that I needn't be afraid of being as healthy and happy as I could possibly be.

So after that I am ready to embrace and love myself and admit that I am queen of the world (uh-huh!). This psycho-therapy is pretty good stuff! I wish I'd done it when I was sixteen.

14 October   Shrinking

I've now moved into the weekly weigh-in phase and I am so happy to say I am now 98 kilos! Ninety-eight kilos! Under one hundred! Woohoo! I feel lighter just saying it. I have now lost 11 kilos. I am nearly halfway there! I rang Crusher and she was so excited. She said she'd measure me at 95 and to make that my new goal. She said if I could lose 11 I could certainly lose three. It seems like nothing in comparison, so today, I totally believe I can do it. Of course tomorrow, when I'm sitting next to my skinny friend and she's eating deep-fried chicken wings and chips, my resolve may not seem as strong. But today I can conquer the world!

I already have more energy to play with Kai and I'm starting to have dreams of me being thin and, hopefully, sexually active. Look, I'm so starved of attention, a wolf whistle from a 200-kilo construction worker would serve as sexual activity. So 95 kilos, here I come!

20 October   A bone!

I've hit 96 kilos and I'm not too sure but I think I spotted a kneecap somewhere around the middle of my leg and I think it might have been mine. It disappeared back into the fat pretty quickly as it hasn't seen much sunlight in the last few years so I'll just have to coax it out with a few more lettuce leaves and a couple of hundred laps.

Two things have happened that have even me bewildered. The first is, I joined a gym. I can't believe I did it. Of course, even I know that joining is one thing, actually using the membership is another. Having lost 13 kilos my fat is not so solid any more. Before it was hard-packed cellulite, now it's the not so attractive floppy skin look. I'm paranoid someone is going to say, 'Hey, nice knapsack,' and I will have to reply, 'That's no knapsack, that's what's left of my gut, let me just get a wheelbarrow for it.' Or that I'll have to roll my breasts up like sleeping bags just so they'll fit into my bra. Euh!

Crusher says it's time to do some toning work on my body. I'm not sure how long I'll be able to stomach the size 6 gym junkies asking if me and my twin (my arse) are finished with both of the rowing machines but I'm going to give it a go. If it's anything like the swimming, I really start to miss it if I haven't done it for a few days. It definitely keeps me focused.

The other thing I did was buy myself a size 16 swimming costume in the hope that in a few weeks it will fit me and not feel like squeezing a watermelon through the eye of a needle (something that reminds me too much of childbirth) and, shock of shocks, it fits me. And it's not even too tight! Okay, so the legs are a little too tight and my breasts are constantly popping out, but it nearly fits and that's all right by me. Especially considering that in the last few years, I haven't even been able to fit into clothes that are supposed to be Free Size. They should have a label saying 'Free Size—except you jumbo, just go and have another burger and everything will be all right! Clothing won't seem as important once you're lying in the cardiac ward at St Vincent's.' No, they wouldn't bother paying the extra money to print the labels. Why waste anything on fat girls? Nobody cares about them!

Anyway, the swimsuit feels good and in a few weeks will fit me perfectly. The funny thing is, I'm not sure how I got here. It feels like just yesterday that even three kilos seemed like the Mt Everest of weight loss and here I am three months later having lost almost two stone. And from this side of the fence, which is nearing the middle, it feels infinitely more possible to lose the next 15 than it did to lose the first. I know it works now. Despite having days off, it works. And not only have I lost weight but I have gained confidence and I feel great. I am totally energised and am already doing more things because I feel so much better about myself.

I remember only four months ago I would get up in the morning, plonk Kai down in front of the television and just sit there for hours on end, with not even enough energy to bother getting out of my pyjamas. Now I jump out of bed, get Kai and myself dressed and go to the park for a long walk or we head off to play group on ice. It's great, Kai has special little kids skates and I hold his hand and we skate around the ice with all the other mums and kids. They make snow and we skate, frolic and play for an hour and a half. Hard work but heaps of fun. We do so much more already I can't wait until I'm at my peak. And he's looking a lot healthier too. He's losing weight as well—not that he needed to lose a lot, but he was getting a little bit too chubby. Now I know he's going to be a healthy, active little boy. The days just keep on getting better. I now believe anything is possible and the key was to just start doing it. And if you don't have too high an expectation and you just do it—keep eating healthily and keep moving—without concentrating on the final outcome, then it just becomes a part of your life. Magic!

My last session with Dr Nutcase was amazing. We discussed my constant need to control the anorexia part of my nature. Some nights I pace the floor debating with myself whether or not to eat, fighting the desire to fall back into the bad habits of the past. She wrote me a list, which I have now plastered around my house.

> false power
> stupid power   } goes nowhere
> destructive power

> Real power is AJ being in control

This relates to the battle of power I go through. Starving myself is a control issue and is false power. It reminds me that I am not being powerful by starving myself and am injuring myself and being destructive. It reminds me to remain positive and truly powerful by being in control of my body and feeding it.

The real goal is health and fitness not reaching a 'number'.

Kilograms do not count. Health is the issue. It is pointless weighing 50 kilos if I'm too weak to speak and near dying. The goal is to fully live my life, not destroy it.

'Numbers' are not indicators of success or failure.

Diets don't work.

Sensible eating and exercise work.

There are many reasons why from week to week I may not have lost kilos and could possibly even have gained weight. Fluid retention, bowel movements, how long since I had eaten, being premenstrual and so on are all things that could have me weighing in heavier than the day before. Making the weight the goal sets myself up for a feeling of failure whereas if I just eat well and exercise, weight will go, fitness will increase and health will be at its optimum.

Everything else I have tried DOESN'T WORK.

It's really good to remind myself of this. Starving does not work. Bingeing does not work. Fad diets do not work. But what I am doing now *is* working and this is the easiest it has ever been. Yes, it is also the slowest but if it comes off slowly then it will stay off. I have changed my life forever. Good eating never ends—it just gets interrupted occasionally by 'treats', which is all about a healthy approach to food and life.

> There are no absolutes. All food has good and bad aspects . . . some choices are better than others; if I falter I can clean the slate and start again.

What happens here is that it all becomes just food. Therefore it is not as exciting if it is not forbidden. If I eat KFC I just do it then return to my 'normal' eating habits. Using the word 'falter' is better than 'failure' because failing sets myself up to feel bad and therefore give up. This way I can simply clean the slate, declare the next meal a whole new ball game and continue on the path. There is no failure because all food is a part of life and eventually 95 per cent of my choices will be healthy and it will be second nature to choose them. At the moment I fake it, but it still seems to be working.

The other day I wanted hot chips. I went out and bought them, had five or six then threw the rest away, not really wanting to let myself down. Because they weren't forbidden, they weren't that exciting.

So where to from here? I'm aiming for 90 kilos and trying to tone that flab.

22 October   Gym junkie (yeah, sure!)

Monday morning:

9.00 am Get to the gym, put Kai in the creche.

9.05 am Met the instructor, a skinny gym junkie. She was going to give me a programme that would help me lose weight and tone the flab.

9.10 am Get on the treadmill to do a fifteen-minute warm-up (not brave enough to tell them that fifteen minutes of fast walking was likely to be a warm-up and a cool-down to coronary land for me).

9.11 am Get a call from the creche—your son won't stop crying. Get off the treadmill (phew!) and go to the creche.

9.12 am Told Kai I would be back in a little while and then we can go for a swim.

9.13 am Get back on treadmill and start warming up.

9.14 am Creche calls and says your son has become so emotional he just threw up on another child. I felt like telling them he'd be all right, it was just the two schooners of beer I gave him for breakfast, then decided better of it.

9.15 am Get Kai from creche, go and float in the baby pool.

23 October   Gym junkie mark II

9.00 am Leave Kai in creche.

9.05 am Get on treadmill.

9.10 am Creche calls. Kai won't stop crying.

9.15 am Go back to the creche. Tell Kai if I get fit then I'll live longer which means he can live at home rent-free for as long as he wants.

9.20 am Kai throws up on two kids and a carer and they suggest he might be better off with me.

9.30 am Go and sit in baby pool again.

Apparently my son prefers my breasts the size of aircraft carriers and if I was a breast-fed baby I'd be thinking the same thing, so I can't really blame the poor boy. I briefly contemplate somehow using him in my routine at the gym, imagine him strapped to the pec deck and realise I'd need two babies to make my workout even and I am just not prepared to breed again. So once more I end up doing my laps in the baby pool.

24 October   Slippery scales

I leave Kai at his usual day care centre and head off to the gym, determined to get this thing happening. A different skinny gym junkie is attending the gym today and she takes one look at my thunder thighs and says she needs to fitness test me first. Oh no, not that again. I remember being so fat I couldn't even have the fat test the day I met Crusher. The callipers wouldn't get around my lump of fat (either on my thigh or on my belly). It was a remarkably tragic moment, really. I didn't want to go there again.

I took a deep breath, threw myself on the bike and

pedalled away, trying to will my heart not to leap out of my chest and hitch a ride to the nearest KFC. Eight minutes and a few calculations later, I am told that I am just a little above average fitness level. It's amazing what a couple of weeks in the pool can do!

I was a bit disappointed to discover the scales I had been using were wrong and that I was 97 kilos and not 96 as I thought. That's why it's important to have good scales and use the same set each week for your weigh-in. I felt a little despondent then reminded myself once again that this is about good health, good habits and fitness, not about what weight I am one week to the next.

She showed me around all the machines, told me how to use them and what parts of the body they worked on. She told me to do three sets of fifteen on most of the machines and they didn't seem too scary once I knew what I was doing. I was pretty much on the lowest weight levels but she assured me I would gain strength very quickly and would be adjusting them up in just a couple of weeks.

It is certainly not the most interesting thing I've ever done but I can catch up on some good Ricki Lake which is on one of the TV sets and listen to some of that new-fangled music the young'uns listen to as they have the cable music show on the other. I repeat to myself, 'Think Elle Macpherson. Think Madonna,' and I imagine my pecs instantly transforming from the wobbling plates of jelly they are to the trim, taut and terrific muscles of a supermodel. It won't happen overnight but it will happen. Okay, I may only be 161 cm tall, which instantly excludes me from being even a supermodel's handbag, but a girl can dream, can't she? Don't answer that!

My workout took an hour and at the end I skipped happily out of the gym wondering big-headedly whether they had underestimated me completely as I hadn't even broken out in a sweat. Huh! Easy peasy! Went to bed feeling thinner and definitely more athletic.

25 October
How much does pain weigh?

Woke up curled in a ball. Couldn't uncurl myself. Someone had put superglue in my joints. The place they call my pecs (the breasts) I have renamed the pockets of pain. My butt feels as if I have gone two rounds with Mike Tyson and, yes, he has bitten off a piece but I'm not sure exactly where from because it's completely numb with pain! My legs feel as if they have been twisted up like balloon animals and I can't even lift my arm to pick my nose.

Surely something was wrong? I rang Crusher and she assured me this was normal and encouraged me to go back and keep at it.

I wondered if, at the end of this, I would be awarded masochist of the year and questioned why the gym instructors weren't dressed in leather and carrying little whips. I did as I was told and forced myself in. Once I had finished my workout I was told that tomorrow would probably be worse but to keep coming as my body would get used to it. Yes, I nodded benignly, and the body would get used to being run over by a truck seventeen times. You would be dead, but your body wouldn't feel it after the third or fourth time.

27 October   Upping the ante

The funny thing is, even though the next day was worse, it kind of felt good. I knew it was actually making my body a better shape and I found a way to be able to move through the pain. Now I'm keen to get back there because when my body feels tired and sore, I know I have done some good work. Do you think I'm ill?

Crusher rang and told me some more interesting info. She told me that your body adapts to the exercise you do. For instance, if I just continued swimming for forty minutes three times a week, I wouldn't burn as much fat off my body as I have done in the last four weeks. The body remembers that is what you do and it stops working efficiently (as a fat burner). You need to vary the exercise, surprise your body, keep it adapting, that way you will continue to burn off a lot more fat. Pretty sneaky, huh? So it's okay to start off gently with laps or walking, but you have to increase the distance or speed and vary your exercise to lose weight and gain fitness as effectively as you can, especially if you are like me and have a lot to lose.

Oh, listen to me, big fitness expert. It's at this point I should admit to having had hot chips and scones with jam and cream on the weekend and far too many beers (you'd think I'd learn). I told Crusher, admitted I'd lost a little focus and asked her for a pep talk. She said that no one else could do this and it was important I don't give up now because if I can learn to get over the hiccups then I will never have a problem with getting fit again, 'cause it will just be a case of living my life rather than being on the diet, off the diet, on the diet, off the diet. She said I deserved a life full of happiness and getting healthy was the first step in that direction.

Okay, no more beer.

At least none for the rest of the week.

29 October   I only read the articles!

I can't believe I did it, but I bought a slimmers magazine. I couldn't help myself. I was just looking at the recipes, wrestling chocolate bars and Chuppa Chups from Kai's hands, trying to ignore his tantrum, muttering things like, 'He's a child of Satan,' and 'He's adopted!' and before I knew it, the woman at the counter was scanning the mag.

There were lots of cute little articles with before and after pictures. Sharon as a beached whale, Sharon as a beach nymphet—but, no, we are not trying to convince you that you are worthless as a big girl! Buy our products now! Dial 1-800 MY BREASTS ARE BIGGER THAN ENGLAND!

Apart from that angle it was not too bad. There were some good recipes in there, and best of all there were lots of interesting facts that I didn't actually know. For instance, it's best to wait an hour *after* you exercise before eating as you encourage your body to burn the stored fat rather than the fuel you have just consumed. Handy, huh? Unfortunately no handy articles on 'How to Lose Seventy Kilos in Two Weeks— The Healthy Way!' And no 'All I ate was fish and chips and now I'm a size six!' But it is inspiring and, like I said, if all else fails, read it at your doctor's, write down the recipes and save yourself five bucks.

9 November   Obsession

This is my third week of being a gym junkie. I had a bad week last week. Could not stop stepping on and off the scales. I did it about fifteen times a day. Struggled with myself knowing that this was unhealthy and not caring because I was obsessing with every little fluctuation. Yes, I did end the week by seeing Dr Nutcase. She recommended I put the scales away and make a deal with myself to just weigh morning and night and nothing in between. She reminded me that I was doing really well and that I had the healthy eating/exercise 'habit' working at a 90 per cent success rate (maybe more). She explained that behaviour was easier to modify than emotions and that is where my hard work lies—the emotional side of eating. Oh goody! It gets harder. That's just what I need to know!

She told me that every time I was dealing with the cravings, it was important to remind myself out loud that I don't eat that kind of food any more. I make healthy choices. Ones that are good for me. She said she knew it sounded silly but if I did this for long enough, eventually I would start to think and act that way. It's a bit like brainwashing. The more I say it the more likely it is that one day I will believe it.

I definitely feel more exposed as I shrink. I am more volatile and whenever I have a fight with someone the first thing I do is walk to the fridge and look for something to comfort me. What am I expecting to find in there? A gorgeous naked black man playing a little harp and offering me a full (and I mean FULL) body massage to calm me down? Huh, I should be so lucky!

The great thing is that there is nothing but healthy food in there so I have to make a healthy choice. If I have a pig-out then it usually consists of two red licorice sticks, four rice crackers, a yoghurt, a mango and, if I still have room, maybe I'll squeeze in a piece of low-fat cheese. Not exactly my feasts of yesteryear, huh? World market prices of cooking oil are at an all-time low!

The other thing Nutcase told me was that when you think you are hungry it is more likely that you are dehydrated. So drink two glasses of water and then see if you are still hungry. I have found this to be true. And the added bonus is, the more you drink, the more you go to the toilet, and if your house is like mine then it is a good opportunity to do some stair work! Aaah! What have I become?!

10 November
Weight: not discussing it!

You are not going to believe it. I'm not sure I believe it! When I was working on the SBS-TV series 'Mum's the Word', the Maggie T clothing company dressed me. They were the only designers who had decent clothing in my size, which was 'Better Get the Lifeboats—This Is the Titanic', more commonly known as size 26. I wore size 24—I couldn't actually button up the shirts but refused to wear anything bigger.

I was riffling through my wardrobe the other day and found a beautiful black suit jacket I hadn't worn in years. I'm one of those people who keep clothes of all sizes just in case one of the crash diets I try miraculously works. I prepared myself for the horror I experienced a year or two ago when I could no longer fit my arms into the sleeve. I did a few bicep curls just to get those extra kilos off (who am I kidding?) and tried the jacket on.

Not only did it fit but I could do the buttons up—something I had never been able to do, even when I first bought it! Then I checked the size. It was a size 16! In four months I have dropped six dress sizes. It certainly explains why the other day, when I bumped into someone I'd not seen for a while, the first thing she said was, 'Oh my God, AJ, where's your arse gone?' I screamed and said, 'Oh my God, I left it on the bus!' No I didn't, I'm just being silly. I slapped her on the face and said, 'Bitch!' I mean really, what else was I going to say to Grandmother? Seriously, though, it *is* quite strange because it really hasn't been that hard. I guess the key has been to just keep going.

I'm enjoying the gym, it's not high heart rate stuff but it is changing the shape of my body. Crusher told me not to focus on my weight as at this stage I am losing fat and building muscle. Muscle weighs more than fat so I'm just adjusting to that change at the moment.

I read an interesting piece of information in one of the men's mags the other day (I was just reading it for the articles, honestly!). They posed the question 'How do you make fifteen kilos of fat look attractive?' Their answer: 'Stick a nipple on it!' Well, now that I'm only 30 kilos overweight (as opposed to 45), all I need is an extra set of nipples and I'll find the man of my dreams. Of course, we'd never be together because I'd be travelling with the Wild Cats strip show, but at least I'd get a lot of interest from a lot of men . . . most of them bottle-fed boys, I'm sure.

I am very excited because I have finally re-entered the world of fashion. Okay, so all the fashions might look ridiculous on me . . . a 90 kilo woman in a skimpy glitter t-shirt emblazoned *Princess* is not quite how Fergie would have dressed, even though she was capable of some major fashion sins herself. But I can go into *some* shops and know that *some* things will fit me. Of course, the wafer thin sales assistant will assure me that the skirt does not make my bum look big and she would be right—it's my bum that makes my bum look big. But at least it's shrinking. And on the good days, I know now that it is simply a matter of time until I go down a few more dress sizes, reach my goal weight and then just maintain.

I wonder if Kai will remember me as a fat person? I guess he'll see photos, but hopefully he'll only ever know me as a healthy weight. Wow, now that's something to aim for!

I need to refocus a little, get strict on my snacks and eating times. I need to make sure I do have a snack. I also need to make sure I only have the one snack. I have found myself being a little free with my grazing—a sure-fire way to not lose weight.

11 November   What we tell our kids

Had a great session with Dr Nutcase. We talked about how I have a negative image of myself. I grew up believing that I was not attractive. I had a relative who would always tell me how good looking my brother was and how easy his life would be and how, because I was plain, I would have to work really hard in life. It's kind of ironic that that is the way we turned out. I am the absolute workaholic, desperate to prove myself, and my brother is a laid-back guy who lives at the beach, fishes a lot and doesn't really care how much money he may or may not ever earn.

The power of words is amazing. I did grow up thinking I wasn't pretty enough to be a successful person. I grew up not liking myself. I grew up thinking that if I were thinner or prettier then the world would be mine. So when I put on the weight I embraced the hopelessness that I felt when I was a child, because the work involved in getting the weight off seemed too hard. It was only ever quick fixes that I believed would help me. I was waiting for some kind of miracle. The kinds of miracle the weight loss ads promise you.

Now, four months into this amazing change of lifestyle and attitude, I realise that I am capable of anything and that the world belongs as much to me as it does to my brother or the supermodel I see staring at me from the pages of *Vogue*. I am entitled to just as much in life whether I'm carrying excess weight or I'm 'normal' weight. I have to learn to really love myself from within and realise it is only stupid people who put limitations and negative belief systems on others simply because of the way they look. We are all equals and losing the weight is for my peace of mind and for my own good health. Losing weight will not make me love myself any more— I have to learn to do that regardless of the weight loss. They are separate issues.

Nutcase said it was important to remember that I am successful and attractive and intelligent and very capable of doing anything I set my mind to. Just because people told me something when I was a child doesn't mean it is true and doesn't mean it has to come true. I am my own person, responsible for my own life, and the best way to live my life to the fullest is to take it back, bit by bit, first by losing the weight and taking control of my bad habits and secondly by finding belief in myself.

This makes me realise the importance of the things we tell our children. I am so mindful of telling Kai how good he is at everything. He may turn out with an overinflated opinion of himself but I'd rather that than an overwhelming sense of failure and a belief that he'll never be good enough.

12 November   No more double chins

I've noticed my relationship with Kai is changing. We are so much more physically active together. We go for long walks (I can't believe how far he can go before asking me to carry him—and because I've lost his entire body weight, carrying him is no longer a problem), we go swimming so often that he actually throws a tantrum if I say we can't, and we play chaseys on a daily basis. I have so much more energy. I'm looking forward to the day he says, 'No more,' 'cause I know then that I will be at my peak fitness—unless of course it means I am just embarrassing him and even though he loves chaseys I have to realise that when he is forty-five and head of Rochester and Rochester law firm he might not want to play chaseys while trying to conduct the yearly board meeting.

He has now lost his little double chins and just looks like a normal healthy small boy. This alone is enough for me to keep going. There's no junk food in the house for him to eat, all his snacks are healthy and he basically eats what I'm eating, which is low-fat meals, lots of fruit and veggies, and generally wholesome foods. I remember Beansprout telling me it's important for children to have some fat in their diet, but only good fats like cheese, milk, avocado etc. So he has full-cream milk and cheese and I have the low-fat version. I put his full-strength stuff (contraband) on the bottom shelf of my fridge so it doesn't catch my eye every time I open the door. That old 'out of sight, out of mind' thing works every time (almost!).

I still open and close the fridge about a hundred times a day. Not sure what I'm looking for, but a decent man would do for starters. Have thought about rigging up some kind of alarm. Every time I open the door a bell would ring and a loudspeaker would yell, 'You're a fat pig! You're a fat pig! Put the chocolate sauce down and back away now with your hands up!' Instead I look at the little sign I have right at the handle. It says: 'STOP. Think about it . . . Are you being as good as you can?' My, how life has changed.

I've just entered the phase where people are now remarking

on my weight loss. It's been quite strange losing 15 kilos and having no one say anything about it. It was almost as if my fat was embarrassing to them. Maybe they were afraid to mention it. I mean, what are they going to say? 'Gee, you look good, not that you didn't look good before—who wouldn't look good with twenty-five kilos of fat hanging around their neck?' Or, 'Wow, I never knew you weren't a Siamese twin!' Or, 'AJ, please tell me you don't have cancer. Oh, you don't? You mean you've finally got off your fat arse and done something about saving your life? Gee, you look great!' I've been fat for so long I've forgotten what it's like to be thin. It's certainly encouraging to have people notice and acknowledge the hard work I've done. I'm now trying to aim for 90 kilos and under and I'm looking forward to my clothes really starting to hang off me.

13 November   Life on the loo, Part 1

WARNING: THIS NEXT PASSAGE MAY BE OFFENSIVE TO THOSE WHO HAVE NEVER HAD TROUBLE WIPING THEIR BUM!

Here's something you never read in the diet books: I got so fat I could no longer wipe my bum from behind. I wasn't going to mention it, but when I told Crusher she seemed to think I should. Someone who has never had to contemplate the joy of wiping without a degree in the karma sutra and a base knowledge of what it's like to be a contortionist would find it hard to imagine just how tricky that simple task can be.

It happened to me a few years ago and, unlike the

commercials for a certain hair shampoo, it *did* happen overnight. One day I could, the next day it was like reaching around a semitrailer. And even though I knew it was because I'd put on too much weight, it wasn't enough to force me to lose weight. I tried to convince myself that it had always been a stretch, that it was because I had short arms (overnight?!), or that it was okay because in some cultures that was the way everyone wiped. What cultures, I hear you ask? Well, there is a cult near Byron Bay called the Fat Arsed Tit Sag Organisation (FATSO for short) and they do it out of respect for their 160-kilo spiritual leader Roland McOffal, otherwise known as Riverbed Moonstar Mock Turtle Pussy Willow the third (or Jason Smith, for anyone who went to Mullumbimby High). Anyway, I can now wipe my bum without putting my legs somewhere around my head and I am glad for it. Oh, the simple joys!

Something not nearly as exciting but still a treat for me is being able to wrap a standard size towel around my waist. Until now I'd have to roll up the carpet from the bedroom, wrap it round and hope for the best, or use two towels pinned together. I even started buying bigger towels! Now I can saunter through the house with only one, and that feels bloody great. Wow, I'm almost normal. Yes, okay, that might be a bit of a stretch but I'm getting there, okay?

14 November Grrrrrrr!

I'm having trouble. I cannot crack ninety-five. I did, but it's gone back up. Crusher keeps telling me it's because I'm doing gym work and assures me I *am* losing fat, building muscle and that when the fat drops off it will amaze me just how toned my body will be. She said I've reached a plateau and that launching off it will be like being in a landslide. (I'm hoping more for a lardslide!)

She told me to imagine I am mountain climbing and that I reached the summit (my heaviest) and now I am descending. She said I can only take small steps and when I reach a plateau all I can do is walk towards the edge carefully, slowly and try not to fall off and kill myself (I think that's a metaphor for starving myself to get there). Eventually I will find my way off the plateau and again be heading down the mountain (the right way as opposed to the fastest way).

All I seem to be doing on this plateau is stopping to eat the mountain goat and everything that goes with it. You see, I can't in all good conscience blame the gym and muscle weight. I have been slacking off. Only in a small way. I justify it by saying, 'Well, I've been so good!' You know how it goes. Red wine one day, beer the next, a couple of my son's hot chips, a chicken kebab here, some crisps there, and before you know it there'll be a mobile mechanic parked at my gut trying to change the spare tyre. I never eat a lot but I have been snacking more than usual and more than I am allowed. I am going to go back to the food diary, which will keep me honest. I'm not going to eat sandwiches from shops. I will make my own and lay off the grog. Oh dear, where's my nun's outfit? At least cassocks are black and everyone looks good in that, they're baggy so you'd never see my bum and I'd get to drink alcohol all in the name of godliness . . . Anyway, I'll try to be more focused on what I eat, continue my exercise regime (which I know works) and just keep walking towards that inviting edge of 90 kilos.

15 November   Whistle away, boys

Got perved at today. Woohoo! It's really exciting because I am starting to feel good about myself. I can feel my body changing and if I can just get over my plateau then I'll be off and racing towards the 'Can I get your phone number' body range and 'no, it's not for a Fat-A-Gram'.

Went to Crusher's desperate to get through this obsession with what I weigh. I know muscle weighs more than fat. I know I am losing fat. I know I am gaining muscle—I can see that my legs are a different shape . . . well they actually *have* a shape instead of looking like a pillowcase full of cellulite. They are smaller at the knee than they are at the top of the thigh. I can see some definition there. So the intellectual part of me knows that I am losing fat but the emotional side needs to see it on the scales.

Crusher said she wasn't going to weigh me and said that we would just focus on the measurements for now. She said stick with the food diary and see what happens in two weeks. We did the measurements and I have lost 10 centimetres off each of my hips, breasts and waist. So that is all the proof I need. I have lost fat—it has just been replaced by muscle! It doesn't stop me from wanting the number on the scales to go down, but I now believe I am transforming my body.

Crusher told me to stay focused and I'd be a size 14 for

Christmas. Wow, what a present to myself! I still can't quite believe that it's going to happen.

17 November   Fat friends

Zoë's mum rang me all excited as she heard I had been losing weight. Even though I was adopted and therefore had two mothers, one of them is dead and the other doesn't talk to me so Roz is the closest thing I have to a mum. She was very encouraging and, to her credit, incredibly honest. She too has always struggled with her weight and whenever we get together we always discuss our previous diet failures. She said she had just come back from a forty-minute walk because she said she couldn't handle the thought of me being thinner than her because then she'd have no excuse to be fat any more. If I could lose weight then so could she and she wasn't going to let me get to my goal weight before her.

That made me realise that the people around me are going to react in very different ways to my weight loss. It might also explain why another friend of mine (who is also chubby) always brings around fatty food and drink. She wouldn't admit it but she probably likes being smaller than me and if I become thinner (which I will) then she will either have to lose weight or be the fat friend. God, I look forward to that day. Gee, I'm not really a very nice person, am I? But who wouldn't want to be the one the men talk to first instead of the fat chick the stud's not-so-confident friend gets stuck making small talk with. Not that I've got anything against fat girls—I just don't want to be one any more!

18 November   Back on the market

Oh my God, oh my God, oh my God! I went out last night, all dressed up in a beautiful red dress that hugged me around the waist, breasts pushed up (any more up and they'd be mistaken for weather balloons), big hair and just enough make-up—the final result being that I had not one but *two* boys following me around and flirting. And, yes, they asked me for my phone number! In the last eight years, the only time anyone's asked for my phone number is when I've rear-ended them in the car park of my local supermarket.

Woke up with a wee hangover and thought maybe it hadn't happened. Checked my mobile and it had four text messages from the cuter of the two boys. He's a vet, which I hope doesn't mean he's used to dating dogs! My first thought was, oh dear, I've found myself a stalker, but he left a message in French and everyone knows stalkers do *not* speak French. He wanted to do coffee . . . eek! I have nothing to wear! I have no clothes except for all the fat clothes, which no longer fit, and the one red dress I splashed out on the other day.

Then I started to think, what if he sees me in the daylight and realises I'm actually fat? Maybe the darkened room made me look smaller than I am. I can't exactly walk out on to the street and ask a stranger, 'Does my bum look big in this . . . daylight?' What if he wants to go swimming? Then he'll see how floppy my tree trunks, sorry, legs are! What if, God forbid, he wants to have sex? He'd need a search party to find him after drowning in all my fat! Oh dear! And my breasts! Sure, they looked great with all the scaffolding under my dress but in reality they hang somewhere around my ankles.

I stalled him by saying I was working till later in the week. We're going to have a lunch date. Maybe I'll buy another of those dresses. I can't afford it, but what other option do I have? The charity shop would be good but I'm not sure how impressed he'd be seeing me in a purple velvet pantsuit from the seventies. The mere thought of having to get naked with someone other than my son, who doesn't know that my arse only just fits in the bath, is terrifying but enough to keep me totally focused on the Alfalfa Zone! I think I'll go and do some sit-ups.

Please note: I know you may be wondering why it never occurred to me that (a) I have lost so much weight that I just look a little chubby or (b) that he might like women with flesh on their bones or (c) that I look damn good, but you are forgetting that I have a problem with self-image. Even thin I think I look fat! This is something Dr Nutcase and I will be spending a lot of energy on.

I have had another horrific thought. Anyone I date from here on in, especially when I get to my goal weight, will eventually ask to see photos of my past, as normal people do. What if he sees the photos of that fat girl and says, 'Yeah yeah, no really, where are the photos of you?' Isn't it every man's nightmare? Their skinny girlfriend getting fat? Well, if they know I've been fat then won't they presume that I'll go that way again? Oh dear, this weight loss thing gets more and more complicated every day. If it does happen then what are my options?

1. Lie and say I buried my old photos in a time capsule that won't be opened until 3003.

2. Wait till I get to my goal weight, raid my friend's wardrobe of all her eighties and nineties fashions, spend a day dressing up and taking photos and paste them all into albums of various ages.

3. Say, 'Forget about photos, I'm horny, let's have sex.' Very few men would say, 'No, no, I'd much rather look at you when you were nine and in a nurse's uniform . . .' And if they did, I think that would be a good excuse to warn the local child care centres and do the biggest runner of your life.

Having been fat is like saying you were an alcoholic or drug addict or, worse, it's like admitting you're a Christian at a convention full of atheists. 'Hi, I'm AJ and I used to be mistaken for the Goodyear blimp.' My potential husband would have to change his vows to, 'For thinner or fatter.' Maybe he'd make me sign a prenuptial agreement promising I won't put on weight again. Wedding presents from his mates would be lifetime memberships to Jenny Craig and free sessions of liposuction. Every anniversary would start with a weigh-in and reminder of what I used to look like.

Anyway, I shouldn't stress too much, we're only going out for coffee! And joy of joys, today I weighed in at 93 kilos! I can see the edge of that plateau and IT WILL BE MINE.

19 November
Seeing is not necessarily believing

I said to Dr Nutcase, 'I need help' (as if she didn't know that already!). I cannot see the weight I have lost. Like every female on this planet I am sure I am bigger than I am. I look back at photos of myself when I was anorexic and I swear I was not that thin. I remember how big I thought I was and it just doesn't match the image I see in photos.

So now, 16 kilos lighter than I was four months ago, I look in the mirror and I still see the same body. And even though I can see my body changing shape I am still convinced that I am the same size. I tell myself that the size 14 tracksuit pants I am wearing are marked incorrectly and that they are really a size 24. I tell myself that the scales are wrong, that my linen shirts have stretched. I know it must sound ridiculous, but I guess this is how eating disorders fuel themselves—an altered body image (A nice way of saying I'm screwed up in the head.).

Dr Nutcase explained that this is an emotional response and not based on any facts. I have to find a way in which I can begin to see and accept the changes to my body. She suggested I stop weighing myself (yeah, right) and that I measure myself every week instead. She also asked me to draw a picture of how I see myself. Apparently we are going to do some visualisations and exercises around it. I can see it now. Badly hand-drawn picture of myself in one hand, diet shake in the other, chanting, 'I am thin. I am beautiful. I accept myself and see myself as I am. I am so full of shit

I need a bucket under my mouth to catch the crap.'

Hey, who am I to be cynical? Everything else she has said has worked so maybe this will too.

20 November   Little black dress

Weighed in at ninety-two today and proceeded to ruin my day by eating chips and a sausage roll. I'd probably call that sabotage, wouldn't you? Does it count if you felt guilty after eating it? No, I suppose not. Oh well, as Nutcase says, one meal at a time. There is no right or wrong track.

Went on the date with the vet. Mind you, it was a lunch date, which is slightly less frightening than a dinner date, except in darkness my bum definitely feels smaller. Bought the same dress as the red one, but in black, which means I'm in trouble on the next date unless it's to the gym or somewhere I can wear Winnie the Pooh pyjamas, because I really do have nothing else to wear.

Anyway, it was okay and he asked me out again. Which I guess is a good thing. We'll see . . .

21 November   Gotta love the gym!

Ninety-one, ninety-one, ninety-one—lardslide here I come!

22 November   Demons

Filmed another interview with the Lifestyle Channel. My band and I played at the Basement and they filmed me doing my big girl song and a poem I do about the abuse I experienced as a child. We talked about it on camera (backstage) which was a bit uncomfortable. It's one thing sharing your demons with a friend or a therapist, but telling all of Australia is a different concept altogether. Anyway, I just told myself that if it helps one person get their life together, then what is a little shame and humiliation? The best thing was that my beautiful red satin corset had to be pulled in inches, so there is definite shrinkage of the hips and tits! Woohoo!

23 November   What the?!

The vet stood me up for a dog that had pierced its bowel with a chicken bone. I mean, really! Fancy standing me up for a dying dog. I know it's his job but let's get real. Saving the family pet is not nearly as important as possible sexual relations. Sex is a rare commodity and should always come first!

With Kai at his godmother's I didn't know what to do with myself. Walked around the house thinking about chocolate (love substitute) or going for a swim but it's raining and freezing cold so it just wasn't enticing enough. I couldn't go the gym to do a workout because I did one yesterday and unless I work on different muscle groups I have to wait 48 hours between sessions so my muscles can recover (sounds like a good excuse, huh?). And that's when my whole world just came crashing down on me.

I stood on the scales and they said I was ninety-four. I know Crusher and Nutcase say don't focus on the numbers but I can't help it. Decided to drag out the Denise Austin workout video. It was mild aerobic exercise just finding the video—it was under the lounge, along with three socks, four pens and a Japanese soldier who didn't know the war was over. Took it out of its security sealed plastic cover (well, I've only had it for five years) threw it in the VCR and pressed play.

Oh my God, the eighties were a special time, weren't they? I never realised that fluoro leotards looked so bad! And why did leg-warmers and headbands go out of fashion? Denise was beautiful, and even though she looks like she's never thought about anything that goes into that naturally skinny body, I too believed that I could look that good simply by doing what she does. After all, she did smile at me and say she believed in me and she should know—she's a professional!

Worried about my leg, I was relieved when she said I could do the low-impact version—same exercise, just lower to the floor. Wondered if low to the floor could mean lying down and simply watching *her* do the work. Did that, noticed the carpet was filthy, stopped the video and vacuumed.

Remembering the number 94 I went back to the lounge room and pressed the play button again. The warm-up was pretty easy, then we got into the aerobic section. There I am in my lounge room bouncing around like a wounded epileptic one-legged elephant. I vaguely recall that I was once a dancer but can no longer move my arms and legs in time. At least in aquarobics, my body is submerged under tonnes of water so most of my flailing goes unnoticed!

I may have looked stupid but my heart rate was up and I told myself that meant I was burning fat! She kept telling me to smile but I couldn't find a good reason to. And anyway, if you use only seventeen muscles to smile and thirty-four to frown, surely I'm doing a bigger workout with a sour expression on my face!

Then it started to heat up. Denise promised I was losing inches. Yeah, I was losing inches all right. Every time I jumped up and down my apartment shrunk three inches underground. I live on the first floor, but I'm getting closer to ground level every step I take. I was doing all right until we did the star jumps. After tripping over my breasts I squeezed them back into the bra and tried again. This time they went somewhere over my head. I persevered, jumping up and down on my lounge room floor when suddenly I heard a dim banging noise. I jumped over to the TV, turned the volume down and realised the lady downstairs was banging on her ceiling with a broom. Apparently she doesn't want 94 kilos jumping up and down on her ceiling. Made a mental note to remember this video at midnight the next time she starts hammering her pictures into the wall. Who knew aerobics could be used as revenge?

Thank God I was saved by the floor exercises. I did most of the sit-ups . . . okay, half of them and about half of the leg exercises . . . okay, about a third of those. But at least I did something! I didn't bother doing the cool-down as by this stage I was incapable of moving, too exhausted to call the ambulance and too embarrassed to even contemplate doing an aerobics class in a gym. Not just yet. I might look for a video that was made in the nineties. Maybe the moves and the fashions have improved.

24 November   One meal at a time

Craving chocolate. I know it's because I haven't heard from the vet. Trying to turn it into a positive thigh-firming exercise i.e. he hasn't called me 'cause I'm fat so if I lose weight then he and many more will be lining up at the door.

And it has become obvious to me that my arse has decided to set up camp on this plateau. I think I'll make a feature wall of my thighs and use my bum as the back patio, because let's face it: nothing else will cast a shadow as big as my arse. And where to put the jacuzzi? Between my breasts perhaps? That way I could install a camera, have a bath and make a porno movie at the same time! I'll be rich! Then I can afford to have liposuction. But what to do with the fat? I hear Venice needs to reclaim some land. Maybe I can send it there.

I've spoken to a few fellow Alfalfa Zoners and they are going through the same thing. No one warned me the plateau would be so tough. I remember the first few days were hard, and then it was okay until the six-week turnaround. But those days were nothing on this.

Having reverted back to the food diary I am eating well. I went to a conference the other day and even took my own lunch, only just managing to bypass the beautiful smorgasbord with a devil on my shoulder whispering, 'Go on, you only live once!' But I was really good and that night avoided the alcohol *and* the dessert table. It was an $80 plate of salad and rice but I know my thighs will thank me and that's all that counts, isn't it?

On Crusher's advice I am varying my exercise—gym,

swim, aqua and walking. And I can't believe it but the other day I did a twenty-minute jog. Okay, it looked more like a stumble but it wasn't walking and I didn't end up with black eyes, so some things have changed.

All I can do is just keep on it and trust that at some point the muscle weight will stop increasing and the fat will continue to decrease and so the weight on the scales will start to go down again. I desperately need a measure. Crusher's hard to get hold of this week so I'm bumbling around blindly. But I just need to remember—one meal at a time. If I eat three meals and three snacks, limit my fat *and* exercise, I will lose weight. I don't need to miss meals or do anything drastic, which is what I would normally do. This is where I cue the voice of Dr Nutcase: 'Diets don't work—healthy eating and exercise does.'

25 November   High on the hills

One plateau for sale or rent. Owner must vacate as soon as possible. Plenty of room—would suit the Von Trapp family. No pets as I would probably deep fry and eat them.

I think I'm suffering from altitude sickness. Or is that attitude sickness? I think I'm 92 kilos but I also think that it could just be temporary because it all depends on when you weigh yourself, doesn't it? I mean, it's the ultimate dilemma. With shoes or without? With clothes or without? In the morning when you definitely feel lighter because you wake up so hungry you could eat your child before getting out of bed? Do you weigh pre or post poo? I always weigh pre and post and am always disappointed, expecting to have lost at least half a kilo. I had locked my scales away in the laundry, only bringing them out once a day, but up here on the plateau we do things differently and that could mean weigh-ins four or five times a day. Just give me a pig's head on a stick and I could call this plateau home! I am Lord of the Thighs.

Haven't had this craving for a while . . . KFC. They're advertising extra crunchy skin and as I've admitted before, the skin was the only thing I ate. I can't watch the commercials. I have to change channels but every now and then I am like a moth to a flame and I just have to watch the ads. Have made a deal with myself. Be really strict now, and when I get to 88 kilos I can have some KFC. Hopefully by then I won't feel like it but it feels like a good deal to have made. And it's only about four kilos away.

Having lost 16 kilos I am back thinking that I haven't lost any weight at all. I drew the picture of myself and Dr Nutcase said I drew it much fatter than I actually am. She made me stand up in front of her and she walked around my body pointing out that I had a waist and that I was wearing clothes that three months ago I couldn't have fitted into.

'Yes, but this dress makes me look thinner than I am!' I reasoned rather pathetically.

She shook her head and said she wanted to see my measurements and that she would make a graph out of them. She said I needed to tell myself that I choose to have two different thought processes—sensible or silly. Sensible thinking is that *I have* lost weight, my clothes no longer fit and it's not because they've suddenly stretched in the washing machine (yes, I did think that!). It's because I am considerably smaller than I was when I started this thing (six dress sizes ago). I have to acknowledge that I am more than halfway to my original goal of losing 30 kilos and the optional extra 15 kilos will be dealt with when I get there.

Silly thinking is convincing myself that I have not lost weight, thinking I am not losing it quickly enough, and focusing on what I still have to lose rather than on what I have lost.

Yes, well, that's sounds easy enough on paper but in reality all I can do is eat well and try not to think about the half a packet of jellybeans I ate yesterday afternoon. I feel like I've fallen into an episode of 'Survivor', only I've eaten my entire tribal council and now there's no one left to vote me off!

26 November   Choc-Anon

1 pm: Have had a breakthrough psychologically. Nutcase asked me how much weight I had lost. I said 16 kilos, then she gave one of those groovy little exercises she'd been alluding to. My mission was to go to the supermarket and load into my trolley 16 kilos of potatoes. I was to try to lift those potatoes all at once (something I failed to do) and then to think about those potatoes being strapped to my body and to realise that this is what I have already lost. Then I was to realise that by simply doing what I have already done, it is inevitable that I will lose another trolley full of potatoes—I mean, fat from my body.

The benefit of this exercise is that you really start to accept the changes you have made to your body. And when caught in the trap of thinking one kilo is not enough—or even 16 kilos is not good enough—when measured out in potatoes or rice or whatever you choose, it is in reality a lot of weight to lose (or to have already lost). It gives you a different perspective and it's one that has worked for me. It's no wonder I now find it easier to carry Kai. Before I was flat out walking 150 metres to the corner shop, let alone carrying him as well. Now I can grab him and run around the block. That has got to be a good thing!

1.30 pm: Chocolate. Chocolate. Chocolate. Please don't let me be premenstrual!

1.45 pm: Craving chocolate. Chocolate covered sultanas. Frozen Mars Bars. Chocolate mud cake. Chocolate chocolate chocolate. Haven't had a craving like this for a looong time. I think the last one was the Pizza Hut incident. I am moving into some dangerous territory. I'm sure it's because I haven't heard from the vet since he ran away to save Fido from its pierced bowel last Saturday night. Oh well, back to basics. Just think forward to the next meal . . . which will not be chocolate!

1.55 pm: Trying to think how I can wrangle it so that eating chocolate is allowed. Chocolate on a Lean Cuisine? Chocolate-covered carrot sticks? Chocolate laxatives? No, I'm afraid that is one industry that has let women down badly. Until they can come up with a no-fat chocky bar then they are conspiring to keep us all fat, which probably works for them because when we're fat we give up and think there's no point so we eat more chocolate, then no one wants to date us and we eat chocolate instead of finding a man, then we get depressed about eating so much chocolate and the only way to feel better is to eat more chocolate and . . . oh my God, it is a conspiracy!

2.07 pm: Maybe I am premenstrual and then it would be okay to have just a little bit because obviously my body needs it to prepare for the trauma of the days to come. Uh-huh!

2.09 pm: Since the beginning of time men and women have turned to certain vices to make their lives less miserable. For men it is beer. For women it is none other than sweet, beautiful brown and sometimes even white chocolate.

2.11 pm: Okay, that's it. I am desperate. I hereby declare the first ever meeting of Chocoholics Anonymous open. Please repeat after me the Twelve Steps of the newly assembled Choc Anon:

1. We admitted we were powerless over Chocolate—that our lolly bags had become unmanageable.
2. Came to believe that a Chocolate greater than cocoa could restore us to sanity.
3. Made a decision to turn our will and our lives over to the care of Chocolate.

4. Made a searching and fearless inventory of our chocolate stash.

5. Admitted to Chocolate, to ourselves and to another human being the exact nature of our cravings (chocolate-covered sultanas, chocolate bars or chocolate drinks).

6. We're ready to have God remove all defective chocolate from our fridge, cupboards and bedside tables.

7. Humbly asked God to remove all calories from chocolate.

8. Made a list of all the chocolates we had eaten, and became willing to make a meal of them all.

9. Made direct amends to people we had covered in chocolate body paint, except where to do so would injure them or otherwise make them unattractive.

10. Continued to take personal inventory and when we were wrong promptly admitted we had underestimated our chocolate intake.

11. Sought through prayer and meditation to improve our conscious contact with Chocolate as we understood It, praying only for knowledge of Its will for us and the power to carry that out (without being caught).

12. Having had a spiritual awakening as a result of these steps, we tried to carry this message to Chocoholics and to practise these principles in all our affairs.

I don't feel so bad now. Knowing that there are other people in my dilemma gives me strength. Remember: one step at a time!

2.17 pm: Okay, this was entirely beyond my control (yeah, right, I hear you snicker). But it was my friend's birthday and she brought around her birthday cake and I couldn't *not* have a piece because that would mean her wish wouldn't come true and how could I be responsible for the ruination of her dreams?

Oh sure, she was being responsible for the ruination of mine by bringing the chocolate mud cake into my house in the first place, especially knowing that I *am* in the Alfalfa Zone, but it's okay for people to ruin *my* life. I'm used to it.

Did I really just say that?

It was a classic moment of sabotage but I didn't have to eat it, did I? She didn't force the cake into my mouth. It was in my mouth before she had a chance to get through the door. I'm amazed the plate and knife didn't go in there as well. The good thing was that I literally only had a sliver and when she asked if she could leave the cake here I said no. She then threw it in my bin but determined not to have the temptation in my house I made her take it outside and put it in the rubbish bin on the street.

So in my new life of making healthy choices, I did well, as previously I'd have had half the cake and finished the rest for breakfast. At least I sated my craving for chocolate with the smallest amount possible (other than having none, which in reality was never going to be an option).

4 pm: Oh dear. It's back. It's like heroin (not that I know from personal experience). One taste and I can't stop thinking about it. Looks like it's back to Chocoholics Anonymous. Now where did I put those twelve steps? Oh, I covered them in Nutella and ate them. Goody. At least I've digested the information.

27 November   The new plan!

Have considered hiring a dog sled team to try to drag my arse over the plateau but realised I'd have to explain to the RSPCA why seventeen dogs died of exertion.

This is my plan. It's four weeks until Christmas, at which time I'm sure to do a lot of bargaining with meals. So I have made a deal with myself. A strict plan. Nothing extra! I stick to my eating plan of three meals, three snacks. I get up early and eat first thing to get the metabolism firing. The only mid-meal snacks I will have are fruit or yoghurt. Normally I have a range of things, jelly snakes, pretzels, red licorice, sardines on rice thins, muffins, pikelets etc, but while most of those are low in fat, they are higher in calories than fruit (not to mention them just not being as good for you nutritionally) and less satisfying.

I will also be totally strict and have no margarine, not even Weight Watchers. I will drink little to no alcohol (oh God, did I really say that?) and all lunches and dinners will be prepared with as little fat as possible, and I'll avoid food from restaurants, cafes, sandwich shops etc.

I will try to increase my exercise which I find difficult being a single mum with no close family support but what I *can* do is on the days Kai is at kindy, I'll do a workout and I'll do a swim as well. On the off workout days I will do a swim and go for a walk with Kai, thus adding another thirty minutes on top of what I'm already doing. I know I won't have to do this forever, but to get me off the plateau this is what I need to do.

When I get hungry, I will drink three long glasses of water.

I will not buy any tempting foods for my son or myself. I will not go into shops that sell hot chips (my weakness). The only food in my cupboards will be healthy and low-fat. I will not go near any shops if I have not eaten. I will eat first then shop. I have pasted signs with: 'Stay Focused! Under 90!' all over my house—on the fridge door, bathroom mirror and lounge room wall. I will not have any dinner parties and therefore be tempted to eat more than I should or drink more than I should. I will no longer have a life.

I know it sounds pretty extreme but it's not really. It's a matter of choices. I want to be less than 90 kilos by Christmas. I will have more than enough to eat, I'm a single mum so I don't have a life anyway, and I want to give myself a healthy body for the New Year. Sure, I won't be at my goal weight (yet!) but I will be under 90 and 80 will seem that much closer and I will know I have managed to get over one of the greatest obstacles in dieting, oops, I mean Alfalfa Zoning—the plateau. I'm sure this is where most people give up.

Well, I couldn't live with myself if I gave up because it's not really that hard. It's not a sacrifice, it's a gift. Giving myself a healthy body, a more active lifestyle, a longer life, a more physical relationship with my son, a good figure I can be proud of, an ability to go into a shop and not have the mirror laugh back at me or sales assistants say, 'I'm afraid we have nothing in your size—Tent City is that way!', or just being in control is the greatest gift I can give myself and seems the world compared to giving up a few drinks and the odd packet of chips.

So here I go.

28 November   Yeehaa!

90.6 kg! I know weight doesn't matter, but let's be real—it does! No matter how many times you go to the shrink, what we weigh means a lot. We've been brainwashed by the fashion mags that weight *does* matter. So today as I joyously weigh myself, I can see being under ninety is just around the corner.

I stood on the scales and couldn't believe my eyes. I changed the batteries to make sure they were working. Then I stood on them five more times to make sure I wasn't dreaming. I was 90.6 kilos! If my son was old enough to call the local mental hospital he would have 'cause I jumped around the room like a . . . like a . . . like a fat girl who realises she has lost 18 kilos and is beginning to believe she might *not* be fat for the rest of her life!

Then I stood on the scales with my two year old whom I can barely lift and weighed seven kilos *less* than my starting weight. I've lost nearly twice his weight! My, how things have changed! I lifted him up again and wondered how I managed to carry that much weight on my body. It's amazing I haven't had a heart attack.

29 November
The body or the sausage?

Okay, so the day started off well. I had my toast and yoghurt for breakfast, banana for snack, salad roll, muesli bar and apple for lunch and then I went to The BBQ. There I was, stomach rumbling, steely determination being chipped away by the pungent waft of offal and sawdust (otherwise known as sausage). I could hear the sizzling, spitting sound that wonderful thing called fat makes as it hits the hotplate. Looked down and realised it was the sound of my dribble hitting the hotplate and not the sausages sizzling away. Oh dear, I knew I was in trouble. Left the cooking area. No good, the smell was following me around. It was like a bad song caught in my head. There he was, Elvis, microphone made out of sausage in one hand, burger in the other, crooning, 'Viva, Lust Sausage . . .'

Told myself I was not hungry, I was thirsty. Drank two litres of water, nearly drowned, pulled my head out of the dog bowl, then somehow found myself once again standing at the BBQ, Rain Man-like, counting the sausages. 'Four hundred and thirty-two. Four hundred and thirty-two sausages on the BBQ. Four hundred and thirty-two sausages on the BBQ and none for me! They don't serve sausages on Qantas! They don't . . .'

Walked away again. Started reasoning with myself. Cue the voice of Dr Nutcase: I don't *need* the sausage, I *want* the sausage. I deserve a healthy body. What's more important? A good body or a good sausage? No, don't answer that, AJ! If it's this hard now, what's it going to be like over Christmas? I'll have to tell my family that they are to have no lollies, no nuts, no chips, no ham, no pork, no chicken . . . oh my God, I'll be Scrooge McDuck. It'll be the last time I'm invited for Christmas.

Ate a banana. Tried to imagine it was a sausage. Dribbled on a stranger. Paced back and forth. Tried to do a deal. Said I wouldn't eat dinner—but I know that is unhealthy eating and

I made a deal with Nutcase and myself that I would eat all my meals. Bargained and said I'd just eat a salad for dinner, and that was the mistake because before it had a chance to even hit the taste buds it was gone and almost instantaneously I could feel the fat coursing to my thighs.

Still, I thought, it's only one sausage and it's not going to kill me. And the day would have been okay had I not then proceeded to finish Kai's peanut butter sandwiches, had two vodka and cranberry juices, and topped my disaster of a day off with two spring rolls and a seafood laksa—the strangest looking salad I have ever seen.

This has to be sabotage. I must be afraid of getting thin. That's the only thing that makes sense. That or I have absolutely no resolve, which I know is not true because I have lost 18 kilos. No, it must be fear of being thin.

What could possibly be bad about being thin?

Reasons I might not want to be thin

- When doing comedy I might be mistaken for the microphone.
- I'd no longer be approached by Fat-A-Gram companies telling me I'm going to be the next big thing.
- When with a new lover he'd say, 'Oh, how cute, you've got freckles on your chest! Oh sorry, they're you're breasts!'
- Have to run around in the shower to get wet.
- When at the park, dogs would try to bury me.
- Would have to go out with guys like Gary.

Hmm, better talk to Nutcase about it this week.

30 November   Cravings

10 am: Oh God, weighed in at 91. I'm sure if I can just get to 89, everything will be okay, it will be the magic number and suddenly I'll be focused again and the weight will magically drop off. Was it this hard at the beginning? The time and weight seem to have flown. I'm having a crisis and I feel all alone.

I guess that's where places like Weight Watchers come in handy. But I can't stand the thought of paying someone $15.95 a week to weigh me, sigh and shake their head at my total lack of control.

Today is going to be a good day. I'll go for a long walk with Kai and I will stick to the plan. Honestly, I will!

2 pm: Talk about cravings cravings cravings. I have become obsessed. All I can think about is pizza, hot chips, chocolate, beer, fried chicken and spring rolls. This has to be sabotage. Can't get under 90 kilos. Will I ever? I won't believe I'm off the plateau until I hit 89. Aaah!

Have decided it is time to hit the cookbooks again. It must be a taste thing. I'm bored with the same old food. I need to find new foods that are low fat but interesting and tasty to eat.

1 December   Location! Location!

I am moving house and it is quite strange saying this but I am moving into the street where my gym and pool is. I never thought I'd see the day when real estate became attractive because of the closeness of my gym. What has become of me? Next I'll be discussing the virtues of carrot sticks versus celery. Hmm, I think not.

6 December   Life on the loo, Part II

Moved house. Didn't get to work out much this week although I did have a great case of the spew and poos. As I was conversing with God down the toilet bowl I couldn't help but think of my next weigh-in with a little degree of hope. Maybe this will help me crack the 90 barrier. I guess that's the old bulimic in me. I can't remember what I found so good about throwing up all the time.

7 December   Why not?

Ninety point five. Damn! Not even a legal spew can get me over the edge. Oh well, head down, bum up, focus on the goal, work out, and eat well. Crusher assures me the edge is near. Maybe only a week away. I can't help but add up all my numbers, presuming I wanted to lose a kilo a week, and think I'm three weeks behind. I was supposed to be 89 at the end of November! Then I reason with myself that those figures were calculated *before* I broke my leg, and considering I was bedridden for six of those weeks I'm not doing too badly. Oh well, one step at a time, even if it *is* with a limp.

My gym is having a Christmas party and after weeks of looking at the sign and scoffing, I was in the pool doing aqua when the teacher asked me if I was coming. There I was, weightlessly floating in the pool on a beautiful blue-sky day, I felt gorgeous, perhaps even athletic, and I wanted to go to this party and have a great time, partying on with all the other people who are just like me—into fitness. So, in a moment of waterlogged stupidity, I agreed and handed over the cash. Twenty-five bucks.

Maybe it's a good thing. I'm not too sure. After all, this is the new me. New house, new clothes, new body. All I need is a life and I might even find myself a new man. I've committed myself now so I'll just have to go and have a good time. Party on!

8 December   How embarrassing!

Oh my God! Did I honestly think that going to the gym Christmas party would be a good idea? It started off well. I got all dressed up in the flowing princess frock. I looked good! Caught a cab, thought I'd have a few drinks (only a few and only vodka and soda!). Halfway there it dawned on me that I was going to a nightclub where I knew absolutely no one. Okay, I knew the instructors . . . well, if knowing them means being the object of their looks of pity as I half drown in their pool. What was I doing? No, I reasoned, there will be people from my class. Yes, people I've never spoken to apart from saying, 'Excuse me, did you just wee in the water or was that me?' No, gyms are funky places, places where people have joint interests in fitness. It makes us part of one big club—the club of health. It's going to be all right, I tried to convince myself as I hesitantly stepped inside.

And there I was completely out of my depth with not one single flotation device in sight to save my sorry arse. I headed straight for the bar. I needed a drink to get me through this. I ordered a double vodka and soda then turned around to survey the room. I knew no one. I couldn't even recognise the instructors out of their gym uniforms and when I did they were all huddled in their nice little my buns are tighter than your buns group. I looked over at the dance floor—maybe there was someone from my class. It was then I remembered most of the people in my class were over fifty and were all probably at home getting ready for bed. I was in trouble!

There I was in my to-the-floor flowing princess dress and what were 99 per cent of the women wearing? Handkerchiefs! Hankies tied around their tits! I just wish I was joking. I think their pants had been spray-painted on. Blonde hair was the order of the day, tans were luminous and I realised with horror that I had fallen into my very own nightmare. I was trapped in a room full of skinny hankie-wearing gym junkies—the kind of girls who do . . . aerobics! And I want to do classes with these people?

I needed an escape plan. I couldn't just walk out, not only because I had just walked in but also because I hadn't finished my drink. And had it not been ten bucks then I could easily have left it on the table and done the biggest fat-burning runner of my life.

I sat down at a table very aware that I was ALONE. I looked very single and all of a sudden I felt fat again. I thought if I could talk on my mobile then it might look as if my friends were late and I was waiting for them. Pretended to talk on the phone, sipping madly at my drink, cursing the double as it was too strong to down in one. Then my instructor spotted me. She bounced over in leggings so tight I could see what she'd had for breakfast. 'You came,' she cried. 'Great! I won't interrupt you,' she said, pointing to my mobile, then bounced away to join the pack of instructors.

Anyway, foiled by my own plan, the drink now finished, I had *no one* to talk to. I knew I would vomit if I watched the skinny girls throw themselves around the dance floor one more time. My big night was well and truly over. Without looking back I was out of the nightclub, into the bottle shop and back home with my low-fat beer and a packet of salt and vinegar chips. And, yes, I know I shouldn't have had them but that was a horrific incident and I needed some comfort food.

I will never ever ever go to a gym thing again. I'm dreading going back to class because I know the teacher will say, 'What happened to you?' and then I know I will have to say 'I got scared' or lie. At least having a kid gives you a permanent excuse for having to go home early. 'My son had a temperature!' Which isn't even a lie! He did have a temperature—it was normal!

9 December   Bugger!

Ninety point eight! Damn those chips!

Is it just me or does everyone who has put on weight avoid anyone they knew when they were thin? Especially ex-boyfriends. Especially ex-boyfriends who are with their new girlfriends.

Actually, it's not just ex-boyfriends that I avoid. All the actors I have worked with are all high on the list of people I hide from when crossing the street. Friends from high school are next on the list—in fact anyone and everyone I knew when I was thin I manage to avoid like the plague, even resorting to ducking behind pot plants so I can't be seen. I'm afraid they either won't remember me or don't recognise me because they knew me thin or, worse still, would be so embarrassed for me that they wouldn't know what to say. But let me just say that this reasoning is not totally unjustified.

I bumped into a comedienne I hadn't seen for about five years and the second thing she said to me after hello, was, 'How come you got so fat?' Of course I should have used the old line, 'I might be fat but you're ugly and at least I can lose weight.' But the reality of the situation was that I didn't have anything so witty fly from my mouth. I blamed pregnancy, my failed relationship and I may have even thrown in some child abuse for good measure. That was one of the defining moments for me (please note it took more than *one* defining moment for me to actually get off my bum and do this thing!). I couldn't continue to live my life making excuses for what I had done to myself.

Anyway, as the weight has come off I have been imagining all these wonderful scenarios in which I bump into one of them, saunter past sexily, look them in the eyes and whisper, 'You wish . . .'

So today, as I was walking through the supermarket in my sweaty tracky daks and ten-year-old t-shirt, hair lank, oily and plastered to my face but modelling my new and improved gym body, I ran smack bang into an ex. I brushed myself off, looked him in the eye and ran away as fast as I could. Huh, there's nothing like progress.

But I do look forward to the day when I can once again hold my head high, be proud of myself, feel comfortable and confident and not be ashamed of my body. Of course this isn't just about the body. This is the stuff I have to work on with Dr Nutcase but as we uncover the layers (excuse the pun) then we are getting to that stuff.

Anyway, to kind of make a point (was I?), on days when I don't want to go to the gym I think of all the people I avoid and use that as an incentive. I want to be as confident as I could possibly be and that means being happy with the way I am. Gym and the Shrink. Gym and shrink. Huh, I never thought of the shrinking image of the body vs actually seeing the shrink. Funny that. Go to the shrink, get well on the inside and shrink on the outside. Spooky!

10 December   Four doors from fitness

Walked down the end of my street to do aqua today. What a joy it is to be so close. I also discovered there are beautiful walks along the harbour, so I'm going to put Kai in the stroller and take him for sunset power-walks, particularly on the days I don't have child care and can't get to the gym.

I did it. I threw away all of my fat clothes. Well, I didn't throw ALL of them out just in case I go on one of those current affair shows. Then I can show them my before and after clothes. My only problem now is that I don't have any money to buy new clothes but I have my two new dresses, and a lot of tracksuit pants, so until I have some money to spend those will have to do. It's funny really. When I look at the scales and see I've lost 19 kilos, I have trouble actually believing it. I remember when I started here in the Alfalfa Zone, a friend told me about his flatmate who had lost 20 kilos. At the time, I didn't really think I would even get that far as I've failed every other time and I've never had to lose as much as I do now. I truly believe that for me to put on that weight again I would have to be in so much denial I'd have to be committed.

12 December   Again

Just popping down the street to do a bit of a workout. Teeheehee.

14 December
Dr Nutcase's famous five

The first thing I said to Nutcase was, 'You have to help me with my cravings!' I explained that not only am I plagued with them but also whenever I weigh in closer to 90, I almost automatically want to go out and eat junk food. I also explained that, sometimes, referring to the techniques she taught me (reminding myself that food does not lead to happiness, repeating that I am in control, remembering that good food and exercise are what works etc) just isn't enough and no amount of simple explanations, no matter how good they sound, are enough to stop me from eating the crap food.

I asked her if it was sabotage and she said it might be. She said that I seemed to fluctuate between extremes in eating habits. All or nothing. I go from bingeing to starving. The starving she related to something called 'the feedback phenomenon'. This is where you are dieting and suddenly people start noticing, they heap praise on you, you feel good, you get more attention, you feel good, people start flirting with you, you feel good, people ask how you look so good, you feel good. Then what you want to do is increase that response and do it quickly. You try to make it happen faster because what you are trying to do is get the praise rather than get your body and mind working well as a healthy unit. You are simply trying to feel better by getting people to notice your dramatic (and possibly unhealthy) transformation.

The other aspect, the bingeing, was explained another way. So much of our lives and happiness revolve around food. If we take the breastfeeding situation as our first feeding experience, it is generally a good one with lots of comfort, love, language and so on all thrown in for your dinner entertainment. Then we have birthday parties, Christmas, celebrations, picnics, dates . . . Even just a meal time for most people is a time for getting together and being with your family and friends—a happy occasion for a lot of people. So food becomes a source of happiness, be it the food itself, the preparation, the presentation or simply the ritual of eating.

Take, for instance, my passion for hot chips. It's not just any old hot chips. It's the old-fashioned chunky chips wrapped up in butcher's paper. You rip the end open, let the steam rise out and caress your nose (oh my God, my mouth's watering) and you dig in and eat them, burning your fingers and mouth on the first few chips, and it is almost a religious experience for me. Growing up in a small country town, fish and chips were a rarity that we usually waited months to enjoy, so for me there is a lot of happiness in that greasy little parcel. Add to that the fact that those meal times were when we were having a big day out in the nearby town (our closest fish and chip shop was 35 kilometres away) so they were never marred by fights and arguments which generally happened a lot in my home, particularly at meal times, which were about the only times my parents actually got together.

So when I weigh in I either feel the need to sabotage that or I want to make myself feel good (celebrate) and up until now the only way I've known how is by eating, rewarding myself with food and rewarding myself with bad choices. Cast your mind back to my first or second week in the Alfalfa Zone. My food reward was a battered sav. Battered savs directly relate to the Royal Easter Show and everyone knows how good that is as a kid (and for those non-Aussies who don't, it's a kind of big agricultural fair). Fatty food was my happy food and this was before the invention of the Happy Meal by you-know-who (note the meaning that goes with that . . . you are eating the *Happy* Meal, so this food will always make you *happy*). Why can't they also have the 'You've just been dumped by your boyfriend meal deal'? Or the 'Haven't Had Sex in Twenty Years Combo deal'? With both of those you get absolutely nothing on the side.

Nutcase made me list the top five cravings I get. The big five hit list of food I fantasise about and struggle not to surrender to. This is my list in order of preference:

1. Hot chips. From my favourite fish and chip shop where they have the old-fashioned thick chippies, cooked well, with salt and BBQ sauce, wrapped up in butcher's paper. Hmm. Rip the end off, inhale the oily potato aroma and eat them even when they're so hot they burn your tongue. Bloody delicious.

2. Pizza. Well, you know the struggle I have with that. Pizza Hut or gourmet seafood pizzas from my local pizza shop. Love 'em!

3. Sausage rolls. The ones with the flaky pastry and, for a nice surprise, meat rather than sawdust. Covered in tomato sauce they are bloody beautiful.

4. Then of course there is KFC. It's only the skin I like but you can't just eat that and leave the flesh, because I come from the Eat What's On Your Plate era. A three-piece pack with chips would suffice at the moment, but as I've said, I have been known to buy and consume an eight-piece or more pack.

5. Chocolate. Ah yes, the good old chocolate craving. White chocolate is my fave but I'm not fussy. Anything in chocolate would do me. Time Outs, Kit Kats, Picnics, Crunchies, Smarties, ooh why go on, the lust, sorry list, is endless. Anything that is chocolate is all right by me. I remember once being so premenstrual and so broke even the chocolate-covered dog biscuits started to look okay.

So my mission, should I accept it, is to create alternatives to these foods and create new rituals of happiness that in time will replace the old ones.

1. Hot chips. Fat-free wedges. What I am to do is make it an experience with Kai. We will cut up the potatoes, cook them, wrap them up in paper and walk to the park at the end of our street and eat them. That way creating a new and happy experience around a similar yet healthier food.

2. Pizza. Healthy pizzas on pita bread. I will experiment with different ingredients. I will find out whether ricotta can go on pizza and if not I will use a little low-fat cheese. Yummy!

3. Sausage roll substitute. That one is going to be a little difficult but I need to find a recipe for stuffed filo pastry. I could do spinach and ricotta triangles in the meantime and look for something with perhaps lean mince or chicken in it. Once again, I need to put it in a paper bag with some sauce and go to the park or the pool.

4. KFC. Okay, so this one is the big challenge. Will check the Internet but in the meantime I will do a skinless roast chicken and have friends to dinner to enjoy the healthy food rather than seeing the healthy food as something I have to keep private or hidden. My new healthy lifestyle is a wonderful thing I can share with my friends—that way it will reinforce the fact that this is a good way to live and that the other way is not really living life to the fullest. The other alternative is to do chicken legs with honey and soy marinade and cook them in the oven. Provided I don't eat about ten legs, then that is a healthy alternative as well.

5. Chocolate. I have low-fat fudge brownies by Betty Crocker and White Wings do a pretty awesome fat-free chocolate muffin. Nutcase reckons that Nestlé have a diet chocolate mousse that is only 50 calories, so there's an allowable chocolate fix I can have. To create a happy ritual around it I can cook the muffins/brownies with Kai and have a little tea party. Then I can individually wrap and freeze the rest for those moments of weakness, of which there are plenty.

So if I create these new rituals, not only will I sort myself out but I will also be giving Kai wonderful memories of fresh healthy food thus ensuring (hopefully) that he will look at food in a healthy manner and never have to de-programme the way he looks at eating like I have to. He will see it as a positive experience and will have that as a foundation for future eating habits.

Then we talked about Christmas. I told her I was worried I will go crazy with food, as there would be lots of temptation. She took me back to the food = happiness explanation. All the Christmases with my adopted family have been celebrated by eating so much there is little to do but sleep or vomit, sometimes even both at the same time. Our family Christmas lunch usually consisted of roast pork, roast chicken, leg of ham, two kilos of king prawns, roast veggies, lots of gravy, Christmas cake, pudding, ice cream, apple pie and custard. On top of that we had nibblies like lollies, chips, fruit, peanuts, cabanossi, cheese, crackers and God knows what else I may have blocked out of my memory. They were pig-out fests. Everyone was so busy eating there

AJ's fabulous low-fat pizza

1 round of pita bread

1–2 tablespoons tomato pizza paste

250 g seafood mix (calamari, mussels, prawns, scallops, baby squid, fish pieces)

2 cloves of garlic, finely chopped

red or green pepper strips (if you like)

3–4 mushrooms, sliced

¼ onion, sliced

1–2 teaspoons fresh parsley and chopped chives

3 sun-dried tomatoes, chopped

50–100 g lite cheese, grated

(Add any extras you like: tomato, chilli, pineapple etc)

Preheat the oven to 200 degrees. Lightly dampen the bread with water, using a paper towel. Cover the bread with the pizza paste, scatter the remaining ingredients over the bread, then top with cheese and place on a baking sheet in the oven for about 15 minutes. Eat and enjoy. This is totally delicious and can be made for dinner parties.

It can be frozen after cooking. Serves 2; contains 8 g fat.

was no time for fighting, so we all had a good time. Some Chrissies when I've been on my own I've eaten a whole chicken and about ten baked potatoes and a bucket of gravy.

So going somewhere I don't have control over what food is around me is a daunting prospect, particularly if everyone else will be gorging themselves.

The plan is to be prepared. Once again, work on having a great family Christmas, with good food and not too much, thus creating a new Christmas memory that is not based around the consumption of gross amounts of food. I will ring Helen (my stepmum—my birth father's wife, to be exact) and ask her what she's cooking for Chrissy lunch and ask if she would mind if I did some cooking or brought some of my own food. Knowing there will be ham, I will buy lite ham. I will cook roast chicken and have the breast. I will cook the veggies in the oven with no oil. I won't have any gravy and I will also take my own snacks like pretzels, rice crackers and fruit, that way eating allowable foods rather than food full of fat.

I will need to find a gym and make sure I go regularly and keep up my swimming. I will buy some lite beer and try to temper the drinking as much as possible. Hopefully, if all goes according to plan, and knowing that in some cases I will crumble, at least being prepared will mean that I always have good choices close to hand rather than having the excuse: 'It was Christmas, the shops were closed and I had no choice.'

It made me feel less anxious and certainly more in control. If I can get through Chrissy without making a pig of myself then I will have made progress in my eating habits.

It seemed a really obvious solution but when you're caught up in the pattern of what you've always done you feel a certain amount of powerlessness. That's why I like going to Nutcase. She just looks at it from the outside and simply states what sounds like reasonable common sense. Ideas I can totally accept and include in my life. She makes it sound easy. When I say that to her she smiles mysteriously and then says, 'Yes, but you didn't get a good start and you are simply doing what you've been taught. Now you are learning a new way of life.'

She finished the last session for the year by telling me I had done an amazing job. Assuring me I wasn't insane, she said she believed in me and that she knew I would do well over Christmas and that she would see me in the new year.

I left feeling I could overcome the enigmatic power of the roast pig leg. Low-fat Christmas dinner here I come . . .

16 December Feelings

Oh my God, I was in my local shopping centre doing a last-minute Christmas shop for Kai when I got a call from a friend who is off to a funeral tomorrow. She says this guy's from out of town, a real mover and shaker in the theatre industry, and I just go cold. I don't know why but I then say to her, please tell me it's not so-and-so, and she says yes, he was killed in a head-on collision on Tuesday. I burst into tears. I realise one of my dearest friends is dead.

Got off the phone and without thinking walked straight to the food court. Found myself staring zombie-like at the muffin shop. Then I circled the donut shop, the cookie house and all those beautiful brightly lit self-serve all-you-can-eat Asian buffet shops. I was in trouble. I knew I wanted to comfort eat but I also knew that I would feel even worse afterwards. Dr Nutcase talks about learning to recognise the bad behaviour before the event and making a better choice. This was it. This was the moment of truth. I knew this was a test.

I could hear the reasoning going on inside my head. *Recognise, Challenge, Distract.* But one of your best friends has just died. It won't kill you to have some junk food. *I don't need this food.* I've been so good; one meal will not make any difference. I'm in shock. *This food will not make me happy.* This food will make me happy. *I don't use food as a comfort anymore.* Spring rolls, dim sims, sweet and sour pork and fried rice *will* make me happy. *Being* healthy *will make me happy. Dim sims will make me fat.* Dim sims don't have head-on collisions and leave you devastated at the loss of their life. *Dim sims will keep me fat and unhappy and put me back where I started.* Hmph! I hate it when you're right!

I circled the food hall three or four times. And then I realised that this moment could be a defining moment (what, another one?) in my eating habits for the rest of my life. This is where I make the right choice and I remember it—if my friend can't live his life then I will live mine and live it well by honouring myself. I walked over to the not so brightly lit healthy sandwich counter and ordered a grilled chicken and salad sandwich, no butter, no mayo, on whole-meal bread.

Halfway through the sandwich I realised I was not very hungry at all. In fact, I actually felt quite ill. It was then that I realised I was *feeling* something. I was sad and pained at the loss of my friend and instead of smothering it with food I was actually *experiencing* it. And even more amazing was that it wasn't killing me. I didn't need to smother my emotions with food. I could meet them face to face, deal with them and honour myself at the same time.

I still felt incredibly sad at the death of my friend but I felt better for having made a good choice and I knew I would feel even worse had I made an unhealthy decision. I had a choice and I made the right one! RIP DB.

89 KILOS

(196 lb)

17 December   Guilty!

Goodbye plateau, goodbye arse. I have finally hit 89 kilos. I have now lost the grand sum of 20 kilos, which is two-thirds of my original goal, and if I lose another ten that means I am more than halfway to having the perfect bod. I seriously thought I would not make it this far. Five months, 20 kilos, a broken leg, absolutely no sign of a man in my life, but I am an Alfalfa Zone legend!

I have never done this much work on my body before. My legs are totally transforming. I can see how good they are going to look as the fat is starting to drop off. A friend came over last night and said I look like I'm a third of the person I was. Someone else made a passing remark and called me muscles, referring to the muscles forming on my arms. Even when I have lost weight before, I've still been floppy and flabby. Particularly because starvation causes your body to eat muscle first and fat last. But as I've been working away at the gym (on the plateau) I have been creating a well-sculpted body that has been hiding underneath the fat. Now that my muscle weight has stabilised, I am back to stripping fat and the body that is emerging is one I have never owned before.

The time has passed so quickly and on the whole it feels like it's been easy. Yes, there are aspects that I struggle with daily, but in the bigger picture this is easier than I imagined it to be. By adopting the 'day at a time/meal at a time' approach, the journey seems to have happened in the blink of an eye. I know that in another four and a half months' time it will be my thirty-third birthday and for the first time in my whole life I will be healthy, happy, fit and have the body I have always dreamed of having (almost anyway). Just like that (well, maybe not *just like that!*).

I know that there will still be plenty of obstacles along the way, some of them old, some of them new, but I will deal with them the best way I can. I have Nutcase and Crusher to help me so, taking a step at a time, I will get there. And the best thing about it all is that by the time I get there, I will have broken so many of my old eating habits that living my life will be a lot easier because choices will be part of my life and it won't be hard to eat well in the morning or a struggle to not eat hot chips five times a week. New habits will be in place and most of the time what I am eating won't be an issue.

I can't wait for that time because I truly feel as if I've had my life on hold. There's so much that I do not do because of my weight and negative self-image. I want to go back to dance classes, I want to climb the Harbour Bridge, I want to go skinny-dipping with a group of friends, I want to do a black and white nude photo shoot. I want to get an agent and go back to auditioning for acting roles. I want to meet a man who tells me I am the most beautiful woman he's ever known and I want to believe him. I want to eat a pizza and not be worried about someone looking at the fat dribbling down my arm or be paranoid that they are thinking, 'Any wonder she's fat.' I want to tell someone I used to be fat and have him or her not believe me. I want my son's friends to think I look too good to be a mum. I want to be the Mrs Robinson in my teenage son's life (except without the sex bit). I want to buy a bikini! And own a G-string! Actually, I don't really want to own a G-string. I can't stand the thought of a little piece of thread stuck up my bum as an excuse for a pair of underpants. What good would they do with a pelvic floor like mine? I have had a baby, after all.

I remember promising myself that when I got to eighty-nine I would have some KFC as a reward, but I don't actually feel like it. I'm wondering whether the next 10 kilos will be as tough as the last 5 have been or whether it will get easier again. I'm also interested to see how different the changes to my body are as the next few kilos come off. I'm sure the next five will be more noticeable than the last twenty. As there is less fat, the body emerging from within is quite a different shape.

Anyway, off to do some laps!

11 pm: Of course, I needed to jinx myself. I had a stand-up comedy gig to do, was running late 'cause Kai's babysitter didn't turn up, hadn't had dinner, was absolutely starving and then I drove past Red Rooster and I just had to go in. Maybe I've had some magnetic chip implanted in my brain that compels me to enter every single establishment where fat is the number one product! Had I not mentioned the stupid 89 kilos = fried chicken deal I had done with myself, I probably wouldn't have been as tempted (yeah, right). It's always after a positive weigh-in that I do this shit—AAAH!

I know better than to leave the house at meal time without having eaten or taken some food with me. I know there are limited healthy options out on the road and, given my history, I know I will fall into eating junk food the first opportunity I get.

18 December   Penance paid

9 am: This morning I weighed in at bloody ninety again. And no, I didn't eat 5 kilos of chicken but it does make me feel more guilty than I should. Nutcase tells me not to feel guilty and not to beat myself up but to simply get on with the job of eating well and exercising. Yeah, easy for her to say. She doesn't know what it's like to be my size. She doesn't see her beautician try to stabilise the table with a forklift every time I go to get my eyebrows done. I am going straight to the gym and will not leave until I have done thirty minutes on the treadmill, forty of weights and five hours of berating myself for one day being all *holier than thou this is a defining moment* blah blah and then heading straight to the fried chicken shop. I definitely think I am afraid of getting thin.

4 pm: Well, I think I more than made up for the chicken. As well as the treadmill and the gym, I did thirty minutes in the pool and an hour of aqua. That was my punishment although Nutcase would not like me saying that. She would say that it is natural to eat the occasional junk meal and to simply move on from it. I did pass a Macca's today and remembered back to when I was working in radio and my lunch and dinner at least four times a week was them and Burger King, so I *have* come a long way.

Sabotage your sabotage

- This sounds ridiculous, but try not to keep too much cash on you at home. You can't order pizza if you can't pay for it! This really worked for me.

- Watch the size of your meals. There's no point going low fat if you eat three times as much food.

- If you are not losing weight, go back to your food diary and make sure you are not snacking in between snack times/ meal times.

- *Never* skip meals. It slows down your metabolism, which in turn will keep you fat.

- Make sure you have breakfast. When you go to bed, your body goes into fasting mode and when you wake up your blood sugar is low, so it will be harder to resist sweet, fatty snacks.

- If you must have light cheese, buy the pre-grated variety and freeze it. Take out only what you need.

- If your kids and/or partner have full fat food, store it on a low shelf in the fridge. Out of sight, out of mind.

19 December Ow!

I am so severely hungover. I went to a big Christmas party and had way too many vodka martinis. The best thing was that the man who taught me how to starve myself was there. Last year, when I was fat—sorry, *obese*—he had so much to tell me about how successful he was and he couldn't help mentioning how fat I had become and he wondered what had happened to me, apparently he was quite worried, and in one beautiful moment he even came out with, 'People don't believe you used to look so good.' I can't believe I didn't punch him out. I cannot believe I ever loved that man. God, I have come a long way!

This year, as I looked reasonably attractive and mildly fabulous (even if I do say so myself) he could barely look me in the eye. I'm sure he was threatened by the fact that I looked great (that's my story and I'm sticking to it!). I was in high-powered flirt mode and I was getting a lot of interest—oh, okay, well maybe not a lot, but some. A bit more than none and a lot more than last year. And it wasn't just from the waiters! I'm not that big a tipper.

It was so much fun. Could have had a boy in my bed, we did a hell of a lot of kissing, but somewhere in the midst of the martini rush I got all scared and ran away when he went to the bar to get me a drink. That little bucket load of insecurity came pouring out and I panicked, thinking he would wake up and realise he had slept with someone who was actually fat. I can't quite believe that my body is within range of attracting the opposite sex. At least not anyone stable enough to not want to handcuff me to the bed and cut up my body parts and put them in a box. Yes, well that might be a slight exaggeration, but even though I can see the changing shape of my body, the emotional side of me still believes I am really really fat.

Trying to sober up this morning, I attempted to do some laps but there was so much alcohol in my system it made me a danger not only to other swimmers but to myself as well. The alcohol leaking from my body was making all the little children drunk. Suddenly all the little boys were standing around their mummy's boobs chanting, 'Drink, drink, drink'; the girls were in the toilets crying on other little girls' shoulders and everyone was saying, 'I love you . . . honest, I do. I love you . . .' Kept sinking and drifting all over the lanes. Decided I was safer on land.

Went into the gym and proceeded to sweat out another bottle of vodka as I did weights to compensate for the extra calories I drank last night. I knew it was bad when five Russians lined up next to the treadmill, holding shot glasses under my armpits. Oh dear, my head hurts. At least I still weigh 89 kilos. There's nothing worse than having a binge and then going up in weight as well.

21 December   90 kilos?

You may well wonder what I am doing up here back on the plateau at 90 kilos. Yeah well, I thought I'd left my arse up here but no, it was actually following me down the hill. Of course, being back up here has nothing to do with what I did in the last few days. It wasn't the calories in the copious amounts of alcohol I consumed, nor was it the greasy bacon and eggs I had to have to get sober . . . now I'm really wondering what the hell I'm afraid of.

The guy I kissed at that party rang me and we are going to do the email thing. I was absolutely terrified. I wanted to say, 'You do know I'm fat? Maybe you've mixed me up with someone else. Maybe you didn't look close enough. Maybe my boobs were so big you couldn't see beyond them?' I am terrified. Thank God I am going away for two weeks. A good excuse not to see him. Now, if I could lose at least ten kilos before we hook up, then everything will be fine.

Am heading up to Port Macquarie tomorrow. Can't wait to see the family and show them my now 25 per cent reduced fat body. I need to make sure I drive *past* Hungry Jack's and not into it, which is what I have usually done. Another ritual I need to break. Jeez, there're so many of them, aren't there? You work on one, get it partly sorted, then you find another. It's a full-time job not thinking about and pigging out on food.

I'd usually start the journey to Port with a couple of bags of chips (salt and vinegar, and Burger Rings). And not the little bags either. They would get me as far as the end of the street. In fact, normally I would have eaten them the night before and would start the next day by licking the salt from the bottom of the bag. I'm such a classy woman!

My first stop, after fifteen minutes on the road, would be the petrol station before the freeway and I'd get a packet of caramel sweets, a Kit Kat, Flake, more Burger Rings, a Milky Way and a Diet Coke because everyone knows if you have a diet drink with junk food the Nutrasweet automatically erases *all* the calories. Honestly, it does. Otherwise I'd have ended up the size of a house. Oh, I did end up the size of a house. Well, it just goes to show how much I know.

Then I'd cruise up the freeway to Newcastle (about 60 kms from my last stop) by which point I would be starving and would have to top up my fat levels with a stop at Hungry

Jack's for a bacon double cheeseburger, large fries and another Diet Coke (gotta save the calories where you can). I'd need petrol so a quick stop at the servo would see me eating an ice cream and a bar of white chocolate. That would get me all the way to Bulahdelah (approximately an hour up the road) where I'd buy even more Burger Rings, by which point I might as well have donned my Elvis suit 'cause I was doing a pretty good impression of the King in his final days.

Then I'd cruise into Taree an hour later and do the drive-thru of KFC. I'd be too tired to actually get out of my car and walk into the shop—driving and eating take up a lot of energy, you know! Then I'd have one more stop for petrol, which would involve me also purchasing chips and Fruit 'n' Nut chocolate (family block) and I would have a piece of chocolate wedged between two chips.

I'd also move up to full strength Coke to keep myself awake and I would be on my way to holidays (and the heart clinic), which in themselves have been food fests. 'What the hell, I'm on holidays' and 'You only live once' have been favourite catchphrases of mine to justify all-out binges on my favourite crap foods, and Christmas is the worst offender. Christmases as a kid were total food fests, as I said, and we were *all* overweight to varying degrees but that never entered our thoughts as we ate in one day what could have fed an Ethiopian family for a year—maybe even more.

But this time I have my pledge, my plan and a box of diet jelly. Now if I can get through it without putting on 8 kilos, then I'll be okay.

I think about what Nutcase says about food and eating

being emotionally associated with happiness, and that's exactly how I feel. I feel as if I am not going to have as much fun as everyone else because I'll be watching what I'm eating, not gorging myself and therefore 'missing out'. Of course, I'm not counting all the years I've missed out on living my life to the fullest because I've been so overweight and unhappy with myself. But at this moment I wish I could eat everything.

22 December
Do not stop at Hungry Jack's!

So first change of habit: I got up early and prepared healthy sandwiches for the road trip. I made lite ham and salad sandwiches. I packed snacks of fresh fruit—berries and grapes (chilled and put in a chiller bag), sultanas, rice crackers and cold water. I also packed some jelly snakes (not a whole packet, just a few, otherwise I would have had the lot before I'd left the house).

I stopped at Hungry Jack's to let Kai have a run-around in their playground, but I did not step inside their restaurant (can I call it that?). I really needed to go to the toilet but I know what I am like with temptation and stepping anywhere near that counter would see me ordering a double bacon cheeseburger meal deal before they could say, 'Would you like some laxatives with that?'

The newly extended freeway took me around Taree (no KFC!), I stopped once for petrol and no extra purchases, and before I knew it I was pulling into Port Macquarie a junk food free person. Woohoo!

After unpacking my bags I decided I would leave nothing to chance. The first thing I did was shop. I'm here for two weeks, including three or four very festive days of Christmas where there will be all sorts of foods that will put me out of the Alfalfa Zone. Knowing that temptation is my major source of weakness I have decided to compromise. Instead of totally doing without I am going to give myself alternatives. So when everyone is eating Christmas cake I will have a fat-free fudge brownie. If ice cream is on offer I'll have fat free. So plan in hand, this is what I bought:

Weight Watchers margarine	Allen's snakes
Soy Light breakfast cereal	Fruit juice for my cereal
5 Lean Cuisines	Chargrilled 97% fat-free
Diet cordial	chicken breast (frozen)
Fat-free yoghurt	Diet Coke
Corn cobs	Fat-free cheese
Lite chicken slices	Lite ham slices
Weight Watchers peaches	3 tins baked beans
Lite gravy (can you	K-time muesli bars
believe it?)	Rice crackers
Lite mayo	Weight Watchers jam
Asparagus in spring water	Pineapple
Beetroot	Lettuce
Veggies	Fruit
Low-fat fudge brownies	Diet jelly
Sardines in spring water	Pretzels
Wholemeal low fat bread	Low-fat chocolate mousse

And a case of Tooheys low calorie beer Maxim—hey, it is Christmas after all! And Santa's going to need a beer and I'm pretty sure he's on a diet too—otherwise those poor reindeer would all have heart attacks before they got him off the ground. I am here for two weeks, remember, so shut up and give me a break, will you? I got here without junk food so I think I deserve a beer!

I have a great range of foods, all low fat, all very yummy, some easy to heat up, others to go with salads or on sandwiches and some, like the low-fat brownies, that involve the rewriting of my history around food and the creation of a new ritual that is healthy and has happy memories. Kai and I can cook them up so that Santa has a yummy snack to eat after leaving him all those wonderful presents that look exactly like the ones in the boot of my car. Now all I need to do is survive Christmas Day and find a gym and then everything will be fine.

So here I am at the beach. I would have to say that in the last ten years, or since my thighs became the size of German U-boats, I have only been to the beach about four times all of which were nightmares, trying to be as inconspicuous as possible by covering up my body with a muu-muu big enough to envelop the Sydney Cricket Ground and keeping a firm eye out for any whale-watching boats expecting me to birth a calf on the sand.

Well, since I've been wandering around in my swimsuit at the pool (the days of the t-shirt cover-up are long gone) I now have a reasonable tan. I don't get mistaken for a leather handbag but I've got some colour, and I think I'm ready for

. . . wait for it—some *leisure* swimwear! Oooh, how groovy! I sound like one of those sixties fashion voiceovers. Where's the funky lounge music? 'AJ is fashioning a lovely head to toe bathing suit that can double as a dressing gown or even, at a stretch, a tablecloth for the Last Supper. Great for one of those grooovy pool parties!'

I want a bathing suit that doesn't actually look like I've bought it from Muu-Muu's 'R' Us. I want a swimsuit that has people saying, 'Weren't you on the cover of *Sports Illustrated* in January?' In the past I'd have had to answer, 'Actually it was January through to December. It was a full body shot.'

Anyway, oil me up. I'm off to be a beach babe! I'm going shopping.

5 pm: I took a deep breath and entered the surf shop trying to look like it wasn't the first time I'd bought a swimsuit somewhere other than Caftans-R-Us. Grabbed a few different designs, size 16 (the biggest size they have) and squeezed into the mirrored box they call a dressing room. Looking in the mirror I realise with horror that I have a monobrow, which wouldn't be so bad if it didn't go from one thigh to the next. I need a wax. But what to do with the excess hair? Maybe I can farm it out to schoolboys for chest hair when the swimming carnival comes around . . . I don't know.

I'm not too sure about this diet thing. It's a huge industry. First you lose weight, then you need new clothes, and then you need to wax. But you can't stop there. Then you need new underwear, a better hairdo 'cause you actually care about what you look like now, makeup, shoes to go with your clothes, and once you've got everything else, then you want a life. On top of that you then need to accessorise with a brand new boyfriend (forget brand new, just one breathing would be good enough for me) and that's by far too costly an exercise. God, Penguin bars and peanut butter sandwiches were just so simple.

Not content with looking like I was trying to stuff an elephant into a bikini I have decided I like my plain old swimsuit just the way it is. Exit stage left.

I have a bit of a phobia about 'real' gyms. Because my gym at the pool is just a scungy little room off to one side, overpacked with equipment, it is totally non-glamorous. That's one of the reasons I like it so much. The glamour factor is the reason I've never actually joined a gym. Actually I did join a gym once. I bought a six-month membership, went twice and stopped answering the phone when they rang to ask where I was.

So here I am on holidays and I know I have to go, but I am dreading it. They should have gyms just for the fat, lazy and unfashionable: 'Come on down to Grotty's where just thinking about being fit is enough'. There'd be signs around the gym like 'No flannelette—no workout'. Or 'If you don't have the correct footwear—ug boots—then you won't be allowed in the room'. And my favourite would be 'NO blondes!' There'd be a regulation dress code of three inches of bum crack (minimum) and instead of swiping your gym card they'd have a measuring stick which they'd hold up against your arse. Three inches or more and you're in. Less and you have to stay outside and eat pies. The treadmills would have a little donut dangling about a metre in front of you so you were always walking towards the food!

Instead of lifting weights they'd have a row of beer steins lined up along the wall and circuit training would mean you have a beer then a pie, a beer then a pie, a beer then . . . well, you get the idea. Instead of aerobics they'd sit you in beanbags and repetitions would consist of having to get out of the beanbag to get a beer from the fridge. You'd have to do it in sets of ten (or until you finish the carton—a total of twenty-four reps).

Anyway, I have to go, my stepmum bought me a two-week pass and if I don't go they'll know I'm a dropout.

23 December   Jeez

Left Kai with my step-mum and went to the gym.

I can't believe it! It's Saturday but the gym hours are only 9–12 and 4–7, and I promised Kai I would take him to the beach this afternoon. I'm so disappointed I don't get to go today. And I was so looking forward to it. Yippee!

24 December   Lycraland

9 am: Have to go today. No excuses.

1 pm: Oh my God, it was every bit as frightening as I thought it would be. Left Kai with Grandma and Grandpa, took a deep breath and breezed in through the door, sucking my gut in as I went. Front desk manned by anorexic peroxide blonde gym bimbo. Treadmills filled with beach babes and the weights room overcrowded with men whose bodies looked like walnut-stuffed condoms. Home of one of the many Mr Australias (probably on steroids), I was way out of my league.

I desperately wanted to run to the nearest bakery and eat fifteen cream buns but I reminded myself that the only way to a healthy body was through this room as it is the only gym in town and Christmas lunch and too many beers are what lie ahead.

Grabbed an old *Cleo* mag, hid myself behind it and cursed my t-shirt. It would have been funny in any Sydney gym but instead resulted in very strange stares that said 'She's not from around these here parts, Lurline!' Okay, so having a t-shirt that says 'Just dip me in honey and throw me to the lesbians' was perhaps not the most appropriate choice of gym wear considering there was more lycra in that room than in the entire movie *Flashdance*.

Got on the treadmill and freaked out 'cause I didn't know how to start it. It was different to the one back home. Inside my head I can hear Dorothy saying, 'I don't think we're in Kansas anymore, Toto' shortly before another voice interrupts with 'Get your fat arse out of this place before anyone notices you were ever here.' Then a Sly Stallone voice yells, 'Incoming. Incoming Bimbo. Eleven o'clock. Get out, get out. Take no prisoners. Save yourself! Run as fast as you can to a KFC and block it out of your memory.'

Ignored the voices in my head by saying 'Shut up' and then realised the woman next to me thought I was saying it to her. Not a good start, I'm afraid. Told myself it could only get better, at which point the woman on the treadmill next to me moved to a treadmill on the other side of the room.

Asked the woman on the other side how to turn on the machine. She said she wasn't sure herself as this was her first time. Ah, a friend. Together we worked it out and soon I was walking. Felt a little better.

Did twenty minutes as fast as I could walk without falling on my face. Felt even better when I noticed someone with a bigger bum than mine (was it possible?). I wasn't the fattest in the gym, which wouldn't have been the case 20 kilos ago! Then I entered the testostero-zone, otherwise known as the weights room.

I managed to work my way around most of the weights. Only a couple of machines were different to back home so I swallowed my pride and asked the biggest guy there. I figured his testicles would be so tiny after the consumption of so many steroids that he probably never thinks about sex and being a muscle junkie he probably only ever dates toothpicks. So I figured, compared to them I'm the bloody Daintree forest and far too big to consider at all. Surprisingly he was very helpful and friendly so I exorcised that demon as well.

Had a brief moment when I was on what I call the power ball. Those big plastic balls I do my sit-ups on. Two bimbo beach sluts—sorry, babes—wandered by, giggled and gave me one of those looks that said, 'She's sooooo fat. And we're sooooo thin.' I gave them an equally nasty look that said, 'I might be fat but I've got great tits and you'll never have those, not unless you buy them.' Huh, it's amazing how small-minded I can be when I want to.

Anyway, whether it was fear, adrenaline or endorphins, by the time I had finished my workout (one hour and twenty minutes) I felt like I had done the best workout of my life and I couldn't wait to come back! I had faced my fear of the dreaded gym. Bring it on!

Christmas Day is tomorrow. I am desperately hoping that I get through the day without pigging out or crumbling and eating everything on the table, including the Christmas tree and any unclaimed presents. Please, oh God of fat cells, help me control myself!

25 December
Santa has left the building

I did it! I did it! I survived Christmas Day with only a few banned substances. I was quite nervous because I have zero willpower in the presence of foods I like and so far have really only been able to practise abstinence as my form of control. So this was the big temptation test.

I woke up and had cereal and a banana. First meal a success. Then we did the big present opening which took us all the way to mid-morning. Relatives started arriving and there was food on the table. I had my little bowl of pretzels, which I kept very close to me. I managed to avoid the dips and cheeses by constantly having a pretzel in my hand. Drank lots of water.

Then came lunch. I made little prawn cocktails (knowing they were healthy) and kept the sauce to the side. I had one teaspoon of low-fat mayo—everyone else had tartare sauce—and I made sure that on mine there was more lettuce than prawns. Off to a good start.

The main meal was the usual smorgasbord of goodies. I had one slice of my own lite ham. I then had two thin slices of veal rolled roast and a tablespoon of port wine and pecan stuffing. I had my diet gravy (which tasted so good everyone had it), two small oven baked potatoes (wrapped in foil), one piece of sweet potato and some beans. I had two glasses of wine and made sure I had water in between.

When everyone else sat down to trifle I had low-fat chocolate mousse and some cherries. In the afternoon when they broke out the chocolates I had two pieces of the low-fat fudge brownies I had made the day before. I did have three beers in the afternoon (hic) but it is Christmas after all. I also stole about six crisps from Kai late in the afternoon but no one saw me so there were no calories in those.

For dinner I had a salad with one slice of the leftover veal and some diet jelly and went to bed feeling not only pretty proud of myself, but feeling I had taken part in Christmas as much as everyone else. Not bad.

Lying in bed I realised that was the first Christmas in my entire life that I had not absolutely stuffed myself until I wanted to vomit. It felt good. I was lying there feeling the shape of my changing body (some might say I was touching myself up, but I wasn't!) and as my hands wandered over my hip area, I felt a lump. No, I'm not really a man! And no, I was pretty sure it wasn't a cancerous lump—it's been a while but I think I felt my hipbone! Santa had brought me a present after all! Went to sleep a very happy (and little bit bonier) girl.

26 December   I love Santa

Boxing Day. Woke up and with some trepidation stepped on the scales. After a few days of drinking beer with my birth dad and feeling a little guilty for not breaking open a Lean Cuisine for Christmas lunch (yeah, right!) I was ready to weigh 90 again. Instead it said 88.5 kilos.

Started the day with a fruit salad and yoghurt, knowing that I am not through the woods yet. I still have lunch at my sister's (birth father's daughter) house and dinner at my adopted dad's farm. That's going to be the big concern 'cause he's your typical Aussie farmer—120 kilos with a passion for fat. Can't wait for them to see the new me. The last time I saw them I was 109 kilos!

Kai and I did our daily walk along the beach, something he's really going to miss when we go back home. I guess I'll have to drive to a beach and do the same thing. Maybe not every day! Have decided to take a Lean Cuisine to lunch at my sis's house. There are no gyms or pools open today so I have to wait until tomorrow to have a workout, which is a good thing as I am still sore from the other day. The walk will have to do.

Arrived at adopted Dad's house all excited expecting them to say, 'Oh my gawd, I can't believe my eyes . . . is that you, AJ? No, it can't be . . . sorry, have we met?' My dad said nothing and probably wouldn't think to tell me straight up. After a little prodding from me—a few subtle words like, 'So do you reckon I look all right? Do I look like I've lost twenty kilos?'— he looks me up and down and replies, 'Oh, yeah.' And then a little uncertainty creeps into his voice. 'You might have lost a little around your face. I expected more.'

But I was not defeated. At least, not yet.

Knowing he's a man (clueless) and probably doesn't notice things like that (is completely blind) I thought maybe my Nan (his mum) would be sure to notice (women always do). I go upstairs, walk in the door thinking skinny thoughts and suck in my gut. I have just enough breath to utter, 'Hi, Nan.' The first thing she says is, 'How much weight do you reckon you've lost?'

I reply with an impending heavy heart. 'Ah, about twenty kilos.'

She laughs, snorts and says, 'You're kidding yourself if you've lost six.' She turns back to the television and presses the remote control to watch 'Wheel of Fortune'. Wondering how she could say that to me I look a little more closely at her, oblivious to the devastation she has just caused. I wondered when it was I'd last seen her. When I was seven? No, I had visited them three weeks before entering the Alfalfa Zone.

To make matters worse, my brother, who has always done everything better than me, has also been overweight for the last few years, which is the only reason I've attended family occasions, happy in the thought that he too would be greeted by the same comment from my father (every time I visited): 'Jeez, love, you're gettin' fat!' Anyway, my brother turns up only moments after, walks in the door—and he is thin. Not just thin as in 'I'm a healthy weight' but thin as in 'Calista Flockhart looks like a bush pig next to me, I get mistaken as a coat hanger in shops, I need a drip in me, call the doctor, I look like a junkie' kind of thin.

And then he laughs and says, 'Yeah, I must have cancer. The weight just fell off. I haven't even tried.' Don't you hate people who say that? Don't know what happened, the weight just fell off? Don't you just want to buy a bucket of KFC and stick it up their oh-so-skinny bums for saying stuff like that? Wayne's incredible weight loss was the sole topic of conversation (all night long) and my alleged weight loss just paled into insignificance.

As the afternoon dragged on I clung desperately to my pretzels and cherries as Nan, brother, sister-in-law and Dad consumed what could only be described as a mini-skip's worth of cheese, dips, chips, salami, lollies, chocolate, nuts and God knows what else. I'm sure if a calf had wandered by they'd have carved it up and eaten it raw. Oh joyous Chrissy! Jesus has a hell of a lot to answer for.

The good thing (was there one?) about the visit was that I had been prepared and had rung Dad earlier that day to see what he'd be cooking for dinner. He told me he'd be cooking a leg of pork and a ham. Anyway, forewarned is forearmed. I brought a roast chicken with me and watched as my now skinny brother peeled the entire skin off the chicken (Hannibal Lecter style) and with the fat dripping off his fingers, shoved it in his mouth, barely chewed it and followed it with the parson's nose. One gulp and it was all gone. Nearly slipping over in the puddle of water created by my drool I carved off the now skinless breast and put it on my plate. I was starving.

Dinner was ready and I had my low-fat gravy—and surprise, surprise, everyone decided to eat that (not that it's going to put a dint in their calorie-laden meals, I so righteously think)—one roast potato, chicken breast, one piece of sweet potato and some peas. When they had pudding, Christmas cake, custard and ice cream (is it any wonder I was so fat?) I had my little tin of peaches. Obviously they hadn't eaten enough because they then broke open the chocolates and I got out some mangoes. Dad surprised me then by saying he doesn't eat fruit and hasn't since he was a kid. I realised he was absolutely right. I had never seen my father eat any fruit whatsoever. This was the man I grew up with and he had a major influence on my life. That was why I had to force myself to eat fruit. It hit me that this is why it is so important to do this thing properly or Kai will grow up not eating fruit and being overweight and if I do that to him, I would never forgive myself.

Mango treat

Cut a mango into halves and pop each half into a plastic sandwich bag. Freeze. Defrost about half an hour before serving. Serve with mixed berries and some Weight Watchers mango ice cream. Very yummy. Or just eat half a frozen mango as an afternoon snack. It's just like gelato.

I drove back to my birth dad's house and felt okay, a little deflated but good for not having succumbed to the Christmas pig-out mentality. I had taken control of what and how much I ate and I excelled at it and still had a really good time, even if, according to Nan, my thighs are still bigger than England.

27 December   Oh poo!

Gym—one hour. Swim—forty minutes. Did not weigh myself today. What I don't know won't hurt me. I decided I was obsessing enough since Nan's disheartening comments so I thought I'd just give it a break. Instead I woke up at five forty-five this morning. Before you go puking in disgust at my apparent healthy waking up early kind of bullshit I should clarify that statement. Was woken up this morning with the repetition of those words every mother loves to hear: 'Mummy, I've done a poo. Look, it's on my fingers. Mummy, I've done a poo, look, it's on my . . .'

Had cereal and half a mango for breakfast. Am determined to be very strict today. I told my stepmum I would cook my own dinner tonight and that I would be as strict as I could possibly be. Seven o'clock and I was walking along the beach with Kai, chasing seagulls, swimming and jumping waves. I felt like I was doing the after-shot of a Lite 'n' Easy commercial. It's amazing what four months and 20 kilos can do to your life. Earlier this year when I came to Port it was too much of an effort to even walk along the beach. Back then I walked for 50 metres then sat in the sand while my dad took

Kai for a walk. We never even went for a swim. This time it's our morning and afternoon ritual.

Snack—yoghurt and a piece of fruit. Then off to the gym. More gorgeous bodies but I told myself they were all probably really dumb and just got on with the job of transforming my life. I had a lite Subway sandwich for lunch, crackers and fruit for a snack and then cooked myself Hokkien noodles for dinner. Had a low-fat brownie for dessert and a vanilla tea with skimmed milk. Then I took my boy to the local carnival parked at the seaside to relieve bored parents of their hard-earned holiday cash reserves.

I knew this would be a test because I totally associate these types of places with binge eating. I spent most of my adult life going to the Easter Show and bingeing, trying to recreate happier times when I was a child. Before my parents divorced and before I was molested and when I had a tiny little body that could handle the Pluto Pups (ice lollies), hot chips and ice creams. I remember doing the Click 'n' Clack Road Safety Show at the Royal Easter Show when I was twenty-two (I was Clack, the road safety clown—see, I told you I was a professional actress. I've done the hard yards!). Anyway, we did seven shows a day and in between each show I would sneak out of the pavilion and consume a hot dog, cheese on a stick, a toffee apple, three donuts, hot chips and a beer. By the end of the day I not only felt incredibly sick but I had a deep hatred of myself and my total lack of control. However, it was not enough to stop me from doing the same thing every day for fourteen days straight. My nights, of course, were filled with many trips to the toilet. I wish someone had sent me to the

Hokkien Noodles

850 g large uncooked prawns
1 teaspoon peanut oil
1 teaspoon fresh chopped ginger
2 cloves garlic finely chopped
200 g oyster mushrooms, thickly sliced
1 red pepper, thinly sliced
450 g Hokkien noodles
200 g Chinese cabbage, shredded
300 g broccoli, chopped
200 g bean sprouts
1 tablespoon rice vinegar
3 tablespoons oyster sauce
1 tablespoon soy sauce
1 teaspoon sesame seeds

Shell the prawns leaving the tails on. Heat the oil in a wok, add the ginger, garlic, mushrooms, pepper and prawns, and cook until the prawns turn solid white (about 3–5 minutes). Add the noodles, vegetables, vinegar and sauces, and cook until the cabbage starts to look wilted. Serve garnished with the sesame seeds.

Serves 4; contains approximately 8g fat.

shrink then. I could own a house in Double Bay by now, with the amount of money I've wasted on Pluto Pups and laxatives. Ah, if only I'd had shares in offal and sewerage systems!

Knowing that was the history I was struggling against, I made sure I had dinner before we went and drank about four glasses of water to really top myself up. Know what the best thing was? Apart from going home and not being filled full of lard and five-day-old food, the best part was being under 90 kilos, which was the allowable limit for the giant jumping castle I went on with Kai—something that even three weeks ago I would not have been allowed to do. We ran around like mad idiots, climbed the rope wall, slid down the giant slide, rumbled and tumbled. I feel like I'm actually starting to live my life rather than hiding from everybody. Today the world is a good place.

Weighed myself before going to bed and I am 87 kilos. I have lost weight over Christmas. HO HO HO.

28 December   The playing field

The guy I met at the comedy Christmas party is sending around ten text messages a day. Could he really be interested? Even if it is just for sex?

The sales are on and I thought I'd do some clothes shopping. Went to two shops and came back home afraid. Very afraid. After 22 kilos I am still either free size or extra large. God, I hate fashion dictators. And those mirrors. Euh! Might wait a little while longer before getting a new wardrobe.

And how depressing is this? Despite four months of busting my arse (literally) and living off rabbit food (not really) I thought I'd treat myself to the latest issue of one of the many slimmers mags. I thought I could do with a little help to push me past the next plateau (85). I was feeling pretty good about myself until I started reading their articles. Apart from the graph that compares my height and weight and tells me I am still EXTREMELY overweight (what, for a toothpick? Overweight, yes, but the word 'extremely' is a bit . . . well, extreme!). But then I read some of their slimmers' stories. Usually those articles would have me feeling incredibly inspired, but this time the three different stories I read had the women saying, 'I was so fat. I hated myself. I hated my body. I had no life, no clothes and no self-respect.' Their words sounded incredibly familiar to me and echoed my sentiments when I started in the Alfalfa Zone. But as I read their vital stats my heart plummeted to somewhere around my extremely overweight ankles. All their starting weights were between 80 and 85 kilos. I asked myself how I had ever let myself get this big. I am heavier now, even having already lost 20 kilos, than any of these women were when they started.

I feel just as fat and blobby and socially unacceptable as I did five months ago. Life's a bitch and then you become a fat one. Oh well, nothing else for it but to drag my socially unacceptable bum to the gym. Again.

29 December   The Black Hole

Depressed. Very very depressed. Can't get Nan's comment out of my head. Six kilos as opposed to twenty-two. I keep telling myself, 'Don't listen,' but how can I not? Trying to be happy around the family but struggling. Want to not eat. Have to remember the deal I made with Nutcase. Starving won't make me lose weight in the long term. Am going to fight this!

The last thing the anorexic part of me needs is for someone to tell me I don't look as if I've lost any weight. I will not let that side have the final say. I am in control!

Was trying not to mope but I don't think I did a very good job. My stepmum Helen brought me a cup of tea and sat down next to me. She said, 'Don't listen to what anyone else says. You know how much weight you've lost. I can see it. Lance can see it. Don't let it affect you. There will always be people trying to drag you down but don't let them.'

I looked at her in surprise. 'That transparent, am I?'

She ignored my question and showed me a photo. 'I've been looking for this since you saw your Nan. Sorry it took me so long.' She explained what she had in her hand. 'This is you last Christmas. Look at the difference, AJ. You are a completely different person. Anyone who can't see that is just being ridiculous.'

I looked at the picture. I am walking along the beach with Kai and I remember struggling to walk just 50 metres. I have more chins than a Chinese phone book. I am absolutely huge. I'd just come back from a holiday in Byron Bay where I managed not to go to the beach once. Completely ashamed of my body I had spent most of my time indoors. I was so big my shadow could have been mistaken for an eclipse. No matter how screwed up I might be, even I could see the difference between then and now. The proof was in my hand. Everything was going to be all right. Just stay focused and don't listen to what anyone else has to say. Unless they're saying, 'AJ, you look like a goddess, let's get married. My yacht is waiting to take us away!'

Apart from that big black hole in my day and despite wanting to curl up and die, I took Kai to one of those kiddy playlands. The ones with all the tunnels and ball rooms. I have managed to avoid them so far, always saying I had to work whenever any of my friends asked if I wanted to go. Last summer I got stuck in the tunnel at Hungry Jack's in Newcastle and very nearly died of embarrassment. So when my sister suggested we go to one, it was with great trepidation that I said yes. I felt better for having weighed in at 87, but was a little worried nonetheless.

But I have to tell you, I had the best time. We climbed and slid, and bounced and ran around for over two hours. I didn't get stuck once, was fighting the kids for the slides and it was my two-year-old who grabbed my hand and insisted, 'We go home now, Mummy. Please?'

Progress.

Oh God, this guy is is now sending very raunchy emails. Finding out a lot about him. We have three-page raves about all sorts of stuff. It's the usual pre-sex banter—likes, dislikes, a few jokes, the odd piece of intimate information. Men work so hard to get you then they just seem to drop the ball. Maybe I've been shopping in the wrong place. Note to self: stop shopping at the Reject Shop! Note from self: you are way too bitter!

30 December   Iced cake

I've hit an interesting point. Today as I was doing my laps in the pool I caught myself repeating a phrase that sounded familiar. I was saying 'Eighty-five, eighty-five, eighty-five' over and over in my head, fuelling myself to do those extra laps to take me to a forty-five minute swim when all I wanted to do was sunbake. Then I remembered (and it seemed so long ago but it wasn't—a couple of months, maybe) saying, 'Ninety-five, ninety-five, ninety-five.' And before that it was, 'Under one hundred . . .' I remember 95 seemed impossible. Now it's 85 that looks that way. And I guess if I keep going, 75 will feel the same.

At the moment I feel as if I have a handle on my cravings and don't succumb to as many, but in terms of lifestyle there have been lots of changes. I am definitely more active and on good days am much happier in myself. I'm developing a new-found body confidence, which is a long way from where I want to be but a long way from where I've been. Hey, I'm not at the table-top dancing in lingerie stage, but give me time, give me time!

I really want to be 86 for New Year's Eve but I realise there is nothing I can do to enhance that prospect, at least nothing that would be healthy. I either will be or won't be and all I can do is to make my choices as healthy as possible. Have cut back to one beer a day and am being strict about what I eat. Today's food so far:

> Brekkie: Poached egg on toast (no butter), apple
> Snack: Mango
> Lunch: Gourmet sandwich, yoghurt, orange
> Snack: Apple, muesli bar

The family is going to have fish and chips on the beach tonight. I am going to make and take with me a huge turkey breast and salad roll, a piece of fruit and a diet mousse. God, I am so good.

Oh dear, I have just had the photos developed from Christmas Day and maybe the slimming magazines are right. Maybe I am still EXTREMELY overweight. Very depressed. Now I am plagued by doubt and wonder why this guy is emailing me so much. Why is he so interested? Maybe he really was drunk and remembers me thinner than I am. Maybe he thinks I am someone else. Oh God, I just want to hide away until I am thin! This in-between business is no fun at all . . .

5 pm: Not doing too well at the moment. Am still depressed after seeing the photos of me taken on Christmas Day. I guess it's good in one way. It means that Nutcase is making progress on me because I actually thought I'd lost more weight than I have. Am plagued by my Nan's comments and that photo. I realise I am really only halfway there. The reason Crusher set a 30-kilo goal is because if she'd said, 'You have to lose fifty kilos,' I'd have been out of her office faster than you can say, 'Two dozen boxes of Durolax, please!' I wouldn't have gone through with it. Too hard and absolutely impossible, I'd have thought.

But I'm committed now. I could never go back and she knew that would happen. Now as I look forward, I feel completely deflated because even though I look at myself differently, having lost 20 kilos, I realise that most people look at me and still just see someone who is fat, and if they're anything like me, they're also thinking what I think when I look at women who are the size I used to be: poor thing, if only she knew how to take control.

And to make a bad day worse, after seventeen tantrums and a lot of begging I agreed to take Kai back to the carnival. I decided (in a moment of madness) to have a go at this groovy vertical bungee jump. I read the sign and it said you had to be under 110 kilos, can't have any injuries or be pregnant. Okay, so I might look like I'm pregnant but I'm not. Any injuries? Well, apart from the permanent neck and shoulder injury I sustained in a car accident two years ago, there's hardly anything wrong with me, especially if you don't count the recently healed broken leg. And 110 kilos? I don't think so.

So there I am in my new-found body, climbing up onto the trampoline and waiting to be hooked up when the 40 kilo waif-like sixteen year old looks worried and goes and talks with one of the attendants, who then looks up at me and talks to another attendant. Then all three come up to me and ask if I've read the warning sign. I nod and wait for them to hook me up. The twig then says, 'You can't go on it if you're 110 kilos.'

Well, that was the icing on the cake for me. If I didn't feel like Ten Ton Tessie before, I certainly did by then.

I assured them I was 87 kilos but they didn't look convinced. They hooked me up with extra cables, I did the jump (ironically feeling deflated at the same time) and walked away wondering what I could do to feel better about myself. Dr Nutcase is on holidays for a few more weeks so I can't call her. I know this is normally where I would try to starve myself. I just have to stick to the plan, stick to the plan, stick to the plan. Breakfast, snack, lunch, snack, dinner, snack. Diets don't work. Sensible eating and exercise does. Ho hum. Must stay positive.

Oh joy of joys. Just what I needed. Weighed in at 88. No one ever tells you that in the middle of your 'amazing' weight loss your body adapts and suddenly you don't lose weight as easily as before. I hate Christmas.

Live net chatting nightly for hours on end with this new boy. Am now truly convinced he thinks I'm someone else. He told me I am beautiful. Maybe he wears contacts and accidentally had them in the wrong way round, seeing everything smaller than it is. We are definitely going to go out. There's lots of flirting and innuendo. I'm glad he's 400 kilometres away, otherwise I'd have shagged him rotten already. I want to get to know this guy first, develop a friendship, then get intimate. It's too easy to get raunchy over the net.

My brother, sister (birth father's kids) and brother-in-law and I are going out to dinner tonight. We're going to the Hog's Breath Café. See, I told you I come from a classy family—nothing but the finest restaurants for us. Whenever I think of these kinds of places I think beer followed by deep-fried everything followed by beer followed by more deep-fried everything followed by tequila slammers followed by cake and ice cream followed by a very big spew in the gutter at around midnight. Ah, such fond memories. So this one's a challenge. I've been reading the slimming magazines for inspiration. Crusher and Nutcase are on holidays so I am on my own. I want to succeed at this. My challenge is to find and order something healthy from their menu.

I've already been to the gym in preparation for the night. Have had four glasses of water and am walking out the door vowing I won't drink beer and I will order something nice— but, really, who wants to order a twelve-dollar lettuce when you can have deep-fried buffalo wings in ranch style sauce? I mean, whoever saw a buffalo with wings; they are so rare they *should* be a delicacy!

12 midnight: Okayb, sob I mightb hbave had a few too miny vodkas but theywere vbodka and shodas, and no beers piised sorry, passed through my lipsd. Too Brunk. Will talk tobmorrow.

New Year's Eve   Euh!

Okay, slight hangover but feeling okay. In the good choices department, on a scale of one to ten, I did maybe a seven or eight. As I was driving there I was dreaming of curly fries and big steaks and having an argument in my head over who was going to order dinner: the on the way to being thin AJ or the happy to be a fat pig AJ.

Got the menu and spent twenty minutes arguing internally. When my brother-in-law suggested we get the mixed entrée I think I was the first to say 'Yesindeedydoo sir yesiree bring it on little doggie yeeha,' or words to that effect. However, I did exercise restraint. I had one tiny little spring roll—okay, maybe two—one baked potato wedge, no buffalo wings and a third of a piece of crumbed chicken. Oh, and a piece of garlic bread but, hey, I was so good over Chrissy I needed not to think about it for a little while. Yeah, my brain needed a holiday 'cause the weight of my arse was too much of a distraction.

Anyway, I did redeem myself. I wanted to order the steak with everything but I didn't. I had grilled chicken breast with mustard sauce (I asked for it on the side), an oven-baked potato not wedges or fries (boohoo), and a salad with no dressing. The only problem was that the bloody baked potato came out with a dollop of sour cream that I scooped onto my brother's plate (well, almost all of it) and I only had one of the breasts even though they served up two. I had no dessert and went for a walk after dinner. Okay, so it was a walk to the nearest pub but it must have burnt off at least some of the calories!

Too hungover to exercise but will do extra time on the treadmill tomorrow. The body needs at least one day of rest during the week and today seems like a good one to use that excuse.

I know I am not going to be 86 by the new year ('cause it's here tomorrow) and I have realised with only mild resignation that the time has come to start aerobics classes. There's too much talk of reaching your target heart rate, doing cardio, working in the fat-burning range! This plateau thing is not something you just step off. I've read so many stories in those mags about women losing 20 kilos and then slowing down to a loss of about a quarter kilo a week. I've got to keep going. I am not content to stay here. It's all well and good to

Eating Out

- If you are going to a party, take your own nibblies. Pretzels, fruit, veggie sticks, rice crackers and a light dip (if you have to). Carry a bottle of water with you so you are not empty-handed, because before you know it you'll have cracked open a bottle of bubbly and downed five buckets of avocado dip.

- When having a night out on the grog make sure you eat first (so you don't break your leg and end up in a wheelchair for two months!). Make sure you work out that day and the day after to burn those extra calories/carbohydrates.

- We all know ordering a plain salad is boring. Instead, order a chicken salad with dressing on the side. It's about living your life, not going without until you are thin. Everything in moderation.

- If going out for breakfast, pick a cafe that does poached eggs or fruit salad. If you have something like raisin toast, ask for the butter on the side.

- Take control of what you eat. Ask how the food is prepared. For example, sometimes grilled fish has oil poured over it in the cooking process. If you know that then you can request they *truly* grill it *without* the oil.

- The same goes with smoothies. Make sure they don't add the ice cream unless it is low fat.

be on holidays, and I have done well to maintain my weight over Chrissy, but the time has come, once again, to move my arse. My food intake is fine; my metabolism needs a kick-start. So, I am going to go to some classes. But I'd better get back to Sydney first and check with my physio that the broken leg can handle the stress. Ha!

I have decided to add to my daily list of exercise one of the first things Crusher taught me—no, in fact I'm going to add two. First thing I now promise to do every day, and you know how good I am at promises, is three sets of twenty stair exercises—where I step up and down twenty times. It will be interesting to see if I can do them in a row. I remember in the beginning I couldn't even do *ten* in a row. The other thing I will do is the tummy tucks, because I want a good stomach and that's the only way to get it. And I have finally decided I am going to get one of those power balls to do my sit-ups every day. Oh my God, what am I saying?

1 January   Resolution time

AJ's New Year resolutions
(which she will stick to the fridge and ignore until December of next year):

- I will do at least thirty minutes of exercise every day even if it is just a walk.
- I will eat healthy food, full of vitamins and minerals, low in fat and calories.
- I will teach myself to cook one new low-fat meal a week.
- I will do my stair exercises and tummy tucks every day.

- I will have sex as often as possible as that counts as a workout.
- I will find someone to have sex with.
- Someone I don't have to pay . . .
- Or beg.
- Or drug.
- I will not drink alcohol.
- Very often.
- At least not on Sundays.
- I will not pick at Kai's leftovers.
- I will take up a sport—something like all-girl soccer or touch footy or tennis.
- I will not sell all the gear after giving up in the second week.
- I will do the Harbour Bridge climb as my reward for losing 20 kilos.
- When I have lost 30 kilos I will do a scuba-diving course.
- After losing 40 kilos I will wake up and find this was all a dream.
- I will buy a bike and take Kai for rides.
- I will do aerobics classes.
- I will go ice-skating.
- I will wear a size 12 dress for my thirty-third birthday.
- I will have a boyfriend.
- I will get an agent and go to auditions and feel good about myself.
- I will go out to a nightclub and not run away after being there five minutes.
- I will go back to dance classes.

- I will own a G-string, a bikini, a pair of jeans, a pair of shorts (really?) and some yummy scrummy lingerie that could double as a hanky rather than a picnic blanket for the Waltons.

And finally . . .

- Next year I will have a shorter New Year's resolution list.

Okay, so I might not have done my stair exercises or tummy tucks this year (yet), but I did do at least thirty minutes of exercise. I went for an early morning swim in the ocean with Kai and later I took him to the pool and did laps as well. It was very strange not being hungover for New Year's Day. The only people on the beach were left over from the big night before and I don't know what happened to them but I think they'll turn up at the cancer clinic some time later this week. There's nothing quite like passing out on the beach at four in the morning and waking up at midday during a heat wave.

I haven't weighed myself this year either. I'm trying a new tactic. If I am sabotaging myself every time I get closer to 85, then if I am strict in my eating and don't weigh myself for a couple of days it just might do the trick. I don't know, I'm flying by the seat of my pants here. No Nutcase or Crusher for another week.

The boy sent me an email and in it he was very hot hot hot. He was very keen. Any more keen and I'd have had to wipe down my screen with a dishcloth. Anyway, he seems very sweet and offered to be my sex slave. He also reminded me that sex is considered a good workout so I could see him as a kind of personal trainer. Hmm, now there's an idea. It's fun thinking about the possibility of actually having sex, considering this is the first day of the year and it is on my list of New Year's resolutions.

I rang my friend Tara, who is part of a tragic women's soccer team, and asked if I could join. She laughed at first but then said yes. I told her that by the time soccer season came around I would be more fit. She said, 'Don't worry about it. We don't even know the rules. You'll be fine.' So that's at least one of my resolutions in place.

Next stop: back to Sydney and a size 12 dress. Well, I'd better get through fourteen first.

4 January   Oh my God

Tomorrow I am finally catching up with this guy. Am terrified I'll open the door and he'll scream, 'Oh my God, it wasn't you I liked, it was your friend!' Then I'll have to watch in horror as he stumbles up the road, vomiting and tearing his hair out. Okay, that might be a little outrageous.

5 January   It's not me — it's the bod

This is it. The moment of truth. I am waiting for *him* to arrive. I tell you what, there's nothing like the promise of some hot bedroom action to get your eating habits focused. I have been so good. I weighed in at 87 today.

The easy thing about being fat is, if the dates/relationships don't work out you can always blame your body. 'He's so shallow he couldn't see the real me.' Or 'He only likes twigs.' At least I can use that excuse for a little while longer. Then I'll just have to label them losers.

Oh my God, what if he gets a phone call halfway through the date then turns to me and says, 'I've got to go, I've got to save a dog with a pierced bowel'?

Oh God, I think I want to vomit, there goes the doorbell. Note to AJ: play hard to get.

6 January   Getting to know you

Well, what can I say? I may not have played *too* hard to get but I'm sure I can count it as an aerobic workout. I'm sure I burnt off about 5000 calories, and that was just the kissing. We went out to lunch and I ordered a grilled veggie burger, sauce on the side, no butter on the bun, salad instead of fries, no dressing and water. He ordered a burger with bacon and cheese, fries and a Coke (don't you just hate men?!). The best thing about what I ate was that once again I felt good about ordering healthy food, and I didn't feel like I was missing out at all because the food was excellent and I knew that in a week, having chosen that meal instead of what I would normally have ordered (wedges or nachos), will help me get that little bit closer to 85 and then 80 and then 75 and then the 'What, sleep with you? Hahahaha' body size.

So the afternoon progressed and we did a little of this and a little of that and before I knew it we were . . . well, let's just say we got to know each other quite well. He marvelled at the size of my breasts. I think he said they were the biggest ones he's ever seen (he's obviously not done too much net surfing) and I told him they would be getting smaller so he'd better enjoy them while he had the chance. He took my advice and that's when all my resolve to play hard to get went out the window.

Later: Aaah! He hasn't called me! Okay, so it's only been eight hours since he left but you'd think he'd ring me and beg me for more, or thank me for the most blissful day of his life. Although he is a man, and most men only use the phone for phone sex or putting bets on at the TAB. Still, I can't help but get a little paranoid. I keep thinking he just slept with me because he felt sorry for me or he was too nice to tell me I was fatter than he remembered. Oh dear, it's all a bit complicated this lust/love thing.

Now this is where I would normally drown my sorrows and insecurities in chocolate, fatty food or alcohol, if not all of them at once. Instead, I have just gone for a twenty-minute walk. Still feel all nervous and stupid but at least I treated myself well. At least this time I'm not going to eat myself into obscurity, obesity, born again virginity or an early grave.

7 January   Going down

He called! He slept for fifteen hours. Apparently I exhausted him. He called me the Pleasure Machine . . . God, this guy's got all the lines.

And you know what made my day? I weighed in at 86 kilos. Okay, so it was 86.7, but it doesn't matter. It's so close to 85 I can almost taste it, provided I don't sabotage it and splurge on something stupid like alcohol. I love going down to the next number, because I spend so much of my time convincing myself that this kind of eating won't make me lose weight and then I just stick to the plan, as instructed by Nutcase, and then before you know it, I've crept down another notch. Woohoo!

8 January   I've seen the lite!

I need to tell you about one of my old friends from school, Jen. She lives in outback WA. She farms cattle but also works at the local post office. I can never remember the name of the town where she lives so I just call it Wherethefugarewe. She rang me last night and said she'd heard I'd lost about 22 kilos and she was wondering how I did it. Apparently cowgirls suffer from body-image problems too, although I'm not sure how many fashion mags they get up there. I'm sure 'Steer Rustler' mag still manages to put a couple of semi-naked cowgirls in their stories with catchy little subtitles like 'Mandy likes riding people and meeting horses'. Yeehaa.

She said she'd been thinking about going to Jenny Craig and what did I think about that. I thought, what is Jenny doing all the way out in cattle country and what is the marketing strategy for girls on the land? 'Sick of the guys calling out, "Show us ya teats!"? Tired of the local cowboys jumping on your back in the pub every time the mechanical bull breaks down? Lose weight now, don't look like a cow! Call Jenny Craig!' Maybe not.

What I *said*, of course, was entirely different. I told her that I had done JC and as soon as I stopped eating their food I put the weight back on all over again. I told her she needed to relearn how and what to eat. She assured me that she already ate healthily and she just couldn't shift the weight, no matter what she did.

This sounded incredibly familiar to me. When I wasn't stuffing my face with junk food, or gobbling boxes of laxatives, I was usually telling everyone, including myself, that I ate healthily, it was just that I had big bones (yeah, recently transplanted from a migrating whale) and a slow metabolism (that bit was true, but I didn't know how to fix it. I thought it was destined to stay that way). I remembered back to the first days in the Alfalfa Zone, and my food diary. How I recorded everything I ate, thinking I had done really well, and then Crusher came in with her little red pen and gave me a huge list of things I had to change or cut out and another list of foods I had to eat on top of what I was already eating. It seemed impossible.

I decided to delve a little further into what my friend called 'healthy eating'.

This is how our conversation went:

AJ: What *exactly* do you eat?

JEN: Toast for breakfast. Salad sandwich for lunch and salad and meat for dinner.

AJ: What do you have on your toast?

JEN: Marmite.

AJ: Butter?

JEN: Yeah, but it's only for breakfast.

AJ: What about on your sandwich at lunch?

JEN: Salad.

AJ: Meat?

JEN: Yeah, chicken or ham. Today I had silverside.

AJ: Any cheese?

JEN: Yes, but only one slice.

AJ: Margarine?

JEN: Yes, but that's the only other time I have it.

AJ: What about dinner? What kind of meat do you eat?

JEN: Tonight it was crumbed cutlets. Sometimes it's chops.

AJ: Cooked in oil?

JEN: Yes, you have to, otherwise the crumbs fall off.

AJ: What about dessert?

JEN: Nothing.

AJ: Never?

JEN: Tonight I had cheesecake but I don't have that every night.

AJ: What about snacks during the day?

JEN: Well, I had chips today but I don't have them every day.

AJ: Anything else?

JEN: And a Pepsi.

AJ: Uh-huh.

JEN: And a doughnut. But I don't buy those. My boss does.

AJ: What do you drink?

JEN: Just water.

AJ: Tea and coffee?

JEN: Yeah, but only two or three a day.

AJ: With milk?

JEN: Yeah, but it's only two or three a day.

AJ: What about exercise?

JEN: I don't have time.

. . . and so on and so on.

It could have been me saying all those things. I explained to her that it's not just a case of only one or two coffees or only one or two doughnuts or one can of Pepsi. I told her one can of Pepsi would exceed her recommended calorie intake for about half her day. I explained that the reality of what she is consuming is that unless she cuts out fat and sugar from her diet, she will *not* lose weight. I told her she could have between 1200 and 1600 calories per day and between 30 and 60 grams of fat. Whether she liked it or not, and even though they were only one or two a day, the doughnuts, cheese, Pepsi, full-cream milk, butter, chips and meat cooked in oil all have to go. No excuses.

Then I told her it was really simple: she had to eat more. Eat more food but less fat. I explained that she needed to convince her metabolism to speed up. Her body needs to know it will be fed constantly so it doesn't store what she does eat as fat. She then needs to train her body to burn the fat she has already stored by exercising at least three or four times a week.

I told her about the breakfast, snack, lunch, snack, dinner, snack eating plan that I have been using, and told her she needed to eat four or five pieces of fruit a day, and at least one serve of low-fat dairy. I could hear her saying, 'Uh-huh, hmm, yeah, yeah,' and I could see her staring off into the distance counting her cows. If you tell someone who has not only always struggled with their weight but who has tried and failed at every conceivable 'diet' known to humankind, to eat *more*, they will *not* believe you. I didn't believe that if I ate more food (better choices) then I would lose the weight I have lost. But it *has* worked. I have now lost 23 kilos and all I have done is make good food choices, eaten regularly and exercised.

I said her boss probably prefers her fat and that is why she feeds her up on Pepsi and doughnuts. I told her to tell the woman that if she wanted to buy her things then she should get an apple or a diet chocolate mousse instead. And then I told her it was crap that she didn't have time to exercise. I am a single working mother with no support and I find time to do it, so I know she can too. I told her to get up an hour earlier and go for a swim. I told her she could do it and that it was easier than it sounds and not to worry about whether or not her kids will like the food she cooks. If they don't like it they can cook for themselves—I mean, they're nearly four; if that's not old enough to use the deep fryer then I don't know what age is. Sometimes I wish I wasn't so subtle.

Anyway, she hung up the phone and I know she didn't believe me and she was too far away for me to be able to inspire her but hopefully, when I next see her and I'm half the size I used to be, that will convince her that it works. Every woman who has noticed my weight loss has said, 'What's your secret?' And that's the strange thing. There is no secret. We are brainwashed into thinking thin thighs in thirty days, a dress size in a week, lose weight with this thermonuclear jet blaster burn the ring out of your bum milk drink pill—only four hundred and eighty dollars a week. Lose weight now, ask me how! *There is no bloody secret.* Just good, low-fat low-cal food and exercise.

Oh my God, I just realised something so horrible I need to have a bit of a sit-down. I have become a Born Again Dieter. The next thing I'll be doing is chaining my exercise bike to people's front fences, door-knocking and asking if they want to buy a copy of the best-selling bible for dieters, Weight Watchtower magazine. I'll be asking people if they believed in Bod. And explaining that if they turned to Bod they would see the light . . . that is, the lite-fat food that had been put on this earth to make us thinners see the error of our weighs.

9 January   Take a load off

One of my New Year's resolutions was to go to aerobics. Well, I did it. Okay, I didn't actually *go* to aerobics but I did walk past a class, which is almost the same thing. The room is your typical fishbowl, haha, let's laugh at all the fat people kind of deal. One of the very reasons I don't want to do it. I was walking past on my way to the kiddy pool (and, yes, I did have Kai with me) when I noticed a class with only about ten people in it. The first good thing was that there was not a size 10 gal in the house. No leotards, no shorts, just plain old tracky daks and t-shirts—Australia's national uniform. And even better, everyone was lying down. Now that's my kind of class. The teacher is one of the other instructors and I know she's nice so she wouldn't yell out, 'Come on, lardarse, one more set. Now move!' I also know she has really bad taste in music, which means I love the stuff she plays so at least I know there'll be no techno. The last thing I need to recreate is a nightclub scene. Euh.

It got my mind ticking over so I went and got a programme and looked up what kind of class they were doing. I had a look at the time and there it was: A LP 1, which meant absolutely nothing to me. I went to the little index and read:

A—*Aerobics* (duh!)

LP—*Lite Pace aerobics designed for the new and/or mature participant* (walking frames chained to the bike racks, thanks). *The moves are simplistic and easy to remember exercise combinations* (particularly for those with Alzheimer's, 'cause we just do the one step for forty-five minutes). *Ideal for friends and family not into the 'gym scene'* (no lycra—just tracky daks and bum cracks). All right. My kind of class. The numbers go from 1 to 5, with 1 being basic (translated: for the skills challenged) and 5 being step aside, Strictly Ballroom, here come the Aerobettes. So I suppose if I'm going to actually honour my New Year's resolutions, then that's the class to start me off. Oh God, please don't let them play 'Flashdance'.

Have asked my friend Tara if we can swap kids—one week I'll have hers for the day and the next week she'll have mine. We'll do it on Wednesdays, a day neither of us have child care, and that way I can squeeze in an extra workout a fortnight. In two weeks I have my updated fitness assessment and get a new gym programme.

One interesting thing I have discovered recently is that if I watch television, read or work while I am having my meal, then I tend to want to eat more. However, if I make a big deal out of it, like sitting down at the table, getting a glass of water and taking my time with it (slowing down, as Nutcase advised) then afterwards my brain recognises that I have had a *meal* rather than interpreting it as a *snack*. Sitting down and focusing on the meal somehow makes the food last longer and keeps the cravings away.

10 January   Numbers

I'm starting to think about 85 (no, I didn't say obsess, although I know that's what you're thinking). How good is it going to feel to stand on the scales and see that number come up? That will mean I have lost 24 kilos. It doesn't actually sound like much, does it? Saying I went from 109 kilos to 85 sounds much better. The few clothes I kept are getting loose but are not what I would call hanging off me. I look forward to walking down the street and having to hold my pants up with one hand. God, I need to get a life. On bad days I still think I look as fat as I did when I started but then I look at the photo Helen gave me at Christmas time and I know I have lost weight. I can't help but compare myself to what I want to be.

I am going out tomorrow and I am going to try not to drink. I am going cold turkey. No more. Never. Not ever. Okay, well, maybe not never—once a month might be okay. Certainly no more until I hit eighty-five. I have an updated fitness assessment at the gym in a week so I want to be my best for that as well. Crusher is back and will weigh and measure me next week and I'd hate her to do the sums and say I'd been slacking off.

12 January   Mad Cow

Went back to Nutcase today. Boy, am I screwed up. I forgot how screwed up I am. First of all she asked how I managed over Christmas. I told her my Nan story and she agreed Nan was an old buzzard to say something like that. Actually, I think her words were 'That wasn't very supportive of her . . .' but I know what she really meant.

I told her I'd lost about one or two kilos, depending on what scales I use and whether it is today or yesterday. She said I did well because most people *put on* weight over Christmas and I lost, so I should congratulate myself on being so controlled.

Then I told her about the boy I had met/dated—okay, had hot steamy sex with! I explained that I had re-entered the dating scene and that I was also back on the comedy social scene and that it was interesting and terrifying at the same time. This is what most of the session was about. I explained that I feel uncomfortable when being approached sexually and that I am either completely overt or I run a mile and act like the biggest virgin on earth. I feel like men are the predators and I am the prey. I remember being highly sought after many years ago and I just couldn't cope. I had trouble saying N . . . N . . . N . . . the word that is the opposite of 'yes'. NO. There, I said it. See, I told you I have trouble saying it. And when they get closer I feel like I can't say that word and then I end up sleeping with people I don't like very much and being fat protected me because fewer people harassed me. I admitted I was terrified and I wanted to feel safe without having to get fat again.

I could see her eyes light up in the way shrinks' eyes do when they have a challenge on their hands. They get that '*Uh oh, it's Glenn Close, I'll just pop out the back and hide my rabbits*' kind of look. She said there were about three different issues in there and that we'd work on them one at a time. She said it was important that I felt like I was in control at all times and to know that being fat does not make me safer or any more protected than when I am thin. I am in control of what I do and I can't make myself do anything that I don't want to do.

She explained that it was quite normal for children who have been abused to act out and be overtly sexual. She explained that I was forced to be that way before I had any concept of what it was and that I did it as a way of communicating. Particularly because my teacher's abuse was perpetrated in the guise of love (which it most definitely was not), I grew up with a distorted perception of how to be intimate with someone—intimate not necessarily *having* to end up in sex. So what I find happens is that I end up sleeping with people that I don't want to sleep with because I don't know how to say no. But more importantly, it's because I don't actually know what I want. I have extreme reactions—overt or church mouse. Absolutes. And as Nutcase keeps reminding me, there are no absolutes. I need to find Me in both of those behaviours and act on what I want.

At the moment I just go with what the other person wants. I need to decide what it is I want. And obviously this would change with each person, but I need to make a general decision about where I stand on sexual/intimacy issues. WOW. Got to have a think about that one because I am plagued with contradictions. What comes to mind first is that I want to feel safe and comfortable and proactive, and I want to enjoy sex and making love but I want it to be with the right people and not with just anyone who asks.

This new boy is different because I actually do like him, but whether or not something more permanent happens with him, there will be other offers and opportunities and I have to learn how to deal with them so that I don't use fat as a defence or as protection. As Nutcase reminded me, fat was never a very good defence because there were still plenty of people wanting to sleep with me. Fat is not the answer. I don't know what the answer is yet but I'm hoping Nutcase will be able to give me the cheat sheets.

I am absolutely starving. I had my breakfast really early today because I have to fit so much in. I dropped Kai at kindy and went to the gym so I could get it out of the way. I made sure I had my snack before working out, did some time on the treadmill and some ab work, then did aquarobics. I've just had my lunch but I am still hungry. I am sitting here drinking water because I know that it takes half an hour for the stomach to recognise that it is full so I know if I rehydrate myself my food will digest and I won't feel the urge to go poking around in the fridge.

Half an hour has come and gone and I am not hungry

now. Feel quite full. I really hate that hunger pain thing and have rarely felt it since being in the Alfalfa Zone. Eating so often there's always a snack or a meal just around the corner, so it's never been that bad but this week I've stepped up the exercise routine by 15–20 minutes (just an extra walk, really) per day, to see if it helps me get to 85 as the weight loss has definitely slowed down again. Since the plateau it hasn't kicked back in to a kilo a week and I know health professionals say a half-kilo loss a week is recommended, but I want to see if it helps shift me into that downhill slide to eighty.

Crusher is back on board and sent me an email saying we'll catch up next week. She was happy to hear I was doing so well (am I?) and said 75 kilos here I come! Seventy-five? I have enough trouble believing I'll hit 85, let alone dropping the bar into the seventies. I guess I live with the daily belief that I will stop losing weight and that entering the seventies is an impossible dream. Am I making myself clear? I don't think I can do it. I do have moments of clarity but the numbers don't seem real. Maybe I was like this in the nineties—I forget. All I can do is just keep going, because there is no way I could go back to life the way it was before. The thought of having a hamburger for breakfast is not appealing. That's not to say I wouldn't love to bite into one at lunchtime with the juicy and succulent bacon, egg and oil dribbling down my chin and arm as I simultaneously stuff three or four hot chips into my mouth. The trouble is, if I eat that food now, I am making a conscious decision to choose fat over freedom, and today I couldn't

Dealing with hunger pangs

- If you are feeling hungry and it's not yet time to eat, drink water. It is likely that you are thirsty (dehydrated) and not hungry. Water can help fill you up as well.
- Never get caught out on the road when you are hungry. Plan ahead. If you know you'll be away from home for lunch, then take it with you because when you are hungry you do not make rational decisions and chances are there will be limited healthy choices available to you.
- Always keep some muesli bars or sultanas in your bag. That way, if you're caught away from home, you don't have the dilemma of what to eat.
- Eat slowly so your body has time to recognise that it is full.
- If you are eating all that you should and still have the odd hunger pang, then carry around some Tic-Tacs or sugar-free chewing gum. Feels like you're eating with little or no added calories.
- If all else fails, eat some fruit. It's low fat and good for you!

do that. Talk to me tomorrow and you might find me in the local milk bar ordering a double serving, but today I choose happiness (groan). Must practise safe eating—always use condiments!

16 January
Yes . . . no . . . yes . . . no . . .

Anyone who reads this must think I'm a total schizophrenic. One day I'm saying, 'Oh yeah, I'm in control. Yeah, I've lost weight.' The next day I'm saying, 'I wish I had control. I haven't lost weight.' It's like being a bloody yo-yo. At least Nutcase said that was normal and that eventually (apparently) it will feel less and less like that. I can already see that's true because in the beginning every meal was a struggle, now it's only occasional days that I have cravings. So hopefully one day it will not be much of an issue at all.

One of the best things about losing weight is that having a bath is a pleasant experience again. When I was at my heaviest, having a bath was like trying to squeeze a bull elephant into a foot spa. Now there's actually room to move. Very yummy. There's almost room for two . . .

20 January   Fun at the pool (not!)

There I was having a pretty good day. Kai was having a day with his dad and the boy was due over in a couple of hours. I'd weighed in at 85 (.6) and even though I didn't quite believe that it could be so, I did feel lighter. I'd done a quick session at the gym so that when the boy arrived I'd be that extra bit gorgeous. But then he rings and says he'll be a little late. No problem. I skip heartily to the pool to have a bit of a swim. There's nothing like a little exercise to give you that healthy glow. As I walked to the edge of the pool a group of five little kids looked at me, puffed out their cheeks and openly laughed at me.

Then they turned together, whispered, giggled, pointed at me again and laughed. I was fat again. How could I put on 100 kilos in sixty seconds because of a few six-year-old brats? I stood there wondering what I could do to them that was legal. I thought about telling them, 'I've put a curse on all of you and you're all going to die on your fifteenth birthdays, hehehehehe!' Then I realised I couldn't do that because they were just six and by the time they reach fifteen they'll have forgotten about my stupid old curse. So I paused at the edge of the pool for a while, now too embarrassed to enter the water, afraid of emptying it should I jump in. Then I told them that Santa didn't exist and that when the tooth fairy left money under their pillows, it was because she was planning to rip the souls out of their six-year-old bodies and send them to hell forever. They looked at me in shock and I laughed before diving into the water, making sure I splashed them with my laughable oversized thighs. Who says I need therapy?

Then I got a text message from him saying he wasn't going to make it after all. And that made my day a total tragedy. God, I hate the world!

21 January   Protection racket

Email. It's just so damned quick. And once it's gone it's gone and you can't intercept it at the other end, or go the post office and bribe someone to take it back out of the box. God, I hunger for the old-fashioned days of being able to take back what you say.

See, I got all paranoid and worried that this guy didn't really like me, and that I was too fat to have a relationship. And now on top of telling him that I didn't mean it when I said I didn't want to do the wild thing anymore, I'm going to have to tell Nutcase as well. There's a big comedy benefit coming up and knowing that he and I would both be at it I expected him to say, 'Look, I know we're *doing it*, but can we pretend we don't know each other that night? I am a free agent, you know. And you are too fat for me to openly admit I've actually been with you.' Of course, I'm probably totally underestimating him but I have trouble letting go of the 'I'm too fat to be anybody's love interest' perception.

So I sent it and as soon as it was gone I regretted it. What I should have said is, 'I really like you and I want to see more of you and perhaps entertain the possibility of having a relation-ship with you' but instead I said 'It isn't going to work out, I can't sleep with you anymore. If I do I'll end up hating you.' Ha, for a writer, sometimes I can be incredibly inarticulate.

I know I am trying to protect myself. Before I have used food and being fat, now I have neither of those so I feel like a tap-dancer with no legs. Aaah! Losing weight is so hard on so many levels. Men! You can't live with them and you can't hunt them down and shoot them either!

Later: Can you hear that? That's the final nail being driven into the coffin of this 'relationship'. He emailed me and agreed we should just be friends. Ho hum. At least I can find some cold comfort in the fact that it was me who said it first. Pity though, he's very cute and such a good kisser! Oh well, onward killer bod, onward.

Have pretty much kept to my NY resolution of not drinking. Not that it is reducing my weight at all as I weighed in at 86.6. I've also gone for a walk every single day. I now take the stroller and when Kai gets tired he sits down and I push him up horribly steep hills that have me turning blue in the face. Our afternoon walks have become a kind of a ritual. We wander around our suburb discovering new parks. Who needs a personal trainer when you can have your two-year-old turn and throw the killer of all tantrums if you don't get off your bum and go for a walk NOW!

I want my body to change NOW. Not in four months or five months. NOW! It feels like I've been doing this forever. I find it hard to believe that I'll ever actually get there. It doesn't feel real. Nothing I can do about it, though. No way I can give up. Not this far into it. It's all the way to the new AJ.

Craving chocolate—total love substitute. If I eat one bite of white chocolate and one bite of dark, does this mean I am having a balanced diet? Just trying to forget you-know-who but I have to tell you what he said to me. If we were to just be lovers, he didn't want to be my friend. But if we were to be friends, then we couldn't be lovers. Some choice, huh? Thinking about what Nutcase asked me about what *I* wanted in regards to 'relationships', I settled for friendship. Wonder if I can change my mind?

No, I don't want to, really. I've thought about it and

because I haven't believed in my body being beautiful I have offered sex far too early in the game to too many people. I want to be loved for all of me. My body, my brains, my generosity of spirit, my talent and the fact that I am the only woman I know who can stick a balloon up her nose and pull it out of her mouth. I want to hold off on the intimacy stuff and find someone who actually wants to be with me, someone who earns my trust enough for me to open my heart up to them and feel good about it. Of course this relies on the rather impossible notion that there is a decent single man left in the world—no, sorry, the universe—but, hey, I'm an optimist, it might just happen. I wonder if there's life on Mars . . .

I can't believe I seriously contemplated driving my car to the end of the street to do a workout today (all of 150 metres). It reminds me of the bad old days when I used to drive around to the corner shop if I ran out of milk. Anyway, it was raining and I feel rotten. Might have something to do with a heavy heart and thighs to match. The last thing I wanted to do was go to the gym today, with stupid reasoning like 'nobody's going to enjoy my body anyway'. Then I told myself that *I* could enjoy my body and if I keep going then I won't be able to use my body as an excuse, so if the boys don't like me then it's because of their complete and utter lack of taste and absolutely nothing to do with me and that made me feel a lot better. So off I trudged in the rain and, while still feeling rotten, I do kind of feel a little bit better. Nothing a good bottle of vodka couldn't temporarily remedy, but I am off the grog!

I've been pretty good, actually. Only had one glass of

champagne and we're two weeks into the year already. Oh my God, maybe I feel so bad because I'm detoxing. Maybe I'll start to see pink rabbits and little green men. Oh no, that's what I saw last time I drank myself stupid. Oh well, my hips might thank me in a month's time, even if my heart won't.

23 January
Whatever you do, don't look down

All right! Super fitness here I come. I have just tried Kai in the creche again and he stayed. Yay! Lite Pace aerobics here I come! It's going to be so good to do those extra classes during the week. If that doesn't get me over the second hump then nothing will. Am feeling so incredibly frustrated. Weighed in at 87 again. The temptation is to cut back on food but Crusher has told me to stick with it. She keeps saying it's because I am toning my body and building muscle and that fat is disappearing from my body. My aqua teacher today said, 'AJ, you're really losing a lot of weight. You're looking really good.' I told her my frustration at not losing on the scales and like everyone else, she said not to focus on that. She said she could see I am getting a good shape and to focus on working out and eating well. God, if only someone would say to me, 'Oh no, there's this magic trick you can do, you'll lose the weight overnight and it's so easy.' But I hear my inner guru speak again: 'Magic tricks are simply illusions. Hard work is real and lasts forever.' Maybe the aerobics classes will get me over what I am now calling the second plateau.

A friend of mine asked me how much I weighed and when I said 86 she said, 'Wow, you're only ten kilos heavier than me.' That amazed me because she has a great body, so maybe my goal is not that far away after all. You get sucked in by all the magazines and their trendy little graphs about what is the right weight for your height, but she has a healthy, good looking body and she's not much taller than me, so maybe there is some light at the end of this tunnel vision.

One of the girls in my aqua class is about to have her stomach stapled. She's a big girl and reckons she's tried everything. She asked me if I'd ever considered it. In desperate times, when I really believed I would never lose weight, I did consider it but knew I could never afford it and, secretly, that would have been admitting that I had absolutely no power over my life.

Besides, the thought of someone opening me up and stapling my gut just terrifies me. Not to mention being at work and having to double as the stationery cupboard. 'Sally, have you seen the staples?' 'Yes, they're in AJ's gut, and while you're there could you get another ream of paper and a cappuccino machine?' You'd get so sick of explaining to customs officers that, no, there's no bomb hidden in your lower intestine and you don't understand why all those fridge magnets are sticking to your gut. And if you stapled your stomach, how would you accessorise—pierce your liver? At least when people asked how you'd lost weight you could simply say, 'Oh, just a staple diet!'

The Bridge Climb is booked for three weeks time. That's the day I do my final interview with the Lifestyle Channel.

I'm annoyed that I am not going to be at my goal weight for that but I guess near enough is good enough. I also wish that they were going to continue following me around because even though I've lost a lot of weight, I'm going to lose so much more and the next ten kilos will make me look so different to the way I look now. But I have to let that go and understand that the weight I am doesn't really matter. The most important message this show will deliver is that over-weight people need to get healthy, that it is possible to do it and not wait for some magical cure, and your life can change dramatically in so many ways, just by losing a little bit of weight (okay, a lot, but it's how you feel about yourself that matters!).

I've decided my reward for getting to 80 is a facial. Gee, we've come a long way from the Pluto Pup reward system, haven't we?

24 January   A star is born

What a day! Weighed in at 85. Actually 84.5 but I'll say 85 to be safe. Then I had my gym update. I have lost 13 kilos in twelve weeks. Yeehaa! Christmas included. Woohoo! The instructor looked at my measurements and was amazed. He said in all his years as a gym instructor he had never seen such amazing results. I have lost 18 centimetres off my hips! Eighteen! No wonder I can now fit on the swing seats in the park. I had to pull out my 30-centimetre ruler and hold it against my hips just to see how big that difference is. It's huge. More than half the ruler!

He went through all my exercises, fixed up a few things I was doing wrong and gave me a few more to do. Then he talked to me about burning fat and the plateau effect. He said the body needed the plateau to get used to the change in weight. When I thought about it that way, it didn't seem so annoying and actually made sense. He said that my body has probably adapted to the exercise I've been doing and now it was time to consciously burn fat. I do this by getting my heart rate to a certain level and keeping it there, thus burning fat. They calculate the heart rate for each person by taking your age, weight and height. I have to get my heart rate at 110 beats per minute or more. I calculate that by checking my pulse and counting the number of beats over fifteen seconds. Then I multiply that by four and I have my heart rate. You can do that or buy a groovy little gadget called a heart rate monitor, which consists of a strap that goes around your chest and a watch which shows your heart rate. I'm going to get one of those. I love gadgets!

Anyway, apparently my target heart rate is equal to that of a 45-year-old woman—at thirty-two that's not so good. Three more months of hard work and it will be better. They call the kind of exercise I need to do to burn fat 'cardio'. That basically means increased heart rate. He gave me exercises on the treadmill, bike and a weird machine called the cross-trainer—something I have managed to avoid the whole three months of my gym training.

He also said I should be moving up to heavier weights and should push myself a little harder than I am already. He said I had adapted and that aqua was now too easy for me so I have to come to the gym first and do an hour of cardio/weights before aqua. The cardio will set me up in fat burning mode and should keep me there through the weights and aqua thus burning my body fat. He also recommended I do aerobics classes. He said the one-hour walks I do in the afternoons with Kai would not actually burn fat now that my fitness level has improved. He said they'd be good for my health and well-being but as a way to lose weight they are no longer that effective. Only cardio and weights will do that for me now.

The other thing he said was to focus on 75 but to know that 75 will still be too big for my height and that once I get there I'll probably want to go to sixty-five. I didn't want to hear that. Sixty-five just seems absolutely undeniably impossible. Not going to think about that! Going to just focus on 80, then 75, and see how I feel when I get there. He also said the next ten will be the hardest to lose. Oh goody! Something to look forward to.

Anyway, my fitness and stretching had improved, he was totally impressed with what I'd done and when I left I felt pretty good about myself.

My measurements:

	Three months ago (first day at the gym)	Now
Chest	108.5 cm	99 cm
Hips	131 cm	113 cm
Waist	97.5 cm	96.5 cm
Thigh	64.5 cm	60 cm
Arm	36.5 cm	33.5 cm

Eighteen centimetres off my hips—I am a legend. I keep thinking about that number. I have decided not to focus on seventy-five. On Crusher's advice I have decided to concentrate on 79, which was my original weight loss goal. She says I need to congratulate myself and acknowledge the huge effort I have put in, and to recognise the achievement for what it is. Sure, I know that I won't be happy there but five months ago I set out to lose 30 kilos and I have nearly done just that. When I get to 79 then I can reset my goals and target weight loss but for now, I'm heading to seventy-nine.

30 January
There's a masterpiece in there

Weighed in at 83. This new cardio business has dropped two kilos off in a week. Nutcase will have a freak-out if I tell her 'cause she's keeping an eye on my kilos in case I lose too much too soon. I rang Crusher and she told me not to worry. She said because I'd been doing weights and because muscle is very dense (heavy), I've been adding weight while losing fat. Now, by changing my exercise routine, I have stepped up the fat burning and shocked my body back into losing weight. She told me I need to keep changing my exercise programme along the way to keep my metabolism firing.

She said to enjoy the next two weeks because there will be rapid weight loss but then it will settle back down. She urged me to keep up the weights and had a great explanation of how that was changing my body. She said to look at my fat as a layer of velvet and that underneath I am sculpting the most beautiful body I have ever had or ever imagined I could have. At the moment the work is going on under the velvet covering and is being kept from view, but as the velvet comes off in the next few months I will be amazed at just how good my body is.

31 January   Operating room

Oh God, I just can't bring myself to do the aerobics classes. And anyway, I could keep that for when I need to change my exercise routine again (in another two months!). I know it was my New Year's resolution, but there's plenty of the year left, thank you very much.

Had a good session with Nutcase. We talked about how, now that I'm losing weight, I'm feeling more exposed and vulnerable. I'm afraid of getting hurt and I don't have as much fat to hide behind or use as an excuse. She said I had tried to sabotage the romance thing and that I had tried to control the outcome. I had decided he didn't like me so I told him it was off. It's like ending a relationship because you're afraid of being alone. Yep, I am crazy! Good thing I've got a shrink.

She said I can't control what other people do. I can only control what I do (I can?). She agreed that I could have gone in more slowly, but she also said that was okay and all I could do was go forward and change my behaviour next time. I could be with him and if it developed then I should let it happen and not decide whether or not it has a future but to just be in the moment. She said I had major abandonment issues (being adopted, mother dying) and that it was normal to behave that way—to push people away for fear of losing them. But she explained that I could learn a healthier approach to life, one that wouldn't have me being alone in order to protect myself (or being fat to do same). She said I could look at dates as a toss of the coin—50 per cent will work and 50 per cent won't. She told me to enjoy each one in the present time and not to worry about whether or not it has a future because most people don't think, I am looking for a relationship, he looks like he'll be good. People get to know each other first, spend time together and then at some point either find they are in a relationship or decide they want to spend more time with that person and then make that extra commitment.

So my objective from now on is to keep myself a little precious, hold back a bit, spend time with this boy and/or whoever else I want to spend time with, and to just take each moment as it comes and not over-analyse it. She also recommended that next time I want to send an email, I write it, save it, read it later and perhaps edit it before sending it.

Anyway, I got home and sent an email explaining to him that I was trying to control the outcome, that I did actually like him and would like to spend time with him.

He sent an email back saying that was good, and that he liked me too and if we were in a different time we might have a relationship together. I didn't say anything about that as I am not thinking about that, I am just going to get to know this guy a bit more and see where it leads.

I feel safer already, coming out of the fat and into 'open heart surgery', which is what the dating world feels like. I remember being hit upon by so many people and I felt scared. Now I feel safer for having Nutcase to guide me.

1 February   Ready . . .

Many emails and lots of late-night net chatting from the boy. We are seeing each other at a big comedy night tomorrow. I think that's going to be weird. Better look like a goddess!

2 February   Set . . .

Tonight's the night. In fact this is kind of like my coming-out party. Everyone from my old stand-up comedy days will be there and I intend to look fabulous. I feel a bit like a lab rat in a controlled experiment. I'm going back into the scene that actually made me want to be fat. Will I want to run away? Will I be able to handle the scene? Will I want to go home and get fat again? Will I sleep with the first person who says, 'Hi, what's your name?'

I don't know, but I *am* going to look fabulous. Have a nice new frock with shoestring straps that shows off the boobs to the max. I have a good tan that in ten years I will regret having, my hair is now blonde and I am 83 kilos, which is two kilos lighter than Kate Winslet when all the mags said she was fat though she actually looked gorgeous. So I am telling myself 'think Kate Winslet', and my breasts will look so good no one will notice my hips (even though they are now also highly reduced).

I just hope I don't come home with another broken bone. Unless, of course, the bone I break is not mine. Disgusting!

3 February   She's back!

What a night! I truly felt like Cinderella at the ball (and it only took me four hours to get ready!). I have avoided this scene so much since I got fat, afraid that's what people would say—'Jeez, AJ, you're so fat! What happened?' When I have come back into the scene, most people I knew avoided talking to me and I did likewise. I felt trapped and embarrassed and totally shamed that I had let myself go. Not so last night.

I was OUT. Not out as in, 'Hi, Gran, I'm a lesbian, this is my life partner Diesel, we've decided to start a family so we were wondering if we could borrow the turkey baster' kind of out. I was out as in 'this is my new life and boy am I gonna enjoy it!' My fabulous breasts were the topic of many conversations, with some old friends asking me to please take them away because they couldn't concentrate. (Good to see the sexual pressure is no longer there.) But I laughed and joked and told them all they would never get the chance to take them for a test drive. I felt strong and safe. I felt like an equal again. And people who I thought had forgotten me came bounding up to throw their arms around me and say hello. Interesting what losing 26 kilos (and gaining a bloody good bra) can do. I wonder whether people avoid you because they are afraid they'll catch your fat if they touch you. 'Yes, doctor, I touched a woman who was fat and woke up with a spare tyre on my gut. Is there a morning-after pill I can take?'

Was asked to be in someone's film as, wait for it, the sexy girl who tries to bring back her dead partner (and, no, it's not a porno film). Realised I was probably heading back into the land of getting gigs in roles other than the funny fat chick or dag. God, just when I think this fitness thing couldn't get any better it does.

The boy and I were a bit weird. Didn't talk much. When he left he lightly punched me on the arm and said, 'See ya, mate.' He later sent me a text message saying we'll talk tomorrow night.

It was great feeling good enough about myself to approach all the people I hadn't seen in years. I am so used to being fat that people don't think I'm the same person. When you're fat you don't feel as worthwhile as a thin person. Stupid, huh? In my new-found body confidence I felt I could approach anyone, even comedians I admired but had never met. It was great. I feel like a new woman. I feel so excited by what my future holds. Hopefully, as more of the fat disappears I will rediscover my courage and belief in myself and with Nutcase as my emotional protector I may even be able to take over the world, something I remember wanting to do when I was young and naïve and full of the belief that if you really want it you can have it. 'It' being everything your heart desires. God, who would have thought—a few Macca's meals less and I am ready to conquer the world.

I'm fantasising about getting to a point where I feel confident enough to go back to my agent and say 'I'm back and I'm not going to get fat so get me some gigs—a few leads in some feature films will do.' Ha. I can dream!

But I want to be my best when I do that. I want to walk through the door and see his jaw drop to the ground. I'm coming back and nothing's going to stop me. Well, the few vodkas I had last night might slow down the action, but that was my one allowable night out (I'm letting myself have one drinking night a month, remember).

4 February   Who?

Back on 84 today. It's those vodkas I had the other night. I was a bit tipsy when I got home and wanted to have a midnight munch but I convinced myself to go to bed instead, so I'm glad I don't have that added guilt to follow me around. The vodka's enough. Am craving fish and chips. That's on my Top Five craving list, so I'm going to make wedges and grill some fish for dinner in the hope that it goes away. Everywhere I go at the moment I see overflowing fish and chip shops exuding that lovely aroma of three-day-old fat and the quick hiss of food being dropped into the oil—oh my God, I'm gonna have the wedges for lunch. If I wait till dinner then I'm sure to buckle.

You'll never guess who called me. The vet. The vet with the best excuse to bail from a date I've ever heard. I knew who it was but I said, 'Who? Michael who?' Just to make him a wee bit embarrassed. He reckons he found my phone number in one of his drawers, and thought he'd catch up. Funny how it's the same day 'Mum's the Word' is being repeated on SBS-TV.

He hasn't rung since he stood me up two months ago, then says, all chatty like it was yesterday, that we should catch

(Almost) Fat-Free Wedges

6 potatoes, peeled
1 dessertspoon olive oil
100 g breadcrumbs
1 chicken stock cube, crumbled
1 teaspoon mixed herbs
1 teaspoon rock salt (or garlic salt)
1 teaspoon crushed garlic
1 tablespoon fresh chives, chopped

Preheat the oven to 200 degrees. Cut each potato into 8 wedges. Wash and dry them and place them in a plastic bag. Add the remaining ingredients to the bag and shake the bag around until the wedges are evenly coated. Lightly spray a baking tray with cooking oil. Place the wedges on the tray and cook in the preheated oven for approximately 20 minutes or until golden brown and deliciously crunchy.

I served these with a dash of sweet chilli sauce and, no, I'm not going to recommend you have them with sour cream as that is full of fat and defeats the purpose of making them almost fat-free!

Serves 3; contains 1g fat.

up for a drink. I laughed and I can't believe it but I told him that I didn't think we had much in common and that I wasn't very interested in him. He laughed and obviously didn't believe me because he sent me seven text messages while I was watching the reruns of my huge arse on the box.

I was so depressed looking at myself but then my friend Alicia pointed out that I shouldn't be depressed 'cause I don't have that body any more. I realised I wasn't as depressed as I had been the first time it went to air because I felt like I'd never get out of that body, that I'd be trapped by my eating habits forever. But this time, I'm on the way to having exactly the body I have always dreamed of having. So when we shoot the next series, everyone will think they fired me and hired someone thinner.

One of the mums at Kai's child care centre keeps saying to me, 'I can't believe how good you look. I just can't believe it.' Which loosely translates as, 'I can't believe how bad you looked before.' Funny.

5 February   Temptation

Hah, just when I thought I was cruising along, two things have happened. One is the urge to skip meals. It's like a little devil sitting on my shoulder, whispering into my ear: 'Do it. Go on. I know you can.' I think, go on, no one will notice, it might make you get there faster. I just reason with this voice, knowing that I will not keep the weight off if I lose it rapidly. Will talk to Nutcase tomorrow. At the moment I make sure I stick to the plan, six times a day.

The other thing is the opposite: the desire to eat junk food. It could be that it's time to do the shopping because there's limited choices in the house so I think, what can I buy, then start imagining all the crap I want to eat. Or I could just be a bit bored with cooking the same food all the time. Must be time to find some more recipes. Will ask my friends—the non-alcoholic non-two minute noodle eating thin ones. Hmm, doesn't leave many people. Better get on the net.

I am totally confused about the guy. We talked on the net for two and a half hours last night and two more in the wee hours of this morning, as I was caring for my bravely vomiting two-year-old child. It was intimate, matey, intimate, matey. On again, off again. The whole thing's been a merry-go-round. He told me he was coming over, he didn't come over, I told him I didn't want to see him (I did) and he said he didn't want to see me either, he said he liked me too much, I said the same, he told me he was seeing other people for sex, I told him I was seeing someone else (I'm not) so he told me he was seeing someone else the very next night. Racked with guilt about stretching the truth (okay, all-out lying) I admitted I made it up to make him jealous. He told me he saw the other person 'cause he *was* jealous. I told him it was 'cause he told me he had plenty of people he was 'seeing' so I said . . . oh God, it's all a bit demented, really. At least I have an excuse. I'm seeing a shrink and am learning this new healthy 'relationship' thing, not that I have a relationship with this guy. If I mention that word he'll be so far out the door it's not funny. I think I've got a bit of work to do before I'm ready to get into a healthy relationship, or even an unhealthy one for that matter. But at least when I do, I won't eat myself to death or singledom.

Why can't I meet a man who has his shit together? Why can't I get my shit together?

7 February   The twilight zone

I had the best session with Nutcase I have ever had. First of all I admitted I had had a horrible week filled with making myself eat when I have wanted to skip meals. Obsessing, thinking about laxatives etc. See, you didn't even know, did you? It's very secretive behaviour. That's the thing. All day every day I get this voice inside my head, trying to convince me to skip meals or buy boxes of laxatives. It's really hard not to listen to it after years of living your life that way.

I told her it was like a little devil sitting on your shoulder saying, 'Go on, get some laxatives. No one will know and you'll get there faster.' I told her I felt like I was dobbing on myself. She wanted to focus on that for a while. She told me it wasn't secretive at all because *I* would know. She asked me what I called the part of me that does that (keeps the secrets) and/or that stores all the past memories/feelings of the abuse. I said I named it Secret Person. She said that the only way to get better from all of that is to unlock it and deal with it, otherwise it stays the same and continues to affect our behaviour. So the next few weeks we will be looking at all the bad stuff that happened to me. Oh goody, better buy some Kleenex and a few bottles of red wine . . . maybe even a case.

She then asked me why I had suddenly started thinking that way and what I had done about it. I told her I had made myself eat except for last night, when I just didn't feel very well and hadn't had dinner. She said that was good and better than I would have done in the past because this time I actually ate. Yes, I could have eaten more or better meals but

I did still eat (stuck to the plan) and it is normal not to eat when you feel sick. She said I had done better than I give myself credit for. I also admitted that I was a bit too broke to do a big shop so I'm eating the staple groceries out of the cupboard, which means beans, sardines and rice crackers. See what a glamorous life I lead? She said as long as I keep eating when and what I'm supposed to, then everything will be okay.

Then she asked me about the boy . . . Aaah! Damn! I told her everything I'd done that week. I told her about the 'I've got someone else well I've got someone else too' routine that we did and after she laughed in my face and rang her friends to tell them what an idiot I am, she said it is now time for me to stop trying to protect myself by playing games. I am to speak the truth, tell people how I feel and not be afraid of doing that. I have to stop thinking about what they will do and focus on what I want and who I want to spend time with. If I like him, spend time with him. If I don't, then tell him to hit the road and not worry about what he'll think of me. I mentioned to her that I told the vet to take a hike and she said she was proud of me and wanted to see more of that. Hah, now I have an excuse to tell men to get lost. 'I'm sorry but I don't like you. Go away.' God, I love therapy.

Later: How do you make a bad day worse? It's like people can sense when you're down. My father rings me and we are catching up with the usual stuff when he says, 'How's your weight problem, love?' Not, 'How's your diet?', 'How's your fitness fad?' or even 'Is your bum getting smaller?' but, 'How's your weight *problem*?'

My only problem with weight is that it isn't seen as a beautiful thing. Well, it is in Africa and India, but I am not going to go and live in a country where I have to wipe my bum with my hand just so I can be a goddess! Oh, okay, it could be seen as a problem if I count the fact that being overweight improves your chances of dying prematurely of a heart attack. And of course being overweight can increase your chances of getting diabetes and that can kill you or make you blind. And if you ignore the fact that most of the last ten years of my life have been filled with self-loathing and abuse then I do *not* have a problem.

God, I'm in a dark spot today. I'm tired, probably premenstrual—that or I hate the whole damn world for no good reason—and I feel completely in the nowhere zone. I'm four months in the Alfafa Zone and about four months out from the beautiful bod. The Twilight Zone. Still fat but not as fat as I was, yet not as thin as I'll be.

Oh and to top my week off, I hopped on the scales last night and weighed 86 kilos. Went to bed cursing myself, wondering what I am afraid of (probably talking about the abuse, which is on the agenda in the next few sessions) and vowing I will never weigh myself at night again.

Of course I forget that premenstrual I always weigh more and this morning I was 84, so either I was full of water and other stuff, or the scales were wrong (I prefer the former excuse). Anyway, the end of the day weigh-in session is out and I'm just going to get to the gym and keep working! Once again, all I can say is that the only way out is through, 'cause I am never going back to being fat fat fat, never ever again.

8 February
When good diets go bad

9 am: I'm having a shocker. I saw one of those articles in the Sunday papers where they show a 'normal' person and their vital stats. This girl was the same height and age as me and she was 45 kilos. She looked pretty good and I realised with horror that I am 39 kilos heavier than her. Oh my God. I'm sure underneath her Gucci business suit there was an undernourished Calista Flockhart type body, but dressed she looked okay. Then again a coat hanger covered in a Lacroix dress is going to look okay too. You might keep it in your wardrobe but you wouldn't want to sleep with it.

10 am: Oh dear. Chocky choc choc . . . I must be pre-menstrual 'cause I haven't had a chocky craving like this for, oh, at least a month.

11 am: Maybe I need love instead of chocolate . . . but where am I going to find that in five minutes? Without having to pay for it or go somewhere with a discreet back entrance, thank you very much!

11.30 am: Do you think it's normal to have sexual fantasies about chocolate bars?

11.40 am: I could just have one little bite and throw the rest away . . .

11.50 am: Afraid to cook the low-fat brownies 'cause if I do what I did last week I'll eat the whole tray over three days. No, it has to be a controlled substance.

12.02 pm: Don't think about it. Think about something else, like taking a walk . . . no, I'd have to go past the shops and then I'd be compelled to get chocolate. Um, think about . . . ah, lying in my back yard and staring at the beautiful night sky. Stargazing. Yeah, that's it! I could look at the Southern Cross, the big dipper, the Milky Way—ah, no, not the Milky Way. That's chocolate. Think of something else.

12.03 pm: I've been thinking. Chocolate actually comes from the cocoa bean, doesn't it? So, really, it could be classed as a vegetable and veggies are allowed and recommended in the Alfalfa Zone, so one chocolate frog would equal two pieces of pumpkin maybe? No? Okay.

12.30 pm: Well, this is my last shot. If people didn't put on weight from eating too much chocolate there would be a grave downturn in the diet industries, corset manufacturers, gyms, plastic surgeons, magazine and TV advertising etc, and then there would be huge economic ramifications because of this, so I am in fact saving the world from a recession by buying and consuming chocolate. Not a chance in hell? Okay, I'll have some strawberries. Of course they would taste better with just a teensy bit of chocolate on them. All right, all right, I'll just have a diet mousse instead. But it's not quite the same knowing it only has 35 calories and bugger-all fat.

Much later: Oh God, the worst possible thing has happened. My on again, off again guy has seen me at my fattest. They're repeating 'Mum's the Word' on TV and he saw it. He sent me a text message asking if it was me. He said he didn't recognise me because I look different, but the voice got him. He wasn't sure so he had to ask. Which I guess is a good thing, really, because it means all the hard work is actually paying off.

And he asked if he could see me on Saturday night, which is okay too. At least he didn't run in the opposite direction, afraid he'd catch my fat virus. It's a weird feeling. I'm proud of what I have done but I cringe to think that I actually got *that* fat and that there is a permanent public record of it. What a dilemma.

I'm moving out of my black mood at last. I weighed in at 83 today and am definitely staying away from alcohol. I want to get to 79. My original goal. The magic number. I'm not going to focus on what the mags say I should be or compare myself to anyone else. I am just going to focus on me.

9 February Absolutism

Lose weight now. Ask me how. Gastro! Yes, I know that's already far too much information but I have lost two kilos so it can't be all that bad. Just hope I get better before the weekend. Don't want to ruin my naughty night out. My friend Phillippa has shouted us a night at a fancy hotel, so hopefully it's going to be a good one. If I manage to leave the bathroom for more than five minutes.

I have had *the* most amazing session with Nutcase today.

She has just blown me away. I'm not sure I'm going to be able to articulate it properly because my mind is still whirling with some of the things she said. I explained to her that I know I've lost weight. I can see the number on the scales going down, the clothes getting bigger, I can feel my elbows and hips starting to emerge from the fat and people are really commenting. On good days I can actually see my body changing shape but no matter what happens I *still feel fat*. And I remember when I was sick, no matter how thin I was, I *still felt fat*. I know it doesn't make sense, but no amount of logic or reasoning seems to be able to sway me from that idea.

I thought she would respond by pulling out a rather large syringe and calling in the men in little white coats so they could cart me off to the anorexia farm where they drip-feed you Crunchie bars and cut your fingers off so you can't stick them down your throat. Not so. She said, 'Good.'

I said, 'What?'

She said, 'Good. It's good that you understand that there is no logic to that thinking because that in itself is logical and if you didn't have that understanding then it would be a lot harder to help you. So even just understanding that it isn't logical is a good thing.'

Excellent! I wasn't as screwed up as I thought I was. Then she asked me what fat was.

Hmm. What *is* fat? That beautiful golden liquid that magically turns boring old potatoes into yummy delicious deep-fried wedges, little bundles of joy and happiness that you dip in fatty yummy scrummy sour cream. Also perfect for replacing the boyfriend you don't have. Fat. Joyous fat.

Glorious fat. Fat is eating five chocolate bars and not worrying about the size of your thighs. Fat is the perfect partner. Fat never tells you you're fat. Fat never farts and pulls the bed covers over your head and fat, well fat is . . .

Found myself dribbling on the couch, the clock ticking and Nutcase waiting patiently for my answer. I thought seriously about what fat is for a while and this is what I said:

Fat is
Ugly
Unacceptable
Abnormal
Unsuccessful
Different
Unlovable
Loneliness
Lack of control
Being judged—people look at you and either hate you or feel
    sorry for you.
And it is half living your life—not going places/doing things
    because of the weight.

Then she asked me to describe what thin is. My list went like
    this:

Thin is
Power
Control
Success (I said that twice)

Beauty
Acceptance
Popularity
Desirability
You belong
You are not judged as much

She then asked if I knew that nearly 80 per cent of Australian women are a size 14 or more. So that thin, as in magazine/actress thin, was not 'normal' at all.

Nutcase asked me to think back to a time when I wasn't fat, and to tell her what that felt like. I told her I couldn't remember a time in my life when I didn't think I was fat. I explained to her that by the time I was ten years old, there was immense pressure in my ballet classes to become a twig and I just wasn't one, so even back then I was being given negative feedback about my body. I went on to tell her about how my brother's friends used to call me fatso, and how the girls at school used to tell me to lose weight.

She asked me whether or not I was popular at school. I said I wasn't popular in the beginning but then I had managed to infiltrate and become a member of the popular group.

She asked me how, exactly, I had managed to *become* popular. I explained that I had lived by their rules, befriended someone in the group and edged my way in. I told her how they would constantly tell me that if I lost weight so and so (Gary) would probably go out with me—if you were in the In Group you had to have a boyfriend. That was one of the unwritten rules.

She asked me what it felt like to be part of the In Group. I said it felt great. It felt powerful and it felt as if I was respected (how deluded was I?). It was a good thing to always be invited everywhere, the parties, the shopping centre, girlie slumber parties. I belonged to something bigger than just me.

Then she said the most amazing thing. She said that when I feel fat I'm not really feeling fat at all. What I am feeling is unpopular, unliked, unsuccessful and all the things that are on my list of what fat is. She said it was because at an early age I was taught that *fat* was all those things and because I didn't have an adult figure to teach me otherwise (i.e. that I was a worthwhile human being) then that became my way of thinking.

So, in my world of absolutes, there is either thin (which is happiness, popularity and everything on the good list) or fat, which is the opposite. So no matter how thin I get, unless I deal with each of those things on my list, I will always feel 'fat'.

I have to tell you, I was absolutely stunned. I knew she was right. She then said the reason I want to feel thin is because I believe that if I am thin then I will belong, because I have never really felt as if I have belonged anywhere. I didn't belong in ballet class because I wasn't thin enough. I didn't belong in the In Group because I wasn't thin enough, and I never felt like I belonged in the family I grew up in because I always knew I was adopted. When I finally met my birth family I never felt like I belonged there either, because they had already established their 'family' and I wasn't a part of it. I felt like nobody's child.

I realised that I have spent my whole life feeling as if I

don't belong anywhere and, most importantly, that I have felt like I don't belong in my body because, fat or thin, I have never ever been happy with myself.

Whoa.

Must take a deep breath and let all of that information sink in. I keep getting what can only be described as waves of enlightenment. It makes so much sense. And even though I wish I'd known this twenty years ago, I am so grateful that I know it today. I have no idea what I'm going to do with this knowledge but it feels so powerful having it in my head. What we are going to do is work through each item on the list until I relearn new ways of thinking and dealing with my feelings of insecurity (not belonging).

We started on success, because I had said it twice. She asked me why I thought being thin equated to being successful. I said that as an actress you *have* to be thin. She said what about Camryn Mannheim? I said yeah, but there are just not that many parts for fat girls. I said I was getting more work since I lost weight, so thin was success. She said it was because I was going out more and because I had more confidence that I was getting more work, not because I had lost weight.

I disagreed. I told her how I felt I had lost a part in a film because I was not thin enough.

She said that I judged myself too harshly and took castings too personally. Some people were just not right for the part. And sometimes not even the best person got the job. (That made me feel good.) She also explained that sometimes people had to *put on* weight for their roles . . . Toni Colette in *Muriel's Wedding*. Yeah, I would have liked that role. When that film came out all my friends asked me why I hadn't auditioned for it. I wasn't sure whether that was a compliment or not.

I told Nutcase how horrible the audition process was for me. I couldn't stand the scrutiny of the cattle calls. Lining up with thirty other women waiting and hoping that they'd pick me like you choose a lobster in a Chinese restaurant. Pick me. Pick Me. Yuck!

Nutcase jumped on that so quickly. She said once again it was about belonging, being accepted. I wanted someone else to tell me that I was okay, that I was good enough. Because my parents rarely praised me and because I always lived in the shadow of my good looking, very popular, loved by everyone who met him, sports hero brother, I felt like I was never ever good enough, so when I didn't get the parts I went for I deemed myself just not good enough. Never was, never would be. That's what I decided. That became my truth.

Gee, this doctor is damn good. I knew she was right. I could not deny that she had got it in one. Anyway, she told me I was going to work on this until it was my new way of thinking: to understand that when I feel fat it's not about my body, it's about acceptance. Until then, when I started to feel fat I was to realise that that was not what I was feeling at all but that it is in fact one if not all of the things on my list—in other words, I am feeling unaccepted, unsuccessful and so on. I am going to be a different person by the time she finishes working on me. What a day!

Anyway, I've got a couple of weeks away from therapy (phew!). I've got some comedy gigs all around Australia for the next two weeks, playing a bimbo game show hostess in a corporate comedy show (a job I wouldn't have got a year ago). I'll be living out of hotel rooms—another challenge. Eating healthily on the road. Avoiding the dreaded mini bar! But I'm going to travel with lots of fresh fruit, muesli bars and my brekky cereal, so I won't be tempted to eat from the already paid for breakfast bar.

Poor Kai will get shipped around between his dad, his godmother, Alicia, and Tara. It's not how I want it but what else can I do? Gotta pay the bills. Wish my mum was alive. Free babysitting!

11 February   I want to be a shopaholic

I spent the afternoon shopping, trying on clothes at the huge second-hand clothes market near my house and I bought a skirt and a top, both of them gorgeous. I am truly back in the off-the-rack fashion range. I'm about a size 14 and a lot of things fit me. They were only five bucks and I realised how much it had cost me to buy clothes when I was a size 24. Big linen shirts were always $150 plus. The fashions were atrocious and you had to pay extra dollars 'cause they not only use enough material to make a drop sheet for the QE2 but they have to find the worst designers in the world and that must cost a lot in travel 'cause they really do find *the worst*. Every 100+ kilo woman loves to wear jumpers featuring Winnie the Pooh. It reminds them that the only person interested in their breasts are babies! Oh, and big women just looove floral print. It's kind of like camouflage. People see you standing there in your nice floral tent dress and presume you're the shrubbery. The major problem is dogs marking their territory, but you get so fat you don't care what you look like, so why care how you smell? Or was that just me?

I am looking forward to skimpy handkerchief sized shirts, and dresses that would double as a dishcloth. Just point me to the treadmill and I'm there, baby!

I've been packing my bag for this trip and discovered another difference between obesity and 'normal' weight. Being obese means only being able to pack one piece of clothing that also has to double as a sleeping bag or convert to a backpack. *Or* you have to take five bags, three of which are just for carrying your brassieres. Being much smaller (to date: seven dress sizes and 27 kilos smaller) means I can pack three skirts, three shirts, a pair of tracky pants, a couple of t-shirts and all my underwear in one very small bag that weighs a lot less than what I have lost in body weight. They don't tell you that on the Lite 'n' Easy ads, do they? 'Sick of hiring TNT freight carriers to haul your undies around the world? Don't look like a bus, call us.'

13 February
This is (almost) the life

Kai's at his godmother's. Missing him lots already and it's only been two days. Rang him last night and he said, 'Come back, Mummy, I need you.' Am having mother guilt. How dare I think of my career when my son misses me? Oh well, someone has to earn the money and I'm not yet ready to sell him on the slave market! I'll get a better price when he can lift heavy objects.

Staying at swish hotels, eating well and using their gyms. I feel like a movie star!

14 February   My Valentine

It's Valentine's Day. I'm back in Sydney for two days then off on the road again. Oh, and to make my Valentine's like every other one I've had in my life, I'm single (again). Yes, it's all over. So today while everyone ran around saying how much they love each other, I went to the shops and ate three potato scallops smothered in tomato sauce. As I ordered them, I reminded myself I was comfort eating and that wouldn't make me any happier, but I told my mental Nutcase to shut up and proceeded to eat them anyway. And they *didn't* make me feel any happier, but it tasted good to have some junk food just for fun.

Decided I wasn't going to be miserable so I got dressed up and took Kai out to dinner for Valentine's. He is the current love of my life so why not take him to dinner? Proceeded to drink an entire bottle of wine and ate my way through a huge bowl of creamy pasta. Came home even more depressed than before.

15 February   Lost it

To continue my downward spiral, on my way to Canberra for another of those gigs I had Hungry Jack's for lunch, three glasses of wine for dinner and a bucket of butter on my bread roll. Woke up and had eggs Benedict with a rasher of bacon and only just managed to avoid the hash browns. I am in big trouble. Need to call in the reinforcements. It's as if I am scared of getting to eighty. I am totally convinced that I am never going to make it. Struggling to stay focused. Hah, I'd say I've lost so much focus I'm about to be declared legally blind!

22 February   I need . . . veggies?

Eighty-three kilos. Was so depressed. Rang Zoë and said I haven't lost weight on tour. She asked if I had put any on. I said no. She was very excited. She said, 'Well, that means you've maintained your weight.'

I said, 'Yeah, that's the problem.'

And she said, 'No, that's the best thing you could do.' I grunted, so she explained it to me. She said it was amazing that while being on tour, eating at restaurants every night, having a few drinks and not being able to work out as much as I usually do, I haven't put on *any* weight. Which means when I get down to my goal weight, maintaining it is going to be easy because maintenance is the hardest thing to do, and if I can do it on tour with constant temptation, then it will be even easier at home. It made me realise how different life will be in maintenance. I'll be able to eat out, have a few drinks and really enjoy myself a few times a week. That will be a good time. She definitely made me feel better. Still, I really want to get back into it and get those last four kilos off.

Have rejoined the gym (membership ran out the day I went away on tour). Swam for twenty minutes and was exhausted. I've had the flu (as well as the gastro before that) so feel really knocked around. At least I'm moving again. Am finally back from tour, which means no more expensive hotel dinners and no tempting, freebie, all-you-can-eat breakfasts, no more free beer and wine, and no more nibblies after the show. Thank God. I need fresh fruit and veggies, my daily fix of yoghurt and I need to get back into the gym. I need the energy boost that keeps my eating focused.

23 February Climb every mountain

Feel a bit better today. Got up and had cereal. Filmed my last interview for the Lifestyle Channel. Climbed the Harbour Bridge with the film crew, which was pretty amazing. They hadn't seen me for months and were so spun out at the changes in my body.

In the beginning I set out to lose 30 kilos, and because of their deadlines, that's where the show has ended. I was depressed that I hadn't lost all of the thirty yet, but I did break my leg, which slowed me down, and it's not about what I weigh. It's about the amazing changes to my life. They focused on the fact that I am much more active, definitely more healthy, so much more positive and a whole lot happier.

I wish they would follow me the whole way, including the extra 10 kilos I have decided to lose, but that is just my ego wanting to be seen as something other than fat. It will happen in its own time.

The crew and the producer said I seem much calmer and at peace, and I think they might be right. I don't feel as if I need to perform so much. When you are fat you feel compelled to make up for your fatness and be the life of the party, always being happy, always being larger than life, but when you start shrinking and dealing with all the emotional baggage, you don't need to try so hard. They have decided to change the title of the show from 'The Fat Trap' to 'Larger than Life' (a quote I made on top of the Bridge), which I am very happy about. I cringed when they told me the original title. I thought, I can never tell people about that. Yeah, my latest show is called 'The Fat Trap'. Yuck! Sounds like a huge machine designed to catch fat people . . . a big cage full of fried chicken and Richard Simmons, waiting to work it all off in a lab filled with scientists and rat-like fat people.

Decided I was going to focus on the positive aspect of the show, stopped giving myself such a hard time (I can hear Nutcase saying those very same words) and, hey, I climbed the bloody Harbour Bridge! I did it without having a coronary!

Had a yoghurt for a snack and a bagel with smoked salmon for lunch. Had some fruit this afternoon and made low-fat tacos for dinner. Swam for twenty minutes and realise it's probably good that I'm easing myself back into it. I need to let my body recover from illness, otherwise I'll stay sick. Weighed in at 83 and have decided to go back to the food diary. I need to stick with what works and the food diary keeps me honest and focused. I think about everything I eat when I have to write it down, so starting tomorrow I'm back to square one. I am going to get to 79 even if it kills me. Time to be good. I will not let the fat person win and I will not run away from love 'cause some balding comedian doesn't recognise the goddess I truly am. They say revenge is best served cold. Well, baby, I have just put my boobs on ice.

24 February　Luxury is lite mayo

Okay, have just had the biggest catch-up with Crusher. She agrees that I should go back to the food diary. She told me to fax it to her tonight and she would scrutinise what I am eating. She told me it was time to get serious. I need to get under eighty. I just need to decide to do it, focus my eating and exercising habits and simply do it. She said I'd come this far, the rest should be easy.

She told me to cut out luxury foods such as lite cheese, lite mayo, alcohol, pasta. She said I need to push heavier weights because having more muscle means your metabolism speeds up. Then if I control my food intake I will burn fat very efficiently. I'll be a lean mean fat-burning machine!

She told me it was now time to refocus my goal to 69 because I'm resting on my laurels only four kilos away from my original goal weight. Time to make myself feel as if I've still got a lot of work to do (which I have). She said it was also good to make 69 my final goal. Not necessarily to never get under that number, but to set it as my 'this is the way I live my life and I may or may not be lighter and it doesn't matter'. She said by the time I get there I will be a normal (well, that's debatable) healthy woman who eats healthily and exercises regularly. If I have a binge then I will exercise the day before and the day after and I will just get on with living my life and eat whatever I want, and get myself to whatever size I feel comfortable with. Wow.

I guess this is it. NO turning back. Approximately 13 kilos to go and I am supposedly where I will be for the rest of my new healthy life. Okay, so back to being as good as I can possibly be. As Crusher says: I can do it!

26 February   Team sports? Eek!

This is it. The soccer team is having their first . . . what do you call it? Rehearsal? No. Training session. Tonight. I either have to agree to do this or pike out. It was one of my New Year's resolutions, so I have to do it really. And it's not some fickle decision either. By the time I register, buy boots, shorts, socks, knee pads and health insurance for my soon to be broken other leg, I'll have paid out a small fortune. And they can't even guarantee that I'll get on the same team as my friend, Tara.

Apparently I have to 'try out'. Damn, and I thought I'd managed to escape the audition process. I can see me now, standing in line and them saying, 'Yes, we have the perfect position for you, AJ. Can you just wear this chicken suit and jump up and down whenever we score a goal? The mascot is a valued team member. Honestly.' Either that or I'll wind up being the drinks caddy.

I did try desperately to get out of it. I said to Tara, 'I can't get babysitting.' She said, 'My boyfriend will do it.' I said, 'I can't afford it this week.' She said, 'My dad is treasurer. He'll fix it.' I said, 'I don't know how to play.' She said, 'Neither do we.' I said, 'I'm busy Thursday.' She said, 'Training's Tuesday.' I said, 'I'm only doing it to get a social life.' She said, 'We go to the pub after every game.' I said, 'Okay, I'll join.'

Oh God, all my school sport fears have risen up in my mind. I was never picked for *any* team sport. Lumps of mud were chosen over me. I would be left standing alone in front of two freshly picked teams, everyone looking at the ground, the captains saying, 'I'll pick, um . . . there's an ant crawling up AJ's leg. I'll take that.' At that point the teacher would say, 'AJ, could you run an errand for me?' He'd hand me a piece of paper and ask me to take it to the principal. He in turn would hand it back and send me to someone else and so on and so on until the end of PE class. One day I sneaked a peek at the piece of paper and it read: 'AJ Rochester. Nice girl. Athletically retarded. Please keep busy till 11.30 am. Thank you.'

Giving up on the idea of representing my country at anything other than professional belching, I decided to never, ever play sport again. I talked my way into becoming editor of the school newspaper, a job I fulfilled while *everyone* else played sport, and a writing career began. How noble to think that my love of words stems from a fear of fitness. Have I really just agreed to be a part of a team sport?

Aaah . . . I feel fat! Oh no I don't (refer to list)—I feel *unaccepted*. What if nobody wants me?

27 February   Look out, Beckham!

I can't believe it but I loooved it! I am a legend. Okay, I'm not that good, but no one asked me if I was looking for the local meeting of Overeaters Anonymous so it wasn't a total disaster. Okay, so I couldn't make it all the way around the oval at a light jog and I am the fattest on the team and the sprints make me want to vomit, but apart from that it was fantastic. I loved running around and kicking the ball. There's something about ball sports—I could feel the testosterone surging through my body. Suddenly I wanted to drink bucket loads of beer, go perving at anything with a heartbeat and put an 'o' on the end of my team-mates' names, although it doesn't quite seem to work with girls' names— Rachelo, Leanne-o, Debbie-o. Hmm, better work on that.

Anyway, it was great fun getting to know my team-mates and having a laugh at how uncoordinated we all are (okay, how uncoordinated *I* am). It was fun to go after the ball too, and our coach reckons I've got a great kick (developed on previous boyfriends!) despite having broken my leg only six months ago. Because of my injury, we decided being goalie was the best position for me. The best thing about it is that after four months of this I will *have* to be fitter than I am now, so not only will I have fun but by the end of the season I should be able to jog around the oval at least once without turning ashen white and wheezing like a dying bull.

1 March   You mean I'm not perfect?

My session with Nutcase was pretty amazing! I walked in and said, 'I think I'm about to have a bad day.' She said, 'How do you know?' I burst into tears and she said, 'Okay, well, you may be right. What's happening?'

I explained that I had had quite a few bad days in the last two weeks. Hungry Jack's, too much wine on Valentine's Day and Chinese last night as the final night of touring with that corporate comedy show. Too many free drinks, too much free food, all pre-ordered banquet so no choice and lots of guilt.

She asked me what I ate. I said one spring roll, a small bowl of fried rice and assorted meat and veggies in God knows what sauce. She then said, 'How many spring rolls have you had in the last month?' I said none. She said, 'How many in the last three months?' I said one. She said, 'How many in the last six months?' I said about three all up. She said, 'So, you are going to beat yourself up for having three spring rolls in six months?'

When she put it like that it sounded ridiculous. She said there will never be a time in my life and nor should there be a time when I am eating 'perfectly' 100 per cent of the time. She said life and normal eating habits don't happen that way. Sometimes we can't control the food that comes out on our table and we just eat it, enjoy it and get on with our lives. If we feel the need we add on some extra time in our workout but it is not really worth stressing about as much as I do.

She said eating has become a nightmare for me and I was never taught to enjoy my meal times. I was not encouraged to go out and enjoy my life, so doing things like that makes me feel guilty. She agreed that I could have ordered steamed rice and to remember it for next time but not feel guilty about it. She told me that was being absolute about food. All or nothing. She reminded me I was not to do things in absolutes, which seemed reasonable to me.

I then told her I had seen myself on television last night and had become thoroughly depressed. Channel Nine's show 'Body and Soul' interviewed me about my love of aquarobics and how I've lost nearly 30 kilos doing it. They did those cute little shots of me at home cooking, walking with Kai and in the aqua class and I just looked sooooo fat. And I know you look a stone heavier on TV but, oh my God, I have got so far to go to get to a decent size. I'm dealing with the disappointment of 30 kilos not being enough to make me look anywhere near as good as I want to look. And I hated the interviewer's voiceover saying (as they show me waddling up the street) 'and though she's not at her goal weight yet . . . ' Meaning, though she's still as fat as a pregnant cow she swears by the exercise!

Nutcase smiled benignly as she does and said she thought I was being too critical of myself. She said it had nothing to do with what I look like now, next week or next month because, as she reminded me, even when I was thin I thought I was fat, so what that means is that deep down inside what I am really saying is that I hate myself.

She was right. No matter how happy and joyful and vocal I am about how much I love myself, I know it's a lie. I truly believe I am not good enough and never will be. So many people in my life pounded it into my head when I was an impressionable child that I grew up believing that no matter what I do I will never be 'perfect'. Wow!

Had to digest that for a few days before I could put that down in print. She said I needed to go home and watch the tape a few more times and to make a list of ten good things that I liked when watching myself on the show. She said to watch it with Kai and see how much he likes it. Enjoy him watching himself on TV. Enjoy him watching me. Enjoy the fact that they thought my story interesting enough to put on television. She said that we were going to work on improving the way I see myself so that when I near my goal weight I won't do as I have previously done and decide that too thin is still not thin enough because there is never a point at which I will be happy unless I find the happiness within.

2 March
What New Year's resolution?

All right. Trying to regain focus. Am making sure I eat lots of fruit in between meals. Drinking lots of water. Am off the grog till May (three months—eek!) and am going hard at the gym. I pushed myself so hard today. Have upped the weights so I can't quite do sets of ten. I am going faster on the treadmill and cross-trainer and by the end of a one-hour session I am puffing, shaking and feel good in a weird 'I've just done something good for my body even though it hurts' kind of way.

I read an interview with Elle Macpherson's personal trainers and they said she really pushes herself in a session and so whenever I think I can't push that weight one more time I think of Elle: if she works out to get that shape then so can I. Okay, so I can't grow another two feet (which would probably make me level with her knee height) but the fact that she still has to work hard makes it easier for me to believe that I can make changes.

I'm still *thinking* about doing aerobics but they're on the days when Kai is not at kindy and they clash with my shrink sessions, so unless I choose a class other than the granny one, then I'm sticking to gym and aqua. (Yes, I know it was one of

---

Shake your booty

- Change your exercise routine often. Trick the body so that it continues to burn fat. Keep pushing yourself. Work harder.

- Change the way you do things. Don't drive everywhere. Walk when you have to take the videos back. Park in the spaces furthest away from the shopping centre entrance. Take the stairs. Get off the bus three stops early. Before you know it you'll have done thirty minutes extra exercise per week.

- Join a gym/health club/walking group/swimming pool. Anything to get you going. Or do what I did and start out exercising in your home, move up to walking and then get yourself to a gym.

- Have regular weigh-ins and measurements. The measurements are great when you hit the plateau 'cause muscle weighs more than fat so your weight may stay the same but your body is changing. The measurements will tell the truth!

my New Year's resolutions, but it's still not the end of the year so I haven't technically broken that one yet!)

I also read that half a kilo of muscle burns fat twenty times faster than half a kilo of body fat so when I'm doing weights I think of that and push myself just that little bit further. Muscle burns fat by just being there, so the more muscle I get the more fat I burn.

3 March   I'm doin' it

Eighty-one—at last. I am more focused than I have ever been. No alcohol. No in-between snacking, strict meal/snack regime, and have cut down my portion size to around that of a Lean Cuisine. Working out almost every day. I am going to get there!

4 March   Live fast, die young

Had another huge session with Nutcase. I told her I was feeling disheartened about the 'diet'. She asked me how much weight I had lost. I told her 28 kilos. She said, 'Isn't that what you set out to do?' I said, 'Crusher told me I would lose 30 kilos by February.' She said, 'Well, today is the fourth of March and you're only two kilos away from what your goal was.' I said, 'Yes, but—' and Nutcase went all strict and preachy on me. She explained (not for the first time) in her 'Now listen to me or I'll spank your bot bot' tone of voice that health professionals recommend only a half kilo weight loss per week, and a one kilo per week maximum. She added up the weeks and said I had lost 28 kilos in approximately thirty-three weeks . . . just under the *maximum*. She also reminded me that during that time I had broken my leg, endured Christmas and had been on a three-week tour around Australia. She said I needed to congratulate myself on what I have done.

I ummed and ahed and explained that it didn't feel real. She asked me if I originally thought 'the diet' would be harder than it has been, and I realised that was true. I always imagined a 'diet' to be absolutely no fun, with no treats, no life and no decent food. Along the way I have had great nights out, breakfasts filled with more fat than just one of Luciano Pavarotti's chins. Almost every day I've had a 'treat' of some kind, even if it has been jelly snakes. And it has been easier than I imagined. So the fact that it has happened and has *kept* happening has been a bit surreal. I always expected to discover some kind of magical motivation. But it hasn't been like that—it's simply been a matter of doing it as well as I can and living my life along the way.

I then explained that even though I've lost 28 kilos I am still not happy. I said I was afraid that when I get to 69 I'll think 59 will make me happy and then 49 and then 39, until I coat-hanger my way to starvation and death. She said she didn't think I would do that this time and that I was giving myself a hard time because of the past. She said I had learnt new eating habits and that I should give myself a break and accept that I have mastered the art of losing weight. She then said she didn't think we should talk about what weight I am any more. She wasn't interested in it. She said she wanted to talk about why, after losing nearly 30 kilos, I am still not happy with myself.

I explained that I thought the weight coming off would solve all my problems. I thought all my unhappiness in life was related to what I weighed. She asked me if, when I was anorexic, I was happy with myself. I explained that I wasn't, because I never thought I was thin enough. I used to look at women who were bigger than me and tell them I wished I had a body like theirs. Nutcase explained that what I was probably saying was, 'I wish I was as happy as you are in your body.' She said that I needed to explore why I am unhappy.

She had this great explanation by some famous psychiatrist from the sixties who described the way newborn babies feel. Now I can't remember exactly what she said but this is my spin on it. Apparently babies spend the first three months of their lives feeling as if they are going to be dropped, afraid that they will fall. She said that sometimes, people who have had an unhappy childhood or children who are separated from their mothers somehow retain that feeling. Winnicott was the name of the shrink and he explained it as 'on the brink of unthinkable anxiety'. Some of the resulting feelings are of 'going to pieces, falling forever, having no relationship to the body and having no orientation' (DW Winnicott, *Maturational Processes and the Facilitating Environment*, Hogarth Press, 1979).

When she said that I nearly fell out of the chair. That is how I have felt all my life. Like I am falling. I've lived my life that way—live fast, die young. Which is not how I want to live my life at all. I have been scared all of my life. Scared, unhappy and totally unconnected to my body, and that is why I starved myself and that is similarly why I nearly ate myself to death. I thought that either of those options would make me happy. The thing is, it is nothing to do with the food or whatever weight I am, it is what has gone on in my past, how it has affected me and how it continues to affect me. I have to learn to heal my past and relearn *new* ways to live my life.

If I come to terms with my very painful past then at some point I will start to love myself again and if I love myself and get my eating habits sorted out, I should start to live my life 'normally' and healthily and won't need to find happiness in a bucket of deep-fried chicken wings. I won't feel happy because the scales say I am 70 instead of 82. I will learn to love myself as I am now and eating well will become automatic. The stuff you do 'cause you just do it and you don't waste much time worrying about it.

So the plan of action is: I am to continue my work in the Alfalfa Zone. I am to try not to think about what weight I am, although she concedes that I will still weigh myself until I get to 70. At that point I do not think about it any more. I am to totally ignore the height/weight charts in slimming magazines, as they are someone else telling me what size I should be—from this point on *I* decide what I should look like and not someone else. She also said that there is a whole industry set up to make people feel unhappy about their size/shape/weight. I agreed that if the magazines and TV ads didn't manufacture discontent then women and men would probably feel a lot happier about themselves and billions of dollars would be lost in the fashion, health, diet and beauty industries.

Now armed with the knowledge that losing the weight has nothing to do with making me happy, I am now embarking upon the journey to lose my emotional baggage. I'm probably paying an excess baggage fee and it's probably the reason I can't shed those last few kilos to get me over the second plateau. I guess if I offload that, it might make me lighter and then I'm off over the edge and on my way to 70.

No one told me there was so much involved in getting your life together. God, talk about excess baggage.

5 March   Aaah!

Weighed in today at 83. How could I put on two kilos overnight? I guess that's why Nutcase tells me I should only weigh in once a week. But I just can't seem to do that. Keep telling myself it has to be muscle but I'm not looking like Arnold Schwarzenegger, so I don't know what is going on. Have decided to start running. I never thought I'd say that but I'm going to get on that treadmill and run like I'm a lawyer chasing after an ambulance. I can't make my eating any better than it already is, so if running doesn't get me over this plateau then I'm going to start amputating limbs—that's sure to lose me at least a couple of kilos.

Just read over what I wrote in the first plateau and I realised I have not been totally honest with myself. I am doing exactly the same as I was last time I hit that plateau. I said I was being as good as I could be but that is not true.

I have found myself snacking in between snacks. Not huge amounts, sometimes it's just a cracker every time I open the fridge, or three or four of Kai's chips, or a bite of his biscuit, but in reality, when you add them all up, it's too much. I know I am repeating myself but it's like I've forgotten or like I don't want to admit to myself that I am cheating, which really means I am cheating myself out of reaching my goal. I have to be totally honest with myself if this is going to work so I will go back to the food diary again, will write *everything* down and only eat at designated meal times and *nothing* extra. It seems really basic but it's so easy to think that one little thing won't matter. 'Oh, it's only a roast chicken and seventeen potatoes. It won't make a spot of difference. And I'll do an extra five minutes on the treadmill!'

I fulfilled another of my New Year's resolutions the other night. I actually went to a nightclub. Yes, it was very scary but I did get a few interested looks and had a few not so interesting conversations with other similarly desperate singles. It wasn't too bad except for the insane man who kept tweaking my nose and squeezing my cheeks and saying, in a baby voice, 'You're so cute, you're so cute.' I half expected him to put me over his shoulder, burp me and attempt to change my nappy. All in all though, it showed promise, so I may just do it again.

6 March *No, no, no . . .*

Second day of running. Let me tell you so there are absolutely no illusions about it: I HATE IT! I hate it! I hate it! I hate it!

It hurts a lot. But in a strange, sick, depraved kind of way I *really enjoy it* as well. Never in my life did I think I would ever say that I like running.

What I do—apart from trying not to think about what I look like lumbering around on the treadmill and trying to discreetly tuck my breasts back into their bra every thirty seconds or so—is I run for a minute then walk for a minute, then run again and walk . . . That way I have little rests, get my breath back and am easing into it. And let me tell you, it feels bad. Worse than bad, actually. Try excruciatingly painful, not only through my legs but in my chest and in my head. It's worse than childbirth.

So far all I can do is fifteen minutes (which is eight minutes of running and seven of fast walking), which I am going to stick to until I can run that whole time. When I fall off the treadmill after the fifteen, I am puffing more than Thomas the Tank Engine but I don't know what it is, maybe it's the endorphins or just the feeling that I have really pushed myself out of my comfort zone, but I get the biggest rush and even though I'm all sweaty, red-faced and out of breath and want to curl up and die, it feels good! Huh, very weird! Hopefully this is what will get me over this plateau.

I told Nutcase I had started running and she was very pleased with me. She said it is good to step out of our comfort zones and do something new. I told her that I hated running and she asked me why. I said it was because when I was a kid I always raced against the local Aboriginal kids and they were so damned fast that not only was I always last but they were at home having their dinner by the time I crossed the finish

Staying on the case

- Develop a plan so that you have something to stick to and focus on. Work out when, where and at what time you will exercise. Plan a week ahead. Have your weigh-in or measure as the weekly goal.
- Create a food diary.
- Draw up a weekly eating plan.
- Commit to your exercise by writing it on your calendar or in your diary.
- Sit down to eat a meal. Concentrate on the act of eating. Don't allow yourself to be distracted, because if you do, you will eat and not feel satisfied.
- Set yourself small goals with treats at the end. Facial at ten kilos. Massage at fifteen. Gives you something to aim for.
- Remember the phrase 'Recognise, Challenge, Distract'. Recognise your previous 'bad' behaviour/habit. Challenge it with a new thought process like 'I don't do that any more. I deserve a healthy body.' And distract it by eating something healthy or doing something that takes your mind off it.
- Remember it is simply one meal at a time.

line. Running had always been associated with losing. She said it was great that I had decided not to be ruled by my past, particularly because I am not competing with anyone, and surely I felt good after doing it. I said I had surprised myself and that afterwards it did feel great. I also told her that soccer was excellent and that I was making new friends and having a fantastic time being part of a team sport.

I told her about my night out and the annoying nose-pinching guy and she explained that I was relearning how to live life and that it was reasonable for me to tell him to naff off and get out of my space. She said I had to practise saying no. She said most reasonable people can take no for an answer and if they don't, then I walk away or ask someone to help get rid of them. She said it was important I learn to say no so I can feel comfortable going out and not have to feel as if I have to run away or hide in my fat. So my homework is to say NO. No, no, no. Huh. Easy. Oh well, I'll have an opportunity to practise it on Saturday night. The boy is coming over. Just as friends, no sex. We're going to write some comedy together.

8 March   Yes!

Oh my God, 80 kilos! Reward—a facial! I can't believe it. It was either the running or the all-night bedroom aerobics session I had with the boy the other night. Yes, I said I was going to say no but he said he had decided it was okay to get intimate with (meaning, kiss!) me so who am I to stop lurve from developing? It was so amazing! I saw the sun coming up and thought, wow, I reckon I've burnt at least 7000 calories in the last five hours! Then the next day, joy of joys, 80 kilos! Woohoo. The boy said he'd come over any time I need a workout. Very nice of him to offer really. I think I'll still play a little hard to get (what, harder than I did the other night?). Anyway, just about to change the sign on the fridge to: 'Seventy-five and under'. Here I go. The final stretch!

9 March   The great pretender

It's a strange thing. I feel a bit as if I am pretending that the weight loss has fixed everything in my life, because whenever I bump into people I haven't seen for a long time they are so excited and pleased for me that I feel as if I have to pretend that life is perfect now that I've lost weight. In reality, though, there is still so much of my life that is unresolved and until I work on those things, the desire to comfort eat will haunt me forever. So, as Nutcase has said, this is the time where I shift more than the weight. I guess I am creating a solid ground (psychologically) from which to live my day-to-day life in a healthy fashion backed up by the healthy eating and healthy lifestyle. The session should be interesting this week.

10 March   On being good enough

Nutcase session very intense. Still crying from all that we talked about. I explained how I felt this underlying sadness that has echoed throughout most of my life and that losing weight hadn't actually changed that. She asked me what was making me so sad. I said, gee, anything from my childhood would do. So that's where we started. We talked a lot, I cried a lot and came to the conclusion that all my life I have never felt good enough, never been accepted, suffered serious rejection and have always blamed myself for it. Getting fat gave me a good excuse to live my life extricated from everyone, thus proving that I didn't fit in. Now it is my goal to catch those thoughts and stop them before they control my behaviour. Recognise, challenge, distract.

I am not a freak. I am not unlovable. I am not unsuccessful. I am not unpopular. Sure, I will not always fit in everywhere I go (no one does), but I am not to blame for the horrible things and rejection I experienced as a child. Those things may have shaped me up until now but they do not have to dictate my future. I am to catch those thoughts out (like I did with the comfort eating) and am to remind myself that it was not my fault that I came to believe, as a child, that I was not good enough. I am perfect the way I am, and just because my birth mother chose to give me away, and because I didn't fit in very well with my adopted family, it does not mean that I am not exactly as I should be and good enough for the right people to love me and, more importantly, good enough to love myself.

Nutcase explained that it would be difficult to change these thought patterns, but if I approach it like I did with the eating habits, then I should see some success and in the future I will not feel the need to be fat to deal with the sadness and pain I have felt all my life. The plan is to deal with it and find a place for it that doesn't take up so much space, freeing me up to live a happy, healthy life.

Phew! I think I'm ready for a bucket of beer now. Bummer . . . off the grog! Better go to the gym instead.

11 March   Me and my 'friends'

Welcome to the world of emotional eating. Since hitting on the heavy stuff in therapy I am struggling to eat well. Desperately want to comfort eat. Craving junk food, hot chips, beer and pizza. Add to that being premenstrual and you could say I am having a bad week. Why do women crave those sorts of food just before getting our 'friends'? That's what my mum insisted I call them. 'My friends'. With friends like that, who needs enemas?

I rang Zoë and asked what she does when she has the cravings. She says she eats whatever she wants—'cause she can. God, I hate her! But then she suggested things she did when she was losing weight and I think they'll help. Lollipops are great for handling the sugar fix. They have no fat and take so long to finish that by the time you're done, the craving should have passed. She also said to remember that if I do eat crap, by the time my period came around I would feel even worse because of the guilt. She said to hold out, eat lots of fruit and to remember that the first two weeks after a period is a much more efficient time for losing weight, so use that as an incentive and tell myself that if I am good for the next few days, then after my body has done its monthly spring-clean I will most definitely fall into the 70 kilo weight range.

Of course, I didn't tell her that I'd already succumbed to the fish and chips on the beach scenario. And why did I do it? Because I didn't eat before going out so I had zero willpower and few healthy choices. You'd think I'd learn, wouldn't you?

12 March   Run like the wind

I just did my first outdoor running session. Outdoors, as in away from the safety of the gym, running alongside a bike track with people who can actually run and who don't sound like they're impersonating an asthmatic cocker spaniel with bronchial pneumonia and breasts that look like they might be hiding the lost treasures of the Incas! Okay, it was run, walk, run, trip, walk, get black eye from bouncing boobs (note to self: sexy black bra only good for getting men excited in a nightclub—nothing exciting about two melons swinging dangerously out of control in the park, particularly when passing hairy unwashed council workers who are so slow they stand there with a sign warning you they're slow!). And even though I kept falling out of my bra I felt fantastic and it didn't cost me a cent.

The reason I have decided to take to the streets is that my gym membership has expired and at the moment I can't afford to renew. So my plan is to run three times a week, do soccer training twice a week and swim once a week. I'm going to give weights a rest for a couple of months. The running should see me burning a lot of fat. Then I will go back to the gym and do weights (tone) after that. If I eat well, I should go back to losing about a kilo a week because I won't be building as much muscle as I have in the last few months. The only risk is *not* doing it. So I have to get really motivated. I've got reminders stuck all over the house saying things like 'Go hard! 79. Are you there yet?' and on my fridge I have put 'STOP! Think about what you are doing! Do you really want to wear that on your birthday?'

I heard a great piece of diet trivia today. If you cut out the butter you normally have in your diet you can lose up to an extra 10 kilos in a year! How amazing is that? This morning I avoided the Weight Watchers butter altogether and just had diet jam on toast instead. It's the little things that count.

14 March Start and finish

Well, it's day four of the motivate your own fat arse instead of going to the gym phase and I can proudly declare that I have run every day for forty minutes. Four days in a row! Now don't get me wrong, I hate it. I hate every painful, out of breath, uncoordinated stumbling step that I take, but as soon as I finish there *is* something absolutely indescribably pleasurable about it. I guess you could say that about any painful experience: 'Honestly, the best thing about having my head screwed into a vice was when it stopped.' But running does feel good. All the blood rushes to the skin, I am out of breath, my body is genuinely tired and I know that I have definitely burnt fat. And when those endorphins hit it is the most extraordinary feeling. It feels amazing to have pushed myself into doing something that does not come naturally to me.

And today I felt a change. Yeah, instead of only half hating the whole thing, I now absolutely positively abhor the entire process! I'd rather have bamboo shoved under my fingernails and my eyelashes pulled out one by one! No, I kept saying to myself as I stumbled along, legs aching, 'You will lose weight, you will lose weight, you will lose weight. Seventy-nine, seventy-nine, seventy-nine.' I ran about three quarters of the way (approximately thirty minutes of running), which is a vast improvement. I set myself little start and finish posts: tree to picnic bench, lamppost to house with red fence, red fence to guy with gorgeous arse running ahead of you— faster, AJ, faster, you've nearly caught up, God he looks good, wonder what he looks like in front, ah, damn it hurts when you trip over your tongue! I lengthen the mini sprints as I feel more fit (which is not fit at all). Today I noticed that a couple of times I actually passed the goal I set myself and kept running without even thinking about it, so I must be getting better.

Crusher thinks it's a great idea to have some time off from weights. She said it really helps the plateau effect, totally changing your workout so not only will the running really boost my metabolism and fat-burning efficiency but when I go back to the gym it will be really effective too. She also said it was a real test of my commitment to my fitness, because not having the gym there means I have to be totally self-motivated. She said that if I could totally commit to running four times a week for four weeks and actually honour that commitment then I would be committed to fitness for life. This is my test. She said that if I did this then her work is done and she can leave me to live my life with health and fitness just a day-to-day accepted part of it. Whoa. Life without Crusher? Scary! And yet quite enticing . . .

16 March   Squeezes

Another New Year's promise fulfilled. What has happened to me? I bought a fitness ball and now while I watch my favourite TV shows I do my daily sit-ups (about 150). Birthday one month away, focusing on wearing something fabulous so I have to have a flat tummy.

Oh and, surprise, surprise, guess who turned up on my doorstep last night? The boy. He said he was just in the neighbourhood. He'd forgotten something last time he was here and popped in to get it. Of course it had nothing to do with the fact that he wanted to see me and that I've been too busy to catch up with him over the net. So we had a quick bedroom aerobics session, he lamented that my breasts were shrinking but insisted I was looking really good and I knew it was true 'cause he kept squeezing my bum and making little happy as a pig in mud noises. God, life is good.

Oh dear. What will I do if my breasts shrink away altogether? My humungous breasts have been a large (literally) part of my self-identity for as long as I can remember. How am I going to attract any men? You mean I'll actually have to talk to them? Euh! What am I going to play with when I'm bored? Don't answer that! How am I going to make other women jealous? Oh my God, this could be a national disaster. I can't afford plastic and in any case I don't want my breasts exploding every time I cross the Atlantic.

17 March   Keep on runnin'

11 am: I have just had the most luxurious facial ever. Reward for hitting 80 kilos. Haven't had one for about ten years and I was lying there covered in God knows what, blissed out to the max, and I thought, boy have things changed in my life. Here I am, I've been for a forty-minute run, I'm dressed nicely in a size 14 skirt and a little negligee type top, I'm having a facial and, oh my God, I just might love myself. And better still I might even respect myself. And my body. And wow, I can't believe it but I'm a member of a social soccer team. I have nights out on the town planned, I know I'll have something to wear, something other than a potato sack, I know I'll look pretty good, and I am actually looking forward to, dare I say it, being on the market. Oh my God, I got a life. Plenty of people had been telling me to get one and I have. It feels pretty damn fantastic. Imagine what I'll be like when I lose another 10 kilos (including the five of emotional crap I'm hauling around!). God, everyone should do this!

2 pm: When I moved into my new house in December I went for a walk along the water and looked across at the leafy headland on the other side of the bay. I said to Kai, 'We'll have to drive around and have a look at that. It looks like a nice place to have a picnic.' Today, only three months later, I ran the entire two and a half kilometres there and stood on the opposite side of the bay and looked back to where I live. I was so ecstatic I was yelling and whooping and couldn't stop laughing out loud. The family having a picnic there gave each other funny looks and I heard the mother whisper to her daughter, 'Emily, stay close to Mummy, please.' But I didn't care.

I looked around the harbour foreshore at how far I'd run and realised with only mild horror that I had to get back. My legs were starting to shake but after a five-minute break I felt pretty much as refreshed as when I had started out. And it wasn't as if I'd decided to come this far. Yesterday I just managed to walk/run 1.5 kilometres to the bridge, but today I ran all the way (2.5 kilometres) and was there in half the time. I thought, I'll just run for another ten minutes then I'll turn around. Well, by the time I ran another ten minutes I was three-quarters of the way to the island and I thought, I'm so close, I might as well go all the way.

Of course the trip back was not so pleasant, the legs were aching and turning to jelly, my lower intestine was close to being vomited up but I ran until I felt my insides melting and then I walked the rest. All up I was out for exactly one hour. This could actually become addictive. Did I really just say that? Where's the number for the loony bin?

18 March
They shoot rabbits, don't they?

I hate the Easter Bunny. He/she should be shot. Brew me up a batch of myxomatosis, I am on the warpath. How the hell am I supposed to hit 79 kilos with chocolate everywhere I turn? I go to my letterbox and what do I find? Fifty pamphlets for Easter eggs. Turn on the TV and there it is—flashing ads for those little golden bundles of temporary happiness and instantaneous fat. Invite friends over and what do they bring my son? Little foil-wrapped eggs filled with temper tantrum number three for him and temptation number five hundred-and-fifty-six for me. Oh God, must I go somewhere they don't have Easter? But where don't they celebrate Easter? Afghanistan? Ah, maybe not. Better just control the cravings.

I think I am definitely afraid of getting thin. Battered sav. Yep. Couldn't help it. There I was at the Easter Show, there *it* was behind the heated glass window. It was love at first bite. I'm not eating as well as I could be. A few of Kai's chips here, a red wine there . . . it all adds up and unless I stop it I'm going to be stuck here forever. Still running. Hoping that will kick me over the edge.

19 March   I'm a runner, hear me roar

Okay, I could be in some kind of endorphin-fuelled trip but I have decided to run the City to Surf. It is in five months' time and I figure if I can run four kilometres only weeks after starting to run, then in five months time I will be first over the line. Well, maybe not the first, but I'm ready to run. Book me in! And sure, the ninety-year-old guy who runs every year will probably beat me but who cares? At least I'll have done it!

What has happened to me?

79 KILOS

(174 lb)

20 March   Goodbye bum!

Seventy-nine! Seventy-nine! As of today I have now lost a grand total of 30 kilos! And might I just add that I have managed to do that without going to one single aerobics class! Woohoo! That's 30 kilos in thirty-five weeks. Now it's on to 75, then 70, then I will stop weighing myself and just get on with the rest of my life as a normal (well, kind of) human being. Oh yeah, I have to book a scuba dive—my reward for losing the whole lot I set out to lose.

10 pm: The best thing happened to me at soccer training tonight. This girl on the team said to me, 'What do you do, AJ?' Not wanting to sound like a wanker I mumbled that I work in TV. She asked me which station and I said that I have been working for SBS. Not content with that, she asked what show. I said, 'Mum's the Word' and she exclaimed loudly, 'I love that show. What did you do on it?' I told her I was the host. She looked a little confused. She asked if it was the show that was being rerun at the moment and I said yes. Then she said, 'But the host is a really big woman with dark hair. You're small and blonde.'

I could have thrown her on the ground and given her a snog that would have reached into her lower intestine, doubled back, removed her appendix, cleaned her teeth and had her panting for breath. Well, I might not have been that grateful but I felt good enough to hug her. I explained to her that I had recently lost 30 kilos but she still didn't believe I was that person. She shook her head and said, 'Sorry, but it just doesn't look like you.' I called Tara over to confirm that it was in fact me and she was so surprised she could barely speak.

All in all I would say that was a reasonably victorious moment, wouldn't you? Can't wait to get to seventy-five! Then I could go back to my Nan and have her tell me I only look like I've lost 10 kilos—and by the way, doesn't my brother look good? Wouldn't that be fun? Actually, I think I'd rather have my left breast slammed in a car door, thanks. Not that I'm bitter!

21 March   All men are bastards!

Okay. THE strangest thing has just happened to me. Eight months ago I ran out of petrol in the back streets of Camperdown, an inner city suburb of Sydney. I got out of my car and, at 109 kilos and dressed in what could only be described as a potato sack, I walked into the mechanic's shop that I had broken down in front of and asked if they had any petrol I could buy to get me to the nearest servo. They told me it was against their policy but advised me that if I called the NRMA, they would be able to help me.

Today, in a strange twist of fate, I ran out of petrol at the very same place, except that today I was wearing my little pink boob-hugging top with the Playboy logo and my hip-hugging black skirt. Before I even had a chance to kick the tyres, I had three mechanics out the front asking if they could help. Knowing their policy I mumbled no and asked if I could use their phone to ring the NRMA so I could get some petrol.

In less than a minute, Joey, who wanted to know if I had a boyfriend, had driven his V8 Commodore around from the back of the garage and was sucking on the end of a hose, siphoning off his own tank of precious petrol. I offered to pay. He wouldn't take my money. He asked for my phone number, so I wrote down the number for Pizza Hut and slipped it to him. He stuck it in his pocket and promised to call, winking at me.

I then asked them if they remembered me from last year when they wouldn't help me out and they stared blankly back at me. To their confused faces I called them asshole bastards and drove off with ten bucks worth of free petrol and angry at a world that can be far too cruel. Yeah, good for me now my hips are the 'right' size, but who cares? You'd think I'd be happy about it, but it's just not right! Oh well, at least I got to where I was going. I wonder if Joey will order the meat lovers pizza?

25 March
My old friend, Pluto Pup

Well, I've just had four days of absolute self-loathing. Reading back I noticed that every time I hit a goal weight (99, 89, 79) I have 'celebrated' by losing the plot. And there is no other way to describe my last few days. It started with a date with a married man. A man I am incredibly attracted to, work with and ended up going out with, even though I do not want a married man. The worst thing is that he is exactly my type except that *I do not want someone who is not available!* So we went out, got on the grog, talked dirty, ate risotto and, thank you very much, I woke up (alone, thank God) with carpet on my tongue and my brain cells somewhere in Hawaii.

Then I had to work at the Easter Show. Starving, no food in the house, steak sandwich for breakfast, Pluto Pup for lunch and then the list of crap just goes on and on from there. Three days of foul food and a depression to match. Every time I ate I hated myself and now I wonder whether I was eating the food to *justify* my self-hatred because when I got to 79 it was all going to make me so happy and when that was a totally non-exciting moment I just ate crap so it was easier to hate myself. Oh dear, I am more screwed up than I thought. I remember Nutcase saying that getting thin would not make me happy, and how right she is. I'm glad I made it to 79 but I now think when I get to 70, then everything will be all right. I thought I'd got it, but now I realise I have been in denial that it *really is nothing to do with the weight*. The weight just gives me a good excuse. I have to do the work on the inside.

Weighed in at 80 for a day but came back to 79. Struggled through a run but am feeling focused again. Want to be 76 kilos for my birthday, which is three weeks away. I've just gone back to basics and am nursing myself back to reality. Looking forward to seeing Nutcase on Friday 'cause I guess while it has been really traumatic, it is a fairly major breakthrough. Not happy here, want to be at the end now. Good weight, good health, good self-image, good life, good God I need some Valium. Oh well, an orange will have to do. Maybe tomorrow will be better.

26 March   Sigh . . .

Not happy. Running. Eating well. Just doing it till I see Nutcase. Wish I were someone else. Saw *Bridget Jones' Diary* and realised that is my life except I don't get the guy. Very depressing.

27 March   A poem

Nutcase tomorrow. Can't wait. Seventy-eight.

28 March   Who's got my legs?

It is the strangest thing. Running again and it magically pulls me out of the depression. I don't know whether it's because I take control of this demon thinking or because of the endorphins, but it works a charm. And I caught sight of my legs when I was in the shower last night and I didn't recognise them. I have never had legs like these. My mind does not compute and I had to look at them and touch them and really stare at them to take in how much my body is changing. My legs are starting to be really well defined, I can see different muscles and parts of them are starting to look lean, just like the kinds of legs you see on athletes. And I am no Cathy Freeman, but my legs are starting to look like they belong on someone who runs. It is very strange. Almost like having been in a coma and waking up in somebody else's body. God, pity the person who woke up in my old one!

Went out to dinner with friends and one of the girls

accused me of being anorexic because I didn't finish my meal. I explained that I had eaten enough and that I was really full and had more than I needed anyway. She then enlisted the opinions of the men at the table and all decreed I had not eaten very much.

I asked how not finishing my meal made me anorexic and she pointed out how much weight I had lost. Then I got really angry. I explained to her that it had taken me eight months of bloody hard work to shift that weight and that I was offended that she couldn't give me credit for having done such an amazing job. Not everyone has to starve himself or herself to get thin but some women just don't believe it is possible. I didn't think anything would work except anorexia, but I have been proven wrong and even though it is painfully slow I can hold my head high and say I did it. Not anyone else, no quick fix diet pill or somebody else making my meals, no stupid meal replacement milkshakes or vacuuming of the fat from my ginormous thighs. I did it. I got off my fat and lazy arse and saved my very own life, so stick that pipe up your own skinny arse and smoke it!

Well, after that little speech, the dinner party went all quiet and without ordering dessert the night was declared to be at an end. Note to self: Ever heard of the word SUBTLE?!

29 March   Absolutism, Part II

Nutcase session absolutely heart-wrenchingly serious. Really working on the serious stuff now. Working hard at learning to love myself. Going over a lot of stuff from my childhood (again). Talking about how the teacher molested me and constantly belittled me in front of my fellow students. Dealing with the lack of praise I received as a child and how I felt I didn't quite fit into my adopted family. I was a square peg in a very round hole.

I explained how I had believed, when I set off on this journey, that when I lost 30 kilos, everything would feel all right, when really every thing feels exactly the same. We keep coming back to this point, dealing with it time and again. It's so hard to break the habit of a lifetime. For thirty years I have believed I am not good enough so it may take me another thirty to believe I am.

Nutcase assures me that it won't take that long and that in time I will see a change, I *will* believe in myself. You must keep breaking the patterns of self-abuse and negative thinking and then replace it with a positive thought. She said I need to stop looking for external signs (i.e. weight loss) to feel good about myself. She said I need to really believe that I am talented, beautiful, funny, smart and so on. She told me my homework was to really listen and take on the compliments I receive from others. She said I had a habit of brushing them off instead of saying, 'Thank you' and really taking the compliment on board.

She also told me that I should think about dropping the weight loss goal down to a kilo a fortnight because I needed to understand that this last ten would be the hardest to lose and to make my goal a kilo a week was setting myself up for failure. I had a few tears to shed about watching a preview of the Lifestyle Channel's show 'Larger than Life' (following my weight loss) because I was just cringing, knowing that everyone will see Crusher try to do the fat pinch test when I was just too fat to test. Obese. Naked, stretchmark-ridden gut the size of Uluru hanging out for the world (and any man I might want to get romantic with) to see. Yuck!

Nutcase said I need to see it from this side of the fence and appreciate that it is now the past and that I don't look like that any more. She said that I should be proud of having filmed it and to think of all the people who will be inspired to get their own lives together after seeing that it is not an impossible task. She said that I can't change the past and at some point I have to accept that I was fat (okay, the size of the bloody Opera House!).

I said that I was scared that I would go back there, particularly after that big bingeing session last week. She asked me exactly what I had eaten then picked it apart. Yes, she said, everyone eats Pluto Pups at the Easter Show; it is mandatory—diet or no diet! Steak sandwich for breakfast after a hangover was good because it was protein and therefore exactly what I needed. She thought I was being absolute about the whole episode and thought I was panicking and thinking that the binge would go on forever, but she reminded me that, without her help, I had managed to stop it and continue with my healthy eating and exercise. This is now the way I live my life and she was sure I would never go back to where I was, not with all the information I now have. I am simply to remember *there are no absolutes!* Hmm, that sounds familiar. Anyway, it was completely exhausting but I did feel better for having endured it.

Oh yeah, and she told me I was only allowed to weigh

myself once a week instead of every day as I do now. Yeah, sure! And I'm gonna save myself for the man I marry!

9 pm: Do you think it is normal to lust after your soccer coach? The first few weeks I didn't really pay any attention to him because I was busy having a heart attack due to my total lack of fitness on the field. But now that I don't want to vomit every time I run around the oval, I can see that he is cute. Very cute! It's amazing what that can do for your commitment to training. Before I was last to arrive and first to leave, carefully timing my arrival to occur *after* the sprint around the oval. Now I'm first there, last to leave. I run that extra lap, jump that little bit higher and work that much harder.

Have organised a team-bonding dinner for Friday night, which is simply a thinly veiled attempt to get him blind drunk and totally seduce him. At least if I do I'll be able to work on my ball-handling skills—not that I've ever had much trouble in that department.

Mentioned lusting after my coach to the boy and suddenly he wants to see me Saturday night. God, men love a challenge, don't they? Nothing like the scent of another man to have them pouncing back to prove ownership. Gee, that'd be good—a new perfume that smells like you've been with another bloke: 'Another Man' from Christian Dior. 'Have him waiting at the door. Another Man.' And what if you could buy little packs of men's pubic hair to put in your shower, on your basin and in the soap? That way they feel as if they might not be the only one in your life and have to work a little harder. Maybe I'm onto something big here—better copyright that idea.

30 March   There she goes!

Seventy-six kilos! Oh my God! Six more to go! Woohoo! Rang Crusher to make sure that I was doing everything okay. Two kilos in one week is not normally allowed. She said it was because I had changed my exercise regime again and I was just having a boost but that it will slow down again. She said to make sure I'm eating all that I should be and not to skip any meals. She said the running would burn fat faster than the gym so it was normal that it speeds up at first but I'm not to worry. Gotta love the running!

31 March   AJ Beckham?

8 am: Have my first ever soccer game today. Eeek! Have had nightmares about this day, dreaming of having my teeth or cheeks kicked in by some big butch soccer player who probably has testicles of her own due to the steroids she has for breakfast. I'm wondering whatever made me think this might be a good idea. I mean, what do I do when there's a 150-kilo, six foot, size 18, built like a brick shithouse soccer freak bearing down on me? Oh dear. Nervous is an understatement for how I feel right now. Cold hard fear for my life as I currently know it better describes it.

8 pm: I am a legend! I am a legend! Soccer hero! Classic moment, five minutes into the game I save my first goal, have the ball in my hands then say, 'Now what do I do?' A girl on the other team says, 'Ah you kick it out—to your team members preferably!' I thank her, kick it out and play the rest of the game. Some classic saves, fell on the ground so many times I considered staying there and absolutely loved being thanked and often cheered by my team-mates (I love applause, no matter how I earn it!). Okay, so we lost 2–0 but it could have been absolutely degrading considering none of us have ever played a game of soccer in our lives. Was awarded Woman of the Match! Woohoo!

Then the soccer team one division up poached me. Impressed by my goalie skills they asked if I'd play with them and that was very very scary. Plus the players were bigger, scarier and had a lot more power in their boots. We lost 5–0 and I vowed I would quite happily stay in my little skills-challenged division. Gee, I love sport!

Am focused on being 75 kilos by my birthday! I'm 76 now so if I can just not drink bucket loads of alcohol when I go out tomorrow night then I should manage to make it.

5 April   Hard work

Nutcase. Heavy.

We seem to be going over the same ground at the moment. In tears again, I said to her, 'Will there ever be a time that I can look at myself and not think I am fat?' She very honestly replied maybe not, but she hoped so. It depended on how hard I worked on the issues surrounding that very statement. She said she had seen me work very hard so far and that she could see no reason why this one would be any different.

She started off by saying the term 'fat' is ridiculous because that word alone is totally subjective. Ask an anorexic woman and she would declare that I was indeed fat. Ask someone else and they might say that I had a beautiful body—perfect the way it is. So the first thing I need to do is throw away the concept that there is a certain size that will make me 'acceptable', 'perfect' or 'right'.

She said I need to work on loving myself, breaking it down to loving certain parts of myself because it is only my self-image that is keeping me 'fat'. She reminded me of the list I had made, the one that said fat is unacceptable, lonely, unsuccessful etc. So unless I actively work on learning to love myself, no amount of weight loss will ever change how I see myself. She asked me what I did like about my body. I said nothing. She asked me again. I said my nose was all right. She prodded some more. I said my teeth were pretty good too. My hands, feet, lips and eyes also made it onto the list, not because I really like them but because I didn't dislike them. She told me to make a list of all the things I like about my body and to put it on the fridge and read it every day.

She asked me if I was still weighing myself every day. I said yes, but I had almost cut out weighing myself at night. She acknowledged that I wasn't ready for the weekly weigh-in sessions and recommended I do it a little at a time. So from this week I am *not* to weigh myself at night ever again. Mornings only.

I mentioned that every time I pass a window or a mirror I can't help but see my reflection and be revolted. She said I was only to look in the mirror in the morning, with night-time observations banned. And when I pass a window, I am to look straight ahead and am not to look at myself in judgment. She said that by looking at myself negatively, I am being absolute again. I like all or nothing of myself. Absolutes, as she so often tells me, are a thing of the past.

I explained that I feel as if I will never really be in control. She said that I am in control. I interrupted her with, 'But what about the binges?' and she explained that bingeing, while it might be an unhealthy choice, was not necessarily being out of control. She said every time I had binged I had managed to talk myself back into the Alfalfa Zone. That was being in control. Taking control of the bad habits and not letting them take you over. I thought about all the binges and she was right. Every single time, particularly lately, I have managed to fall back into my pattern of returning to the exercise which in turn brings me back to the healthy eating. I did it. I took control! I am in control of my body! Wow!

She also explained that in my family history I didn't have anyone who let me know they believed in me, who told me how good I was, taught me to trust myself. These are things I now have to teach myself. She said I need to 'mother' myself like I mother Kai. All the things I tell him, I need to teach myself.

She reiterated to me that I am not to blame myself for the difficult times in my childhood. I must not blame myself for being adopted out, for feeling like I didn't fit into the family I was adopted into, for the abuse. None of it was my fault and it is time to start loving myself unconditionally as all those people in my life *should* have done.

Nutcase said I am a beautiful, generous, talented, giving, sympathetic person and anyone who cannot see that isn't good enough to be a part of my new life—the life where I actually come to realise and accept that *I am a worthy person.* I deserve nothing but the best in life.

I then said, 'Maybe that's why I have chosen friends and boyfriends who are never there for me.'

Her response? 'Absolutely. But not any more. Now you know you deserve more. And settling for second best just isn't going to work for you.'

I started to see what she was talking about. I had never learnt to love myself because no one in my family taught me how to do it. I grew up thinking I would never be good enough. Yet somehow, despite all of that, I still managed to stay focused on my dreams and become a writer/performer. And as Nutcase pointed out, that makes me pretty special. And if I can do that against all odds, then learning to love myself should be a breeze.

I also had a damn good cry about 'Larger than Life'. I am going to a party for the launch of the show and it has just dawned on me that thousands of people are going to see me at my fattest, and almost naked. They are going to see my gut, stretchmarks and all! They're going to see me crying on the phone to Crusher about feeling as if I have no control and wishing I'd never started this thing. They will see my weekly confessions of craving Pluto Pups and hot chips, they'll see me after my alcoholic leg-breaking binge and, worst of all, they will see me at the end still fat. Sure, not as fat as I was, but not as thin as I'll be.

Nutcase said I shouldn't be surprised—after all, it was my idea in the first place. I said I understood that but I didn't really think about it at the time, I just did it. And now I know I can't ever take those images away, they will be there forever, for anyone and everyone to see. She said I shouldn't be ashamed of my fat, I should be proud. I should congratulate myself on my bravery and realise that this show might actually save other people's lives as well as my own. After all, would I really have done this if the camera hadn't been following me around? Maybe, but it might have taken me a few more years of trying and failing.

Nutcase said I dwell on the negative too much and I should look at the positive. She said I am to go to the premiere and soak up all the praise, thank people when they say something nice and try to believe the good things people will say. I said I wasn't sure I could watch it all and she said to just do what I felt comfortable with. Most of all, she said, I am to congratulate myself on how far I have come.

Oh my God, I think I need a drink.

7 April   Ouch!

Played my third game of soccer. We lost. I'd be more surprised if we won, or even scored a goal. I figure if we score just one goal during the season then we'll have played okay. Got kneed in the nose. Want to change sport. Perhaps fishing might be more my style. But while the coach is there I feel I can't let the team down so I'll stay for a little bit longer (and, no, it has nothing to do with wanting to have sex with him, thank you very much. It's a team thing—team loyalty, or something like that!).

8 April   Did I do that?

Oh God, I feel absolutely sick about this thing going to air. Dreading any guys I know watching it, particularly any of the guys I have been dating and/or thinking about dating! Aaah! In some ways I wish I could take it back. Can't believe I bared my soul to the world. Sometimes I wish I'd keep my big mouth shut. Still, I am kind of glad I did it. Apart from it paying the bills, I do feel as if it is a good thing to have done, not just for myself but for anyone else who has done the diet merry-go-round, like me. Anyway, the launch is tonight, so I'm just going to grin and bare it (literally!).

9 April   Larger than Life!

Okay, so it wasn't as bad as I thought it would be. Okay, yes it was. In fact it was worse than I thought it could be. A million people came to this party to watch the show (okay, about forty, but it felt like a million!). A few people who hadn't seen me since the start didn't recognise me, so that was nice. Crusher came and held my hand as we all sat down to watch the show.

It wasn't so bad at first but I had to walk out of the room for the gut-pinching fat test. I started to cry and just could not watch any more when they showed me on the phone to Crusher having my six or eight week breakdown. Leaving a room full of teary-eyed people I headed straight for the champagne and didn't stop drinking until the show was over.

Thank God I had to get straight on the net afterwards, so I didn't have to deal with many people face to face. Was amazed at how positive all the net talk was. So many stories of men and women 100 kilos or more saying they were inspired by my story and thanking me for having the courage to share my life with them. On the whole, it wasn't such a bad night. Might wait a few months to watch the rest of it. Doesn't really matter, it's out there now. Nothing I can do but get on with the rest of my life.

13 April   Candles coming . . .

Seventy-five and still four days to go till my birthday! Happy birthday to me! For the first time in a long time I can go out on my birthday looking and feeling good about myself. Not that it has anything to do with the weight.

Uh-huh!

19 April   The beat goes on

Nutcase session. Talked a lot about getting my head around liking myself. She said, 'You need to think about what people probably think about you rather than what you fear they will say about you.' I tend to focus on the negative aspects and then on top of that blow them out of proportion, thus convincing myself that not only do I think I am ugly, but other people think it too, which confirms what I think about myself, and around and around I go on that little self-hatred merry-go-round.

I told her that all week I had managed not to weigh myself at night and hadn't done the big 'I hate my body' mirror sessions either. I was amazed at how much better that made my week. Stopped a lot of the negative thoughts entering my head on an almost compulsive basis. So without the daily downers, the week feels as if it has been a lot better than previous ones. She said it was great to get rid of the negative stimuli and now all we have to do is work on the positive thoughts and then I'll be perfect. Of course she didn't say it anything like that, but that's my take on it.

She also explained that it is our aim to eventually have me eating without any guilt, remorse or major deliberation whatsoever. To just have eating as a daily part of my life that requires little or no thought apart from, 'Oh, it's lunchtime, I'll eat and be done with it.' That seems quite unreal from where I stand but I know I can do it. As she said to me, I have done everything else, so why not that?

Surprisingly, we talked a lot about other aspects in my life like financial responsibility etc, all the things that I have to fix in my life, and once again she said I was fixing one thing at a time. First of all I tackled the weight, then the food/eating issues, then the self-image, then financial responsibilities and then after that we will tackle relationships, by which time I will be the perfect specimen of how easy it is to live your life to the fullest.

20 April   Happy birthday to me

Running like a champion for forty minutes solid. Am going to add another ten minutes from tomorrow. It is the absolute best rush in the world to run that last fifteen minutes. Your skin tingles, your body burns and you feel so alive. I now cannot imagine life without running. I am hooked! Bring on those endorphins, baby.

I have always struggled with not eating extra food in the afternoons or not snacking on Kai's dinner because that is when I am at my hungriest. I have my snack in the afternoon but it's really hard to hang on till dinner time. A friend suggested I have two snacks in the afternoon and it actually works. I have a piece of fruit around 3.30 pm and then I have another piece of fruit around 5.30 pm, which lets me cruise safely through to my dinner time. It's totally fat free and good for me so I don't have to feel any guilt about it and it gives me the extra strength I need not to raid the fridge or snack on Kai's meal.

Went out to dinner with my friends for my birthday. Slinky black silk dress. Once again, friends I haven't seen for months walked right by and, best of all, only a couple of days after the big night out I weigh in at seventy-four! Come on, number seventy!

21 April   The wardrobe

Quite focused and feeling good despite Nutcase going on holidays right when I am making major progress. She's away for a few weeks but I reckon I'm okay for the time being. Have been wearing size 14 for a while now, but even some of those clothes are a little loose in the bottom department. I'm shrinking! Thirty-five kilos and seven dress sizes have come and gone from my body. We are about to start work on another series of 'Mum's the Word' and it's a great feeling to know I'm going to have a range of clothing choices. I am definitely going to wear something sexy and flattering to my new body. Can't wait. Feeling great.

26 April   A whole new world

Seventy-four kilos! Still running like a champion. Am running so far and fast that I am covering more ground before turnaround (halfway time) than I did in my entire runs four weeks ago. Running gets rid of headaches, tiredness, poor eating habits. It is unbelievably fantastic. I run for an hour. Discovering whole new suburbs as I run from Leichhardt to Birkenhead Point (four suburbs away) and back. I run the whole way and I feel totally connected to my body.

Feeling good even with Nutcase away. Am eating like a . . . well-adjusted human being.

27 April   See ya!

Oh my God, I still feel great. Every day feels so good. Could this be what life is going to be like for me? Being in control? Feeling happy and joyful? Communicating my feelings rather than stuffing them down with food? It just seems so easy. Told the boy I've been seeing that I didn't want to 'see' him any more. I deserve more than just the odd sexual liaison. I want more and I'm going to get more. Felt good to say goodbye.

Maybe I'm being drugged and don't know it. Am struggling less and less with food. Healthy choices just seem to be my preferred option. Running is just something I do, not something I force myself to do. In fact, I now feel as if I *have* to go on my run. It makes me feel so good, can't start the day without one.

Do not weigh myself at night. It's always inaccurate as everyone is heavier at night and that makes me unhappy. So why bother? Don't need the grief.

28 April   Get up there, baby

Only weighing myself every three days. That's as long as I can hold out, but it makes me feel good not doing it every day. Feels as if it is not so important. Trusting that my running and healthy eating is doing the job. Feel good about everything else. Nutcase away and who cares? Not me! Happy happy happy.

Crusher rang to see how I was going and she recommended I push myself a little harder during my runs, try to get the heart rate really going, pushing it up into major fat-burning range. She told me to start running up hills. Have so far managed to avoid them but I reckon I'm ready. Will probably half walk, half run them but if it's anything like my progress so far, a little perseverance and the fitness follows really quickly.

29 April   Whose washing's that?

Was just looking at the washing on my line and saw my new t-shirt flapping in the breeze and I thought, 'is that Kai's shirt or mine?' Do I really fit into that? And I do. I bought a pair of tracksuit pants today. Got them home (size 14), put them on and had to take them back to the shop. They are way too big. I am now, officially, a size 12! In nine months I have gone from a size 26 to a size 12. Wow. Any wonder I feel good.

Currently running 7 kilometres a day. Wow!

Soccer this week—a nil-all draw. At least we didn't lose. And next week I'm sure at least one person on our team will score a goal. It doesn't matter though 'cause we're having so much fun. Who cares if we're coming last? Actually, we're second last because I'm such a good goalie (modest too).

30 April   The Pom

Nutcase still away. Just cruising along. Coping well. May have met the last decent man on the planet last night. Was out with the soccer chicks and in he walked. A cute cross between Billy Idol and Spike the vampire from 'Buffy the Vampire Slayer'. Absolutely gorgeous *and* a nice guy. What's wrong with him? Yes, there is one fatal flaw. He's from England and is only here on holidays! See, there had to be something wrong with him. Oh well, who knows what will happen? Just gonna have some fun!

1 May   Fat photos

Seventy-three kilos! Getting closer . . . When I hit 69 I throw the scales away. Nutcase said to do it at 70 but 69 will make my total loss 40 kilos exactly, and that sounds so much better than 39. Hard to believe I'm in the home straight. Blink and here it is. Almost.

Had a bit of a cry last night. Saw a photo of myself (taken last week) and got upset because of the size of my thighs. I can't believe that I still look fat! I know I don't really, but it's just that I want perfection and I want it now! Rang Crusher all upset and she told me to go and get a real fat photo. She said she would wait. I dug up one of my horror ones, the kind I hide behind my bookshelf for fear of anyone seeing them. Got back on the phone and Crusher told me to hold the photos next to each other. I did. She said, 'Are they the same people?' I said no. She said, 'Do you eat what the fat AJ used to eat?' I said no. 'Do you exercise more than the fat AJ used to?' I said the fat AJ never exercised.

Then Crusher said, 'Well, rip that fat photo up now.' I couldn't believe what she was saying. She said it again. She said, 'You don't know that woman any more, you will never ever be like her so you might as well say goodbye.' She also said that in six months I could then rip the new photo up. She told me to pin it to my fridge, put a date on it and then aim for that date. Aim to rip it up when I get to where I want to be. She said it was important to recognise how far I have come and to keep moving on. I said I can't imagine losing another 10 kilos or even getting under 70, and she brushed it aside with: 'You said that when you were over a hundred, and then ninety, and then eighty. Just shut up, AJ, and get on with it. Now rip the bloody fat photo up!'

I ripped it up and it felt great. Goodbye, arse! Forever. Wow! Don't feel so fat now.

2 May   Picture this

Went to the movies with the English boy and he held my hand. I felt like I was in high school again. He's very romantic and very affectionate, but best of all he said the most incredible thing to me. He said, 'The other night, you could have had any guy in that whole room. Why me?' Thankfully I didn't say, well I used to be the size of a German tank and don't actually think of myself as attractive. Or, I was desperate and you looked like you'd say yes. I think I laughed it off but secretly inside I did the Toyota jump and a great big 'Yeehaa!' Life gets better every single day.

5 May   Bend it baby

Absolutely loving soccer. Love it, love it, love it. Am I making myself clear? This is the best thing I have done since . . . since I learnt how to deep-fry Mars bars! Actually, it's better than that because this doesn't make me fat.

6 May   Lift

Started back at weights. Didn't join up, just going casually at the moment. Ouch. Did it really hurt that much before?

Where has all my strength gone? Every time I painfully push those weights I say to myself, 'Burning fat. Building muscle. Burning fat. Building muscle.'

8 May   No fries with that

Nutcase back next week but I feel pretty good. Wish I never had to go back. But I know that if I don't work on all the 'excess baggage' then I'll probably just put all the weight back on. No, in for a penny, in for a pound. Will stick with this until I am one total functioning unit. No matter how long it takes.

And how's this? With Kai at his dad's house for the weekend, I stayed over at my new man's house (can I call him that yet?). He cooked me the most amazing dinner. He said, 'I know you're a health freak, so will a stir-fry with fish do you?' Huh, a health freak. Yeah, that's me. Let me just wipe the Pluto Pup stains from my mouth! Who am I kidding? I have to tell him I was fat. Anyway, I realised with shock that although I am thirty-three years of age, no man has ever cooked me a meal before! Jeez, maybe I should marry this guy.

10 May   The hills are alive

Running a total of one hour now. Up hills, down hills (I prefer down), across hills. I just love running. Why is it I never knew about this before? What was wrong with me? From self: *you were fat and lazy!* To self: oh yeah, that's right!

11 May   The bod and the bike

Seventy-two kilos. The numbers don't seem to mean that much to me any more (Nutcase will be proud). The Alfalfa Zone has kind of become like riding a bike. You don't count how many times the wheel turns every time you ride it up the street. Well, it's the same thing with changing your body shape/size. I know the rest of the weight will eventually come off because I have become like a machine. I eat well. I exercise. I eat well. I exercise. I prefer the healthy choices because they make me feel better and I feel better because I make the healthy choices. It just happens.

Oh well, at least I've got my life back now, better just enjoy it. Speaking of which, am waiting for the boy to arrive. We're going to have a cuddle and watch *Spartacus*. The only tough thing is, he is a total chocoholic. Talk about temptation. I'll just make sure I have red licorice strips and lots of water so I won't get tempted.

12 May   Sabotage!

How is this for totally bizarre? I have a male friend I've known for a long time and I have never been thinner than him. He's a little overweight but only by about ten kilos. Well, since I've started creeping towards my goal weight I have noticed that he has started bringing bucket loads of junk food to my house on our regular back-slapping, beer drinking, footy watching nights. Lollies, pizza, Cherry Ripe ice cream, cheese, fatty dips, huge slabs of cheesecake and beer. He asks if I want him to get me anything from the shops, I say no, and then he arrives with enough fat to deep fry a dozen pigs in. It takes such strong resolve to say no. I usually crumble and have a little but it's certainly not the binges we used to enjoy together. Mostly it's him bingeing and me drinking water. It's not the same and I wonder whether our relationship was just two people getting together to binge guilt free.

I also wonder whether it is sabotage. Maybe he likes me being fat. I talked to Nutcase about it and she said it could well be sabotage. She said that people establish their relationships with people and they don't like them to change. Once the hierarchy changes then the people have to question themselves. I told her I was hurt by the fact that he's trying to damage all the good I've done.

Nutcase explained that it was best just to tell him that from now on my house is a junk food free zone and if he wants to eat that stuff then he is more than welcome to do so but that it has to be done somewhere else. All junk food is banned from my presence.

14 May   Oops

Bugger. Seventy-three. Could be building muscle now I'm back at the gym. Going back to the food diary just to be sure I'm doing all I can. Spoke to Crusher. She said I need to raise my heartbeat to around 160 beats per minute as opposed to the paltry 110 I was at six months ago when first joining the gym. But I am a lot fitter now so I have to make myself go harder and faster.

She said it was natural for the body to almost stop losing weight after such a major weight loss. She said that the body reduces the calories it burns in an effort to keep its reserve of fat. In other words, the body doesn't want to strip all its fat. She said that if I keep exercising and watching what I eat and keep drinking lots of water then it will eventually shift even if it only shifts around a quarter of a kilo a week. The key is to just keep living healthily rather than seeing the weight loss as a goal with a beginning and an end. These changes are for life. I knew that, but it's easy to forget!

15 May   How do I tell thee?
Let me count the weighs

Can't stop thinking I have to tell the new boy I was fat. Don't know why it's important. A part of me wants him to think I've been thin all my life but I know that would be a lie. It's strange . . . if I talk about it I make an issue of it, but if I don't mention it then it becomes an issue for me, 'cause I am constantly 'afraid' of getting busted. Having a friend walk up to me and say, 'AJ, you finally went to India—it's great what a good dose of dysentery can do' is not the way I want him to find out. Damned if I do, damned if I don't. When is the right time to tell him? And how?

16 May   Gym-bo

Seventy-two again.

Am thinking about joining a new gym, a really big flash one, but it is just so bloody difficult. They have thirty-eight different payment options all meant to leave you absolutely broke. There's the off-peak option, the peak-hour option, the off-peak peak option, the staggered payment plan, the upfront payment plan, the not so upfront payment plan, the first month free payment plan (that's where you pay them $200 for nothing but your first month is free!) and on and on it went. Think I'll stick with the one at the end of my street until I win Lotto. Note to self: better buy a ticket!

17 May   Them bones, them bones

How cute is this? These days when Kai wants to have a snuggle with me on the lounge, he goes and gets some pillows to make himself comfortable. He says, 'Mummy, you not as snuggly any more. I need a pillow! You're too prickly now.' How good is that? I wonder if he'll date big women in the hope of recreating that big fleshy cuddle he came to know so well as a little baby.

18 May   Friends, Part II

Rang my junk food saboteur a few days ago and told him I was now making my house a junk food free zone. He agreed that it was a good idea and said he respected my decision. I told him I was too close to my goal and I didn't need to eat that kind of crap food any more and that nothing was going to stop me from getting to my goal. I have come too far to stop now.

Anyway, today he rang and told me he has just joined a gym. Interesting, huh? Knowing I was not going to be swayed back into fatness he has now decided to do something about his own weight. Nutcase was right. People don't like the hierarchy to change. It is now my ambition to reach my goal weight before he does. Nothing like a little bit of friendly competition!

20 May   Olé Olé, Olé Olé!

We won! 1–0. Not only did we score a goal but we won! Better than that was Kai standing on the sidelines yelling at the top of his little voice, 'Go, Mummy. Go, Balmain. You a legend, Mummy! Good save, Mummy.' Everything the coach yelled out, Kai repeated (well, except the 'Mummy' bit). After the game he ran onto the field and jumped into my arms and said, 'You a goalie, Mummy. I'm going to be a goalie too.' I realised then that his perception of me as a person will be so completely different than it was a year ago. And because of how he sees me, his influences are likely to be life-altering as well. Sport and fitness are things that will just be a natural part of his consciousness. So much of what we do is what we have learnt from our parents. So if the very least I get out of this journey is a son whose normal consciousness includes fitness and health, then it has been a journey well travelled.

21 May   Material loss

Monday morning, the day after becoming a member of a goal-scoring, game-winning women's soccer team, I have weighed in at 71 kilos! Two more and I'll have lost a total of 40 kilos. Freaky.

The other day I mentioned to my Pommie boy that I was losing weight (notice I didn't say I have already lost close to 40 bloody kilos off my arse!). He asked me why. I said because I don't want to be fat for the rest of my life. He said, 'You're not fat, you've got a beautiful body!' And then it hit me. I might not be thin but I am definitely not fat any more. 'Oh my God, I can't make jokes about the size of my arse any more. I've just lost ninety-nine per cent of my comedy material.' Oh well, better that than a heart attack.

22 May   Woohoo!

This new boy is incredible. He's so affectionate and caring and loving and gentle. There's so much hand-holding and cuddling and kissing. He rings when he says he will, he tells me I'm sexy and beautiful all the time, he cooks me more meals than I cook my son. He's smart and funny and wants to teach me chess and the guitar, and he doesn't want to change me. He loves me just the way I am. It's been interesting because even if he does go back to England soon (if he can't find work) it's made me realise that I deserve this kind of a relationship. So from now on, I won't ever settle for anything less.

I am now a member of a real, only twelve monthly payments of a pound of flesh and your first-born baby, gym. Phillippa lent me the money so I could get to my goal weight sooner. And, yes, I know I've managed to avoid it until now but the time has come, I am afraid to say, to do some aerobics classes. I don't think the last kilos will shift easily unless I do something different, and that is all that is left. Watch out, Denise Austin, here I come . . .

23 May   Shhh! (Mark II)

Couldn't go today. Pulled a groin muscle. It wasn't mine. Ha ha. Now I know I'm harping on about this guy but after this, I promise I will shut up. I just have to say, he is the most romantic man I have ever known. I decided to introduce him to Kai, and after the little fella had gone to bed and we'd been snuggling on the lounge for about an hour, he took his bulging backpack and disappeared into my bedroom and was rustling around in there for about fifteen minutes. I desperately hoped he wasn't donning a dress and make-up (don't laugh, it's happened to me before). Eventually he called out, 'It's okay to come in now.' I entered my bedroom and could not believe my eyes. He had covered my bed in rose petals, filled the room with red candles, had an oil burner on, and was lying there waiting to give me a massage. As I stood there open-mouthed he added, 'And it doesn't have to end in sex either. You can just fall asleep if you like. I just wanted to tell you how much you mean to me.'

Have I died and gone to heaven? He was offering me a massage and he wanted nothing in return? Unbelievable.

I must be dreaming. Whatever you do, do not, under any circumstances, wake me up!

24 May   Jippy tap-tap

Back to Nutcase day after tomorrow. Have had such a good few weeks, what with her being away and things with my boy. She may have to work harder than usual to have me in tears. Oh well, have to do the (mental) housework. No point having a beautiful house if you're not going to keep it clean.

And guess where I am going tonight? Tap-dancing! Yep, it's time to take the shoes out from the dark recesses of the wardrobe, dust off the cobwebs and make a complete fool of myself. I've picked one of those little out of the way dance academies run by women called Cheryl-Lynne and Valerie. I'm doing the adult tap class and I just know it's going to be filled with sixty-year-old women wearing black leotards with flash razzamatazz stockings and sequin belts around their waist. You know, the kind of women who get filmed by the local news, tap-dancing their way around the state's nursing homes. That'll be me in a year's time. Perfect audience, really.

25 May   Stomping

What a hoot. I had the best time. Michael Flatley I am not. More like Michael Flatfeet but I threw myself into it and loved it. It's been ten years if not more since I have done any dancing, and, let me tell you, it showed. Legs went one way, arms the other, poked someone's eye out with a cane and, yes, the class was filled with oldies but the advantage was that at least they forgot how bad I was by the end of the class. It has made me realise how much of my life I had put on hold being overweight. I stopped doing so many of the things I loved doing because I wanted to hide away. I wish I could get that time back now.

27 May   Another aaah!

Grrr. Seventy-two! Have become a little complacent. Will cut out butter and cheese (again!), even if it is low fat. Will have tea with no sugar or fake sugar. And definitely no alcohol.

It would be so easy to stop here, three kilos from my goal. You start thinking near enough is good enough but I just can't do it. I have to do what I committed to doing. And, yes, these last few kilos have been harder physically to move but emotionally it seems easier because I know that if I stay focused then they will eventually go, even if they take three times longer than the first 30 kilos. I'm tired of thinking about the whole diet thing but I know the 'end' is in my sights and if I push myself that little bit harder, then I'll be where I want to be and I can get on with living my life.

31 May   Can run, can't hide

Interesting session with Nutcase today. Thought I was having a good week until I entered her office. It's always the way. You think you are functioning well and then she pulls you apart and puts you back together again.

We talked a lot about handling the cravings I get. I said I thought I was doing well, being able to ask myself whether I wanted the sausage roll or the good body and being able to walk away from the junk food. She said it was important to acknowledge the craving for what it was. She said it was good that I realised that the sausage roll doesn't actually give me what I want and that not only do I wind up feeling disgusted, but I don't enjoy it and it does set me back from achieving my goals.

She then explained that the craving was important to acknowledge, though, because it means I need *something*. She said that perhaps I was needing nourishment. I replied that quite often my cravings had nothing to do with hunger and she said, 'Not that kind of nourishment.' She said that because I never really had enough nurturing when I was a child, maybe that was what I was after and if I could recognise that desire and fulfil it in another way then it would be more effective and less detrimental to my ongoing happiness.

She also said that when I crave hot food that I might be craving warmth, so to have a cup of tea or something warm. She said I could also create a ritual around the craving. First of all, check that I'm not hungry or thirsty, and then identify what it is that I need and get the appropriate sensory fulfilment (taste, touch, sight, smell). Perhaps as I make myself some tea, I can burn some incense, light some candles and create a ritual that makes me feel nurtured, that way avoiding the eating of the 'banned' substance that doesn't actually make me any happier.

We also talked about accepting my fatness (the past). The

other day my soccer coach told me he did a search for me on the Internet and he came across the 'Mum's the Word' website. He said there was a photo of me that was pretty funny and very different to what I look like now. I cringed when I found out that he had seen it and got paranoid that my boy would do the same. I want to erase all evidence of my fatness. When anyone asks me what I did for the last ten years I will say I was lost in the Himalayas and there are no known photographs of me during that time.

Of course making a TV show about my weight loss and now writing about it is going to make it mildly difficult to ignore that part of my life, and Nutcase is concerned about this. She wants me to accept that without getting as fat as I did, I may never have made all these positive changes to my life. I may have continued to diet dangerously or not diet at all, and that would definitely have shortened my lifespan. I have to accept that being fat is a part of my history and goes towards what makes me the person I am now, and not be ashamed of it. Oh goody, that means I will have to tell the boy sooner or later. Can't hide the photo albums forever.

I also talked about how difficult it has been for me to get under 70, and how, if I was being completely honest, it is because I am not being as strict as I was in the beginning. I think it is more a psychological thing I am fighting because if I want to get over that edge I know I can, but something is stopping me. It's like I am afraid of being under 70 because when I get to my goal I will no longer be fat and being fat is all I have ever known. Even when I wasn't fat I thought I was, so it's all the same. I have developed all my comedy routines around being fat. My whole persona and poetry and songs are all about being fat. If I give this up then I have to start again. And because I use my goal weight as benchmark of my success, I will no longer be able to say I am not good enough, which is what I have said about myself all my life. When I get there I won't know what to do, how to be, and I am afraid. I am afraid of being thin.

Nutcase looked all excited as she does when she is about to pass on a revelation. First of all she agreed that I would no longer have an excuse when I get to my goal. Now I say I am not successful enough because I am not thin enough or that people don't like me because I am fat. It is my excuse. When I get rid of that then all I can blame is me. She said there was nothing I could do about that other than experience it, possibly be surprised at my success, feel the fear and do it anyway, and I might even like it there. She said I almost had to work out which parts of the fat persona I could keep and how much of myself I would let out. Being thinner, I am definitely more exposed. I don't have so much to hide behind. She said I was probably afraid of getting hurt but that the fat didn't actually stop the hurt—I felt it just distracted me. I was so busy hating myself that I didn't have time to feel my pain. She said the future may hold painful relationships and experiences but that they may not be as bad as I think/fear.

I said that, in my past, rejection had pushed me so close to suicide that I was afraid of what might happen. She explained that I do things differently now and I have a good emotional basis to work from and that even though there might be pain ahead, I might surprise myself and find that there may even be less pain, now that I am not destroying myself with food. And that got me right in the gut. I realised that the last ten years had been so painful I had become numb. The only way I could survive it was by becoming a big fat void, constantly topped up with crap food and negative thoughts, crap food and negative thoughts. That's why it feels like I am waking up. I'm finally getting in touch with my feelings and she is right, they aren't killing me. They are not anywhere near as bad as I imagined. She asked me if the fat had actually protected me. I said it hadn't, and it had probably caused me even more pain. She agreed that fat is a very effective protection and that it was time I realised that not only do I no longer need it but that it doesn't do anything for me. Wow!

It was at that precise moment that I knew, without a doubt, that I will never ever be fat again. I never ever want or need to go back to that place. I am safe right where I am and I would rather experience a little fear and maybe a little pain than stuff it all down with bad food and bad thoughts and a body that has death knocking on the door. I feel totally ready to go the next few steps now. I am ready.

1 June   Trendy gym junkie

The new gym, first ever aerobics class. A thing called Body Pump. That's where all the women with silicone breasts get out their bicycle pumps and inflate their breasts in time to the music. No, it's basically lots of weights and barbells lifted in time to the music. Not very interesting. Not my thing, I

Crush those cravings

- If you know you crave certain foods, explore healthy alternatives (like my low-fat pizza instead of a standard fat-filled one) and freeze them so you don't have to order takeaway to satisfy your cravings and you can't use the 'I don't feel like cooking excuse' 'cause it's already done. All you need to do is heat and eat.

- Handle the cravings by doing something to distract you from the obsession. Make a list of things to do and refer to it when dreaming of eating your favourite junk food.

- If you have a craving for something sweet, eat a snack that is substantial first—for example, a piece of fruit or some sardines on crackers. Eat to fill yourself up nutritionally then have your sweet snack because if you are hungry you won't stop at just one.

- Cook up some fat-free brownies or muffins and immediately individually wrap and freeze them for those weak moments.

- Don't buy your kids and/or partner any of the stuff that tempts you. Chances are they don't need it in their diet either so you're doing them a favour.

prefer running, but it's something different and does work on specific muscle groups. I won't become an addict but will do the odd class for a change of pace.

I did take a second to notice the difference between how I felt when I went to Crusher's gym, way back at the start of this thing, and now. Back then I felt so completely fat and such a fraud and totally embarrassed just being in the room with people who all looked like they didn't need to be at a gym. I felt ashamed of having let myself get that way, and I was sure everyone felt disgusted just looking at the size of my thighs. My tracksuit pants were so tight Crusher thought they were tights and I couldn't find a sports top big enough to house my breasts.

Now I look the same as everyone else, I wear a trendy pair of size 12 tracksuit pants, an Adidas sports top that tells me I'm a size 12 and I look like I don't need to spend a lifetime in the gym either. I'm not embarrassed being there, no one thinks I stand out and I no longer actually feel (or look) fat!

Guys I've known for years are suddenly giving me their phone numbers and asking me out for dates. How funny!

5 June   Do up that shoelace

Seventy-one! Not that the weight means anything, of course—but 71! Must have been that pump class!

Have noticed that my fitness level has improved out of sight. At soccer training, I am actually doing the sprints rather than pretending that my shoelaces are undone or that I've pulled a muscle in my leg. I do the runs up and down the field and even though I'm the slowest of the lot, I still manage to make it there and back. Have asked Crusher how I can find out about fun runs because I want to start doing some in preparation for the 14-kilometre City to Surf in August. Actually, I just want the little participants' medals they give you when you haul your dying body over the finish line. I want to drape them over my mantelpiece and brag about them at my dinner parties. 'Oh, the Olympics? Yes, been there, done that! Sorry? Which Olympics did I compete in? Oh wow, look at the shape these breadcrumbs have made on the table. Looks just like Jesus. Drink, anyone?'

Am going up to the Blue Mountains for a romantic weekend away with the boy. Kai's at his dad's house and I am going to sleep in, make love without worrying about waking anyone up, and go for long, quiet bushwalks, have cuddles in the canyons and have every meal cooked for me. Am going to catch up with Zoë (it's been about 30 kilos since I saw her!) and have prepped her not to freak out about my weight loss. I've told her and her mum to say nothing. I know I have to tell him but all in good time. I have to find the right moment. Anyway, see you after the weekend.

9 June   Away with the weekend

Oh my God, I had the best time. It was so funny, though. Caught up with Zoë and her mum and they carried on about how different I look with my hair like that (now that my head is 40 kilos lighter?). 'Oh, your hair just looks soooo good. I never knew you could look so good with hair like that. It's just so different! And I think you've had it *thinned*! Oh, and is your colour *lighter*?' Nudge-nudge, wink-wink, say no more. Then there were the photos of Kai and I that I had to quickly pull out of the album, and it all got a bit ridiculous.

Then we took photos of ourselves out on bushwalks and had them developed and I freaked out at a couple of 'fat' photos. I had a bit of a cry and he gave me a cuddle and said that if I wanted to change my body I could but that he loved me the way I was. Yes, the L-word was slipped in but I was being so self-obsessed that it failed to cause a tremor.

Anyway, by the time we went out for drinks with Zoë and her partner, I knew it was time to cut the crap. I got Zoë to tell him because I was busy hiding under the table trying to cheese-grate the rest of my thighs away. Do you know what he said? 'I know.' I bumped my head on the table and came up to make sure I had heard right. 'Yeah, I already knew.'

'How?' I managed to splutter.

'Oh, there was a photo at your place of you doing some show and you were a lot bigger than you are now so I figured you'd lost weight. So what's the big deal?' Then change of subject, drinking of cocktails and an excellent under-blanket workout. So what *was* the big deal? Who knows!

10 June   Bad mother!

Poor Kai. He's become a sports widow. Somehow he knows if it's a Tuesday or Thursday and late in the afternoon, just out of the blue he'll say, 'Don't go to soccer training, Mummy. Don't go.' Or the other is, 'Can I come to soccer training with you, Mummy?' I tell him he can come when he's older (which will be so much fun) but he doesn't understand. He just sees me as leaving him again! Ah, don't you just love mother guilt!

Seventy kilos. One more to go!

I am going on major shopping sprees at the moment. I don't buy a lot but I love trying on all the clothes. This is the first time I have been in fashion for about ten years! I'm really enjoying walking into the shop and the sales assistant not looking the other way wishing I would *leave* the shop. I even had a woman walk up to me once and say, 'We have nothing in your size.' To which I replied, 'Well, I'll take the thousand dollars I was going to spend on my size 10 sister elsewhere.'

I hold up dresses and think, gee that's small. Do I actually fit into that? I take it into the dressing room expecting not to get it over my breasts and it slides smoothly over the breasts, over the hips and fits like a glove. I look at the tag, just to make sure, and it says size 12.

11 June   It ain't easy

Had a good session with Nutcase again. We launched straight back into the topic of last week's conversation, which was me wanting to forget that I had ever been fat. I commented on the fact that finally, after all this therapy, I *can* accept that I am no longer fat. But what I find interesting is that even though I've always thought myself fat, I didn't really see myself as fat as I was—obese. Nutcase thought it might have been precisely because I always did see myself as fat: I already had a distorted body image, so maybe I had to get really really fat to actually see it as it was.

She asked me if I was worried I would get fat again. This doesn't bother me as much as I thought it would because I know I would never let myself go for any more than a couple of kilos. She asked what I would do to fix it should it happen. I said I would do what I've done for the last ten or so months, but I really don't think much is going to change because it's not as if I go off 'a diet' or a set menu. I'm not really going to change what I eat. My whole lifestyle has changed. I can't eat the kinds of foods I used to consume without starting to feel quite ill. They no longer make me happy. I find happiness in so many other ways I don't need a burger and fries to get it. Most of the food I am eating I will continue to have in my day-to-day living.

I also said I can't believe I waited so many years to actually do this. I said it had been easier than I thought it would be and I wish I'd done it sooner. Nutcase pulled me up on that very quickly. She said it had not been easy. For the last ten months I have counted fat, calories, sugar content and everything I have eaten. I have consciously thought about every meal I have eaten, I have conscientiously stepped up my exercise quota from nothing to running 7 kilometres a day, I have worked internally as well as externally, I have delved into my past, my feelings, my habits, I have totally opened up my life and exposed myself to a complete stranger (Nutcase) and *I have lost a huge amount of weight* (nearly a whole person), but she said it was absolutely imperative for me to accept that it had *not* been easy.

Put that way, I thought, yeah, it has been hard, but I did say I originally thought it was going to be harder. Once again she said it was because I have always worked in absolutes and because I thought it would be 'too hard' I opted for the all-or-nothing scenario. Well, I did the nothing part of that scenario. She also mentioned that it seemed easier now because everyone who sees me can't help but comment on the drastic physical changes I have made. She reminded me what it was like when I had only lost 15 kilos and no one noticed or said anything. She reminded me how hard it was to keep going, because the only person who noticed was me and it felt like I was not making any progress at all. Now, every day is filled with a positive comment from one person or another—it's like the difference between night and day.

She said I have done an amazing job but I shouldn't lose sight of where I have come from because it then erases all the hard work I have done. She said if I could totally integrate that aspect of my life (the fat part) then I may work even more effectively. She said I cannot erase the past, no matter how hard I might want to, but I can use it positively, knowing that in the future, chances are that neither I nor my son will be fat, and that is something I could not have said a year ago. Without that fat person I would not have learnt the right way to eat and metabolise my food. I have learnt how to work my body as effectively as it can.

Wow. Did I really do all that? Any wonder my brain hurts as much as it does.

13 June   Is it really me?

I have just had my wardrobe fitting for the new series of 'Mum's the Word'. For the last series Maggie T clothed me and I only just squeezed into a size 24 (shirts unbuttoned) but I was actually a size 26. This time the Australian designer Andiamo is clothing me and I am a size 10–12. The sales lady held up a pair of black trousers and I said, 'There is no way they will fit me!' The legs just looked too thin. She laughed and said, 'Don't be ridiculous. Try them on.'

Anyway, I did as I was told and they glided up my legs, over my bum and fit me perfectly. Put on the shirt. Fit me perfectly—size 10. I truly feel like Cinderella. Now, as long as I don't turn into a pumpkin at midnight, everything should be all right!

Later: My friend Shaggsy popped around and couldn't believe how good I looked. He said I look completely healthy and alive, 'like your aura is saying "Ta-da!"' Life just keeps getting better.

14 June   Then and now

Sticking to the food diary. It's the only way I stay absolutely focused. I write down everything I eat. I look over it at the end of the day and first thing in the morning. I ask myself if I am going to exercise or if it is a day with Kai, and that's when I make my daily food decisions. If it's a day with Kai then I won't have any treats. If it's a Tuesday (child care day) and I am doing a run *and* soccer training, then I know I can have an ice cream or something special. I'm so close to hitting the ultimate goal, every day makes a difference. I put a sign up on my fridge: 'Every decision makes a difference. Have you made the *right* choice?'

It seems to be working. I get bored, I go and look in the fridge, there's nothing very interesting or tempting there anyway, and then I have a glass of water instead. My skin is almost perfect and I feel really quite energetic (if not actually hyper). What has happened to me?

Looking back at what I used to eat, I realise now why I could never lose weight. Apart from never eating regularly enough to fuel my metabolism, I constantly made choices that kept me hungry and unsatisfied. Even the differences between my first week in the Alfalfa Zone and now are incredible.

First week in The Alfalfa Zone

Monday

Breakfast: Uncle Toby's Sport Plus cereal with peaches in apple juice

Snack: Muesli bar, lime juice cordial

Lunch: Ham and salad sandwich, fruit biscuit

Snack: Banana, two crackers

Dinner: Lean Cuisine, corn on the cob, mashed potato, lettuce, 2 glasses of wine

Snack: Nothing

Tuesday

Breakfast: Muesli bar, two slices of toast with Marmite and butter, glass of apple juice

Snack: Muesli bar, banana, cordial

Lunch: Ham and salad sandwich, fruit biscuit

Snack: Low-fat yoghurt, 2 crackers, 4 lollies

Dinner: Seafood stir-fry with Hokkien noodles

Snack: Nothing

Wednesday

Breakfast: 2 crumpets with butter and Marmite, muesli bar

Snack: Nothing.

Lunch: K-time bar, cup-a-soup

Snack: Tuna sushi roll

Dinner: Lean Cuisine, salad

Snack: Diet jelly

Thursday

Breakfast: 2 crumpets with butter and jam

Snack: Muesli bar

Lunch: Ham and salad sandwich

Snack: Muesli bar, 6 snake lollies

Dinner: Healthy Choice dinner, mashed potato, corn

Snack: 4 glasses of wine

Friday

Breakfast: Banana, crumpet with butter, apple juice

Snack: Pikelet with butter

Lunch: Egg and lettuce sandwich

Snack: Sushi roll, yoghurt

Dinner: Lean Cuisine, corn on the cob

Snack: 2 glasses of wine

Saturday

Breakfast: Scrambled eggs (made with skimmed milk), 2 pieces of toast, pineapple juice

Snack: Muesli bar

Lunch: Ham, cheese and salad sandwich
Snack: Nothing.
Dinner: Teriyaki stir-fry
Snack: Muesli bar
Sunday
Breakfast: Baked beans, 2 slices of toast, 1 piece of cheese
Snack: Banana
Lunch: Ham and salad sandwich, muesli bar
Snack: Yoghurt, 8 rice crackers
Dinner: Veggie cannelloni, 2 potato gems, piece of corn
Snack: 2 glasses of wine

Typical week in the Alfalfa Zone now
Monday
Breakfast: 2 crumpets with lite peanut butter, low-fat yoghurt
Snack: Apple, banana
Lunch: Ham and salad sandwich, apple
Snack: Fruit salad
Dinner: Lamb stir-fry with Hokkien noodles
Snack: Weight Watchers Sweet Temptations ice cream with strawberries
Tuesday
Breakfast: Soy light breakfast cereal with fruit juice, 1 slice toast with Marmite
Snack: Low-fat yoghurt, piece of watermelon
Lunch: Bagel with smoked salmon, lite cream cheese, onion, lettuce, apple
Snack: 2 ryvitas with 2 pieces of low-fat cheese
Dinner: AJ's special seafood pizza
Snack: Apple, mandarin

Wednesday

Breakfast: Pancakes with lemon juice, banana

Snack: Peaches in own juice

Lunch: Chicken salad, frozen mango

Snack: Tuna sushi roll, apple

Dinner: Spinach and ricotta pie

Snack: Diet jelly, a few fresh raspberries

Thursday

Breakfast: 2 poached eggs on toast, plum

Snack: Apple, low-fat yoghurt

Lunch: Minestrone soup, bread roll, grapes

Snack: 1 packet of sultanas, 6 jelly snakes, kiwi fruit

Dinner: Dolmio's creamy mushroom risotto, 2 glasses of wine

Snack: Nestlé diet chocolate mousse

Friday

Breakfast: Baked beans on toast, apple

Snack: Banana smoothie (skimmed milk)

Lunch: Egg and lettuce sandwich, grapes

Snack: Small packet of Parker's pretzels

Dinner: Two grilled lamb cutlets, steamed veggies, pear

Snack: Low-fat yoghurt with blueberries

Saturday

Breakfast: Scrambled eggs (with skimmed milk), 2 pieces of toast, piece of pineapple

Snack: 6 strawberries, grapes

Lunch: Home-made burger (lite mince), no butter, salad on a roll

Snack: Apple, 6 dried apricots

Dinner: Grilled fish, steamed rice and veggies
Snack: Weiss Mango Bar
Sunday
Breakfast: Soy light cereal, juice, 1 piece of toast with diet jam
Snack: Banana
Lunch: Sardines and sun-dried tomatoes on toast, small fruit salad
Snack: Wendy's Choco'lite ice cream
Dinner: Tomato-based pasta, 2 glasses of wine
Snack: Nestlé Diet Mousse, 6 strawberries

On top of the changes in my diet, exercise is a large part of the driving force that strips the fat. I run for 7 kilometres, at least four times a week. I go to soccer training twice a week *and* play a 90-minute game of soccer every Sunday. I'm getting back into the weights and will probably wind up doing about two sessions a week—one of weights and another of cardio. On the days when I have Kai, we usually go for a one-hour walk and when I take him to the park I take my soccer ball and have a run around with it.

Whenever I lose focus a little, I throw myself into the exercise and within a day or two I find I feel strong and healthy, and that encourages me to make healthy choices. It's such a different life!

15 June   Ooo-hoo — medals!

I was getting a full body massage last night (as you do!) when my man stopped to make a production out of kissing all my stretchmarks. I go to complain about them and he tells me I should be proud. He calls them my little badges of honour—without them no one would believe that I have lost so much weight. He says I look like I've been thin forever and that I should be proud of what I have done. Oh God, somebody give this guy a job! Keep him in the country!

16 June   Crusher—the final countdown

Caught up for a coffee (skimmed milk, no sugar) with Crusher and she said, 'I've got a surprise for you.' She reached into her handbag and pulled out a tape measure. I groaned (premenstrual), not wanting to know, but lifted my arms and let her do her thing.

Then she pulled out the list of what I first measured and this is how it went:

	Then	**Now**
Neck	41 cm	33 cm
Bust	125 cm	99 cm
Waist	108 cm	80 cm
Hips	140 cm	102 cm
Bicep	46 cm	30 cm
Mid thigh	82 cm	54 cm

Total lost : 144 centimetres. Any wonder I couldn't fit my arse into the swings at the park!

I was in shock. Then she did her little speech, something I think she's been working on for a while. She said, 'AJ, I want you to listen to me very carefully, because this is the last thing I will say to you other than gee, nice arse, how'd you get that? AJ, you are the master of your own destiny. Congratulations. You rock, sister! You made this happen with determination and the will to become the very best you could possibly be. You made the pledge to me a little under a year ago and you made it come true. You are a total success and an inspiration for me and every woman in the world.'

I laughed that last bit off and she grabbed my hand and very seriously said, 'AJ, it's very important that you acknowledge how hard this has been. You are selling yourself short if you don't accept exactly how hard you worked to make this happen. I remember you crying on the phone to me six weeks in saying you couldn't do this. Well, you did it, sister. Shazam!'

Then she laughed and added, 'So how does it feel to no longer have the largest arse in Sydney and to be a hot babe who stands out in the crowd?' I told her to shut up and have some chocolate cake. She pushed it my way and said, 'You look like you need a good feed. You have it.' We both left it alone, hugged each other and, I must admit, I walked away a little bit taller (and a good deal smaller!).

18 June   Groan

Gym. Run. Gym. Run. Pump class. Run. Soccer training. Soccer game— nil–all draw. Go, you bastard kilo. Go!

Rang Crusher. She reminded me that the last kilos are the hardest because my fitness level is now so high it is hard for me to get my heart rate up high enough to burn fat. She said it was now important to think about just getting fitter, keeping up the weights and changing my cardio workout. She explained that people with higher muscle density and higher fitness levels just naturally burn fat throughout their normal day. So increasing fitness (rather than just burning fat) is what I am to concentrate on. I am to constantly surprise my body. Instead of running for longer times (which is what I thought I had to do) I have to run faster and up hills. She also told me to get on the bike at the gym because I haven't done that and even though I can run easily for forty minutes I will struggle to do twenty on the bike, thus shocking my body into an adjustment phase. Weights are to continue as usual but I am to keep pushing harder weights. If I am not sore the next day then I am to lift heavier weights. Having more muscle density to fat will help me burn more fat. She gave me a million new ab exercises which hurt like hell but I think of what my abs will look like at Christmas and I am doing them without a single murmur of dissent.

I explained that I couldn't help but compare my weight to those of women in the slimming mags—my height but weighing only 50 kilos. She explained that I am working out and getting a wonderfully sexy, slightly muscly (well-toned), strong body. That will always weigh more. She told me to read fitness magazines instead of weight loss mags and to see strong, healthy bodies that weigh more and look great. She said it was better to have definition than to weigh less. 'Throw away the scales, AJ—everyone is different! You look beautiful.'

Any day now. Any day.

It's all in the mind

- Find a support person. Someone you can walk with/talk to/ someone who can ring you every day and ask if you've exercised.
- Set realistic goals. Reward yourself often. Have treats.
- Take it one day, one meal or even one hour at a time.
- I recommend getting a shrink or a therapist. Work on the inside so you're equipped for the work on the outside.
- Be honest, because the only person you are really cheating is yourself.
- If you crack and have something 'bad', then don't stress about it. Simply move on and decide that at the next meal you will make a healthier choice. Remember, there is no right or wrong track. It is all one track. Having a right and wrong track sets us up for a failure.
- Put motivating signs/reminders everywhere, particularly on the fridge and cupboards.

20 June
Any more than a handful is a waste

Every night in front of the TV I do all my ab exercises. All up it's around 300 sit-ups, all working on different parts of the tummy. I keep telling myself, 'Abs of steel by summer!' Hey, by then I might even look good in a bikini! I've started to believe anything is possible! I squeezed my bum last night and guess what? It's a nice, firm handful. Woohoo!

Bumped into a bloke I haven't seen for a few years and casually said 'Hi'. He took off his sunglasses, scrutinised my face and asked, 'Sorry, do I know you?' After explaining who I was, we talked for a while, he asked if I was seeing anyone and asked for my number. Goodness, it's starting to rain men. Lovely.

21 June   Perfection

Caught up with a friend the other day who couldn't believe how much weight I'd lost. When I told her I would probably lose another five or so she seemed surprised and asked me why. I explained it like this. Imagine wanting to build a beautiful wooden table that you hope to become a family heirloom. You do a woodworking course, you buy all the tools and you take a year to make your precious table. Why bother doing all that if you don't bother putting the polish on it? I've come this far, I know how to do it, so I might as well make my body as good as it can be. That will take time and it's all much of a muchness now, but that is why I will keep doing the weights, even when I get to my goal. Just to finish up the edges!

25 June   Touching myself up

I can't help but run my hands over my new body. I have never had muscles like this before in my life. I know I keep saying it, but it really is like waking up in someone else's body. Never have I been able to feel (and see) the muscle that runs from my groin area into my leg. Now there is no fat there, I can see the muscles work as I move my leg. It actually feels lean! And I love catching sight of my arms in the mirror. I have definition. Not big she-man muscles but the arms of someone who goes to the gym. It's very strange and I feel like I have a new toy.

My breasts are still big but they're changing shape. My pecs are taut and hard and a guy at the gym said getting good pecs was the next best thing to getting a boob job. A lot cheaper too!

Found myself putting one of Nutcase's theories to the test. Was craving wine but didn't want to have the extra calories so I decided to create a ritual around the drinking. I lit a fire, brought out some candles, put some music on and burnt some yummy incense. I got out one of my favourite wineglasses and filled it with nicely chilled apple juice. I sat in front of the fire, sipping my juice, chilling out, and it was as good as a bottle of wine would have been. It worked, and with a minimum of extra calories and no sore head the next day. Nutcase is so good!

27 June   Life on the loo, Part III

Come on, arse. Just one more kilo! Trying not to weigh myself every day but it's so hard being this close.

I have a comedy gig coming up in New Zealand. When I finally found my passport and looked at the photo, I realised no customs officer would believe that person was me. Oops, the passport accidentally got flushed down the toilet. Gee, I'd better get a new one.

28 June   Are we there yet?

Feel like eating chocolate. Go for a run. Miss my man, who's backpacking in Uluru. Feel like eating chocolate. Go for a run!

As soon as I pound that pavement I get an amazing endorphin rush and I feel so good about myself I stop obsessing about whether my man will get to stay in Australia or have to go. I refuse to comfort eat. Doesn't make me feel any better. All I need is that natural high and I'm not even tempted to drink (well, almost).

Just keep running, AJ!

29 June   Singin' in the rain

I've started running in the rain. I used to look at people doing that and thought they were mad. But there's something satisfying about not letting the weather get in the way of your fitness. And it's quite refreshing. I feel like a naughty kid playing in puddles. I'm running in the rain, my hair and clothes are soaked, but I'm warm from the exercise and it feels good. The shower afterwards is divine and I find I'm not as cold throughout the rest of the day.

I even bought a running magazine! Crusher said the best

way to find out about fun runs is to buy fitness mags, so that's what I did. It was such a foreign experience, to be buying a magazine about fitness, I felt like a sixteen-year-old kid purchasing a copy of *Penthouse* while his friends waited around the corner from the shop. I do not know this person I have become. But I like her. A lot.

I bought a pair of jeans (size 12). It's been ten years since I owned a pair of jeans. There was no breathing in to do the button up, no lying on the floor and pushing the fat down into the pants and no pulling the shirt down over the top to hide the fact that the button won't do up. In fact, the sales girl said they were probably a little too loose. I just stared and stared at them on me. I couldn't quite believe that it was me in the mirror. I kept looking at where my bum used to be. I kept rubbing my hand over where my stomach used to bulge and I must say it is still a little bit unreal. It just seems like yesterday that I started this thing and it seemed too impossible for it to come true.

I had to buy the jeans and now I'll have to go horse-riding because I know it won't be like what happened last time I tried to get on a horse. Its legs buckled and they had to put me on a bigger horse. Now I know that won't happen to me. Ever again.

69 KILOS!

(152 lb)

It must have been the running mag that pushed me over the edge but I am here. Let me take a deep breath as I say it. Fanfare, please. Sixty-nine kilos! Not 70, but 69 kilos. Forty kilos lighter than I was a little less than one year ago. I have arrived. I stepped on the scales this morning and couldn't actually believe it. I had to check three or four times just to make sure I wasn't standing the wrong way, but every time it said the same thing (69.3 to be exact, but who's counting?). That means I have lost nearly 40 per cent of my total body weight. A few more kilos and I'll have lost Calista Flockhart from my body!

How do I feel? Numb, actually. It's a bit like a fairytale. I can't say that I ever really believed it possible. I just kept going 'cause there was nothing else to do but go forward. And here I am. Someone said to me yesterday that my weight loss was a testament to my self-discipline, but I don't think that is true. I never woke up and had this magical resolve or extra amount of willpower. I just did it a day at a time, a meal at a time. I can't say it's been easy but it hasn't been as hard as I imagined it would be. And the thing is, if you keep going then it just *has* to happen. And before you know it, a year has passed and you are a different person!

Of course, my journey is far from over. I've probably got years of therapy to get through and I may even decide to lose a few more kilos, but it's all one path now. It has become my life. I am in control of my body. Even when I eat crap *I am in control*. Because I now have a firm commitment to eating well and exercising, that will see me through my hardest times.

It's time to throw away the scales as I promised Nutcase I would. My weight will no longer rule my life. I have learnt how to eat. I have learnt that input versus output is the way to get fit and is the only thing that works. Remember: *Diets don't work, healthy eating and exercise does. Nothing else matters!*

It has been a total change of lifestyle. It never stops, because this is my life now. Unlike a diet that has a beginning and an end, my life is now well and truly entrenched in the Alfalfa Zone. I will never leave. I don't want to. This place feels like home. It's safe, secure, gives me structure and focus and most of all it is healthy and I will live longer and lead a fuller life and almost certainly I will teach my child a better way of living to the one he may have experienced had I never taken control.

My man may or may not stay in Australia. If he does, then I think we have a future together but if not, then I know that someone is out there for me and because I feel more confident, I am more likely to go out there and find him. And because I respect myself more now, I will not settle for second best. And most importantly, I love myself and my life so much now it doesn't seem as important to find someone. Yes, it would be nice, but, for now, I'm just enjoying all the wonderful experiences my new life brings to me. There's so much to do, discover and enjoy. Summer is coming and I've decided to learn to play tennis. That and God knows what else lies ahead! It's sure to be a lot of laughs!

Okay, well, I'm going to go now. I've got my usual session with Nutcase and then, well, I think I'm going to celebrate by having a big piece of chocolate cake! No, only joking. I have decided to celebrate by buying myself all new underwear. I wonder if I am a size 10 yet? Huh, never thought I'd hear myself say that. God, life is good.

See you in the City to Surf!

Famous last words

Well, there you have it. Look, I don't profess to be a diet guru. The truth is there are no secrets, no fancy wraps, prepackaged food or special drinks that will get you the size and shape you want to be and keep you there. The only thing that will *permanently* change your body is a complete lifestyle change. There are no quick fixes—well, there are, but they don't last and will only help you put on more weight in the future when you return to your old eating habits. When it comes right down to losing weight and getting fit it is a simple equation. Low calorie, low fat food in reasonable quantities eaten at regular intervals with cardiovascular exercise (and weights) equals fat loss and thus change in body shape and size. Simple, isn't it? And it didn't cost you twenty-six monthly payments of $49.95 plus postage. You can have that little gem for free.

But that isn't the hard part. First you have to decide that you have had enough of being fat. Admit that you are sick of hating yourself, sick of not caring for yourself and sick of using food or fatness as an excuse for everything that is wrong with your life. Then the most difficult aspect of losing weight is starting. It all seems too hard. The goal seems unreachable, giving up your current lifestyle is difficult and seems like it will last forever, and you know what? *It is forever*. It has to be forever otherwise you will never reach your goal and maintain it. But that is not to say you can't relearn to live your life healthily and that includes having the odd junk food day or the occasional fifteen glasses of champagne (or is that just me?). It's finding the right balance that will work for you.

Being overweight means the exercise *is* hard. (Hard but not impossible.) I didn't realise how heavy I was until I lost forty kilos and tried lifting that weight. I couldn't do it! So start out slowly, don't rush in and do too much or you will injure yourself and be back where you started, if not a little further behind. Hey, I began by simply going up and down my stairs a couple of times a day (and that had me puffing and panting). Inspired by a one kilo weight loss I then got into the walking, got horizontal with the broken leg (still exercised), then swam, discovered aquarobics, went back to the walking, graduated to running, then did weights and now I do a range of sports—anything I can find including a combination of all of the above and some just for fun. And you know what? I love it. I have never felt more alive in my entire life. And it's only one year later. One year! One year to live the life you've always dreamed of. How easy is that? Not very, actually, but it *is* worth striving for.

I remember when I started in the gym, surrounded by beautiful people, ashamed of my body and not wanting to be there, but I just reminded myself that the only way out is through and I just imagined the body I would have in a year's time and that kept me going. Remember, you are doing this for yourself and what anyone else thinks is of no importance.

I do fully believe, particularly for anyone who is obese or who suffers from an eating disorder, that it is not just enough to go on a 'diet'. I could not have done it without the help of my psychiatrist. Yes, they are expensive, but some may bulk bill (you will have to discuss that with them) and there are plenty of other places to get help. See your doctor; your local community health centre (they often have free counselling to those in need); and check out your local hospital for any outpatient services or support groups.

Most importantly, don't be afraid to ask for help. Asking for help is simply seeking alternative solutions. I did. The first thing I did was see my doctor who referred me to my shrink, Dr Nutcase. I then rang my best friend's sister (Crusher) and begged her for help. And she didn't just do it for the TV show, she said she'd have done it years ago: she was just waiting for me to ask. You never know until you ask. You can find that same support in a friend. Find someone who wants to lose a few kilos (maybe more). Go walking together, motivate each other. Make a pact to ring each other every day to make sure you have done your exercises. This is what I found most helpful in Crusher—a friend who understood my goal and wanted the best for me. You don't have to pay someone to do that for you, just look around to the people who love you.

You may use the same excuse I've used a thousand times in my life: 'Oh, it's easy for her. She had a personal trainer.' Yes, Crusher did advise and support me through the journey but *I* was the one who dragged my fat arse to the gym, *I* did my sit ups while lying in bed with a broken leg, *I* walked past the lolly aisle while doing the shopping, and *I* managed (on most occasions) to drive past my local fish and chip shop. *I* went running in the rain when all I wanted to do was drink beer and eat battered savs, and *I* was the one who kept going, even when I didn't want to keep going, because I knew the time had come for me to change my life. I was not going to go back to being fat and out of control! With or without Crusher, if I hadn't finally resolved to do this I would not have stuck to it and that's the point you have to get to in your life. You have to ask yourself, 'Am I *really* content to live like this for the rest of my life?' If the answer is no then put this book down (actually, read the next few paragraphs *then* put the book down), throw out all your junk food, create a healthy eating plan and go for a walk.

If you can't join a gym, then hire a personal trainer for one session and ask them to run you through a range of exercises you can do around the home. In a one-hour session they can give you a decent routine for you to stick to until you are ready to join a gym.

If you do have the time and money to join a gym, then swallow your pride and get your big bum moving and you will find a whole new support network. And once again, don't be afraid to ask the girl or guy next to you how something works and what it does for you. If you don't ask you will never know. Don't feel stupid: realise you are smart for wanting the knowledge to make you a better person.

The thing is, everybody is different and what might work for me may not be right for you. I don't have all the answers—no one does—but all you really need to know is: do you want your life to change? If the answer is 'Yes', then go out and find what works for you and just stick with it. Never give up. When you falter (and believe me, you will—you are human after all!), pick yourself up, dust the cake crumbs from your mouth and *just keep going*. There is no right or wrong track—it is one track—health and fitness. You deserve to be as healthy and as happy as you could possibly be so never ever give up. If you don't save yourself, no one else will. You *can* do it. I know you can, because if I can do it, anyone can!

Postscript: AJ Rochester finished 30,431st in a field of 70,000 runners in the 2002 *Sun Herald* City to Surf. Her time was 121 minutes. Shortly afterwards she was seen consuming everything on the menu at the Hog's Breath Café—everything except the fries!

Thank Youse

Thank you so much to Vanessa Williams-Henke from Russell Williams Injury Prevention Professionals who not only allowed me to call her Crusher but who most likely saved my life; even though she will say it was all me, I could not have done it without her constant support, encouragement and belief. Thank you also to her business partner, Dianne Russell (russwill@tpg.com.au).

My thanks also to the following:

Anna Bateman, for wanting to interview me because I was fat and making me realise I didn't actually want to be fat, and to the Lifestyle Channel at Foxtel for filming the whole thing.

Dr ED who, even though she hated it, allowed me to call her Nutcase.

Selwa Anthony, my agent, who plucked me out of a literary competition and made my writing dreams a reality.

Peter McQuade, for coming to the rescue when I broke my leg. It is truly appreciated!

Leash—you truly embody the spirit of generosity.

Flippy—words cannot describe how great a friend you are.

Lou Pollard, my comedy partner—you are an absolute legend!

Nigel Collin from Absurd Entertainment who booked me for work fat and thin.

Alicia, Lou, Tara, Daniel, Juzzy, Simon, Zoë, Simone, Cinders, P.C., Uncle Eno, Uncle Chris and Aunty Ann for the endless babysitting and other shows of support.

Bruce Towler and Helen and Lance Barrett for undying love and support.

Glenn Majurey for funny words 'n' other stuff.

Shaggsy, my lab rat and record producer at brokenrecords. net.au, who ate my dinners despite them being branded 'rabbit food'.

Ziggy—you are a very beautiful man. Love you long time.

Thomas Gray and Gary Whale, my Years 7 and 10 English teachers who I promised, way back then, I would dedicate my first book to (is that good proper English, but?). This is for not only believing I could do it, but for taking the time and energy to convince me.

Fiona Henderson, Jo Jarrah and Roberta Ivers who took my dietary ramblings and made them something I could be proud of. They held my hand and ever so gently guided me through 'the process'.

Oh yeah, and a big squishy hug to Kai, whose life will hopefully be better because it won't be *his* mum who gets stuck in the slide at Hungry Jack's.

Go Tigers and go Manchester United!

Also available in Arrow

The Luck Factor
Dr Richard Wiseman

*The revolutionary book that reveals the four scientific principles of luck –
and how you can use them to change your life*

For over ten years, psychologist Dr Richard Wiseman has been
conducting a unique research project, examining the behaviour of over
a thousand volunteers who considered themselves 'lucky' or 'unlucky'.
The results reveal a radical new way of looking at luck:

- *You* hold the key to creating your luck
- There are four simple behavioural techniques which are
  scientifically proven to help you attract good fortune
- You can use these techniques to revolutionise every area of your
  life – including your relationships, personal finances and career

For the first time, the elusive luck factor has been identified. Using the
simple techniques described in this book, you can learn how to increase
your levels of luck, confidence and success.

'These principles can be used to enhance the amount of good
fortune people experience in their lives ... the research has serious
implications' *Guardian*

'Using Dr Wiseman's scientifically proven techniques, you too can
understand, control and increase your own good fortune' *Daily Mail*

arrow books

Also available in Arrow

The Many Faces of Men
Stephen Whitehead

The book that exposes one of the best-kept secrets of all time – what goes on in men's heads

Ever wondered what a man really thinks when he says 'I love you'? Ever questioned why so many men appear to love their football teams more than their children? Or agonised over whether a particular man can be trusted?

The Many Faces of Men is the first book to lift the lid on masculinity and to disclose the 27 distinct 'types' that make up the male species. In frank and humorous detail, gender expert Dr Stephen Whitehead defines men's inner characteristics and reveals:

- how to predict whether he's a marrying type or a serial seducer
- the telltale signs of an empire builder or a couch potato
- what kind of man makes the best boss
- how to spot a poser

Don't live in ignorance of men. *The Many Faces of Men* is an indispensable guide for any woman who wants an insight into the men in her life, or for any man who wants to understand what makes him tick.

arrow books

Also available in Arrow

Did You Spot the Gorilla
Dr Richard Wiseman

Spotting gorillas is easy – if you know how!

Have you ever regretted missing a good opportunity? Do you feel short of original solutions at work? Have you ever said 'I wish I'd thought of that'? Or found yourself concentrating on the details and missing the bigger picture?

In a recent series of groundbreaking experiments, volunteers were shown a short film of people playing basketball and asked to count the number of passes. Halfway through, a man dressed in a gorilla suit wanders in, beats his chest at the camera and walks off. Remarkably, almost none of the volunteers noticed him.

Would *you* have spotted the gorilla? In truth, we all have psychological blind spots that make us miss the obvious. But the good news is that we can train ourselves to be more aware of the opportunities hidden beneath our noses. In this fun and stimulating book, bestselling author Professor Richard Wiseman outlines the scientific evidence and shows you how to:

- Maximise the opportunities in your personal and professional life
- Come up with innovative ideas at work
- React flexibly to problems
- Change the way you see the world – and how it sees you

arrow books

Also available in Arrow

True Brits
J.R. Daeschner

When J.R. Daeschner first witnessed cheese rolling, he was astounded. As an American who had lived in the UK for years, he knew the British did some odd things. However, nothing could have prepared him for the sight of men – and women – flinging themselves off a grassy cliff in pursuit of a cheese. He soon discovered that Britain has scores of seemingly lunatic acts enshrined as traditions: events with strange names like gurning, shin kicking, horn dancing and faggot cutting.

True Brits is the hilarious account of J.R.'s trek around England, Scotland and Wales, as well as a bit of Northern Ireland in London's backyard. From 'Darkie Day' on New Year's Day to the English summer 'Olimpicks' and Pope burning on Bonfire Night, J.R. uncovers the people and places that make Britain great – and at times, not so great.

In his quest to find out why ordinary people do such extraordinary things, J.R. talks to countless characters, catches them in action and even takes part in the events himself. Along the way, he discovers that many of these ancient pastimes provide insights into 21st-century Britain, including football, francophilia, Page Three girls and Sellafield.

If you think you know Britain, think again…

arrow books

Also available in Arrow

Your Back, Your Heath
Dr Paul Sherwood

Over ten million Britons suffer with back pain. Many more have other health problems that are caused by their backs. There is little offered to these patients other than temporary relief in the form of drugs, largely ineffective orthodox treatments and complementary therapies. There has *never* been a more permanent solution – until now.

In *Your Back, Your Health*, Dr Paul Sherwood explains his pioneering view of the cause of non-specific back pain and outlines his revolutionary treatment, including a complete action plan for the immediate relief of acute pain and a daily five-minute exercise plan to help remain pain-free. He provides undeniable proof that many of today's most common illnesses have their origin in the back. Using his unique holistic approach he examines:

- How to identify your pain, understand the cause and deal with it effectively
- Why thousands of hip replacements and disc operations could be avoided
- Why it is essential children's backs are checked frequently
- Why regular back check-ups could dramatically lower your risk of a heart attack
- Your back as the cause of other diseases including migraine, arthritis, indigestion and ME

Dr Sherwood's methods have helped thousands of sufferers from all around the world and are easily adapted for use by other therapists. At last, you can say goodbye to back pain and its related illnesses.

'How to banish backache for good' – *Daily Mail*

arrow books

Order further Arrow titles
from your local bookshop, or have them delivered
direct to your door by Bookpost

☐ **The Luck Factor** Richard Wiseman   0 09 944324 4   £6.99

☐ **The Many Faces of Men**

   Stephen Whitehead   0 09 946635 X   £6.99

☐ **Did You Spot the Gorilla?**

   Richard Wiseman   0 09 946643 0   £6.99

☐ **True Brits** J.R. Daeschner   0 09 945346 0   £6.99

☐ **Your Back, Your Health**

   Dr Paul Sherwood   0 09 946802 6   £9.99

Free post and packing

Overseas customers allow £2 per paperback

Phone: 01624 677237

Post: Random House Books
c/o Bookpost, PO Box 29, Douglas, Isle of Man IM99 1BQ

Fax: 01624 670923

email: bookshop@enterprise.net

Cheques (payable to Bookpost) and credit cards accepted

Prices and availability subject to change without notice.
Allow 28 days for delivery.
When placing your order, please state if you do not wish to receive any
additional information.

www.randomhouse.co.uk/arrowbooks

arrow books